COOKING
with the
SEASONS

COOKING
with the
SEASONS

Lesa Heebner

Interior Illustrations
Tershia D'Elgin

Cover Illustrations
Mary Heebner

Cover Design
Joyce Weston

BOB ADAMS, INC.
Holbrook, Massachusetts

To Don
My inspiration,
my love,
my man for all seasons.

Published by Bob Adams, Inc.
260 Center Street, Holbrook, MA 02343

ISBN: 1-55850-274-2

Printed in the United States of America

A   B   C   D   E   F   G   H   I   J

Library of Congress Cataloging-in-Publication Data
Heebner, Lesa.
    Cooking with the seasons / Lesa Heebner.
      p. cm.
    Includes index.
    ISBN 1-55850-274-2 (trade pbk.) : $11.95
    1. Cookery. 2. Menus. I. Title.
    TX714.H434 1993
    641.5—dc20   93-29220
                                                     CIP

This publication is designed to provide accurate and authoritative information with regard to the subject matter covered. It is sold with the understanding that the publisher is not engaged in rendering legal, accounting, or other professional advice. If legal advice or other expert assistance is required, the services of a qualified professional person should be sought.

— From a *Declaration of Principles* jointly adopted by a Committee of the
American Bar Association and a Committee of Publishers and Associations.

COVER ILLUSTRATIONS: Mary Heebner

This book is available at quantity discounts for bulk purchases.
For information, call 1-800-872-5627.

Contents

Acknowledgments

Such a long path led to this book! It wouldn't have happened without Julie Castiglia, my agent, whose efforts on my behalf have gone above and beyond the usual. She has been unwavering in her belief in me, knowledgeable in all the business aspects of publishing, and a warm and supportive friend.

Bob and Irene Nishihira and Laura Ann Thompson deserve a special thanks—I guess we did it all for love!

My sister Mary's lovely watercolors grace the cover of this book—as only a sister could, she knew exactly the mood and style that would suit me and introduce readers to the feel of the book. Thanks also to Tershia D'Elgin who created beautiful images to accompany my recipes and enhance the reader's understanding of them, and to Yvonne Nienstadt who worked into the wee hours to compute the nutritional analysis on all the recipes, making all the right qualitative judgments that go into that task. Arlene Sobel, my editor with the very red pen, assured that cooking from this book would be a smooth and clear process. Many thanks for her thoroughness and culinary savvy.

To my friends who loaned their time, talent and support to this book: Bill and Mary Culver, Steve and Christine Dime, Lisa Gordon, Tricia Hays, Nina and Stephen Israel, Evelyne Johnson, Susan Murfin, Diane Shea and the folks at The Silver Skillet. A warm thanks to my Writers Group, Karen O'Connor, JoAnn Middleman, Ann Valades, Janet Kunert, Al Christman, and Connie Stockman.

To my family, including neices Kris Wiechman, who helped me test many of the recipes in this book, Audrey Wiechman, who actually likes my food, and Sienna Craig who assisted at two marathon cooking sessions during much-valued school vacation time, my sisters Toni and Dorothy for their continuing interest in this project. And to my parents Claire and Walter Heebner for their love and encouragement.

Thank you Lynn Edmundson for counting so much, to Lisa Marraro Cole, my stress equalizer and main support system, to Sally Guenther for always believing in me. To Dr. Richard Dahout, whose sound nutritional advice I so value. To Billie Bowen and Carol Cole for their care and nurturing. And to my husband Don, who keeps me cookin'!

Introduction

Some of my strongest ties to the past are my memories of special foods. They're capable of provoking a flood of wonderful sensations, just as the first taste of a summer-ripe peach prompts the gentle feel of salt breezes, the squawking sounds of seagulls, and the provocative smell of Coppertone.

The sight of tangerines on neighborhood trees awakens the spirit of Christmas, of busy days filled with the aroma of fresh pine needles and trays of holiday cookies.

The smell of cinnamon and apples being baked into a perfect autumn pie kindles my urge for oversized wool sweaters and steamy bowls of soup.

And spring's first growth in the vegetable garden arouses memories of frilly new Easter dresses, egg salad luncheons, and strawberry desserts.

These food associations, linked in my mind through years of delicious repetition, are precious to me. You may have shared similar experiences. They serve the purpose that all traditions do—bringing people together with a common bond, a common memory, a source of comfort through custom. This is one of the joys of cooking with the seasons, when foods are linked with traditions we hold so dear.

Cooking with the seasons also allows us to enjoy foods when they are most flavorful, the brightest in color, and most abundant in juice and texture—when they are perfect gifts from nature. At this time they need little adornment or fussing with to impart full, rich flavor. No need to smother fresh asparagus in a fatty sauce, or over-salt a luscious summer tomato. Bare of enhancements, they are at their best, and that's the best for us.

Seasonal foods nourish us in many ways. They not only enrich our lives with tradition and warm remembrances, they also fortify our bodies with their goodness and nutrition.

To create delicious, healthful meals year round, use this book in concert with each season. Trust in nature and the variety she provides. By cooking with the seasons, you will find a wealth of nutritional wisdom and a wellspring of warm and lasting memories.

How to Use this Book

The seasonal recipes that follow are low in fat, sodium, cholesterol, and sugar, yet rich in taste and texture. To achieve these qualities, I occasionally suggest an ingredient that may be unfamiliar to you, such as miso, date sugar, or others. They are thoroughly explained in boxed "tips" alongside the recipe, and in the Glossary (see pages 139-142). More commonly available ingredients are indicated as replacements when possible, however, please do try some of these newer foods as you'll find they bring flavor, texture, and nutrition to the recipes.

Nutritional analysis was computed for each recipe using The Food Processor II Nutrition & Diet Analysis System software program. (Please note that values are approximate.) You will see very quickly just how healthful these recipes are.

Complete menus are suggested at the beginning of each season's recipes. Take note that the recipes in each menu do not always serve the same number of people, so adjust your plans accordingly.

WINTER

The festive winter months fly by so quickly! Activity abounds with family visits, friendly gatherings, old acquaintances renewed. Rush and hurry are tempered by moments of celebration with neighbors, colleagues, and loved ones. Appetites are heartier now, satisfied by thick soups, chicken stews, and pizzas. Since fresh produce is scarce, the fruits and vegetables available, often dried versions of another season's plenty, act as complements to these robust meals.

SUGGESTED MENUS

HOLIDAY DINNER I
Greens Tossed with Cumin Orange Vinaigrette and
*   Candied Pecans*
Roast Turkey*
Whole Grain and Lentil Stuffing
Herbed Tomatoes, Swiss Chard, and Potatoes
*   Parmigiana*
Sugar Pumpkin and Gingersnap Tartlets

HOLIDAY DINNER II
Black Pepper and Fresh Herb Breadsticks
Caesar Salad
Holiday Lasagne
Spinach Fettucine with Parsley Caper Sauce and
*   Pan Seared Sea Bass*
Apple Strudel

SUPER BOWL SUNDAY
Black Bean Chili Nachos
Chicken, Shiitake Mushroom, and Sun-Dried Tomato
*   Pizza*
Fresh Raw Vegetables*
Chickpea Puree and Pita Wedges

VALENTINE'S DAY DINNER
Winter Greens Salad and Pear Vinaigrette with
*   Walnuts*
Orzo and Sautéed Shrimp with Curried Tarragon Sauce
Amaretti Almond Torte

DINNER I
Minestrone di Abruzzi
Crushed Red Pepper and Rosemary Baguette (see
*   page 71)*

DINNER II
Jake's Dinner Salad
Pan Seared Salmon Served with Julienne Carrots
*   and Leeks plus Tangerine Juice*
Baked Potatoes*
Honey Vanilla Shortbread Cookies

DINNER III
Romaine Lettuce with Little Ranch Dressing (see
*   page 37)*
Chicken Breast, Parsnip, and Rutabaga Stew with
*   Sage Dumplings*
Sliced Pears in Phyllo Pillows

DINNER IV
Healthy Fettucine Alfredo with Peas
Baked Chicken Breasts Vinaigrette
Spinach Salad with Lemon Vinaigrette (see page 41)

* Recipe not included.

APPETIZERS AND BREADS

BLACK PEPPER AND FRESH HERB BREADSTICKS

Makes 64 breadsticks

Black pepper lends a nice bite to these flavorful breadsticks. For the herbs, scour your garden for snippings and for edible geranium leaves. Chop them up finely, knead them into the dough, form, and bake the breadsticks. If you have no fresh herbs available, try dried herbs. The proportion of fresh to dried herbs is 1:3, thus 1 TB of fresh thyme is equivalent to 1 tsp of dried.

DOUGH

1 cup water
1 package yeast
1 TB honey or maple syrup or sugar
1^1/$_2$ cups unbleached flour
^{1}/$_2$ cup whole wheat flour
^{1}/$_2$ cup semolina flour or ^{1}/$_2$ cup unbleached flour
^{1}/$_2$ tsp salt or VegeSal
^{1}/$_2$ tsp black pepper
2 TB extra virgin olive oil or Olio Santo (see recipe page 10)

Suggested fresh herbs per ^{1}/$_4$ piece of dough:
2 TB fresh chives, finely chopped
1 TB fresh thyme, finely chopped
2 TB fresh lavender leaves, finely chopped
1 TB fresh rosemary, finely chopped
2 TB rose geranium leaves, finely chopped

1. Heat water to bath water temperature (105° to 115°F). Add yeast and sweetener and let sit for 5 minutes, or until the mixture begins to foam. If it hasn't foamed within 5 minutes, that means your yeast is no good. Discard and begin again with a fresh package.

2. Meanwhile, place the flours in a medium-size bowl. Add salt, black pepper, and olive oil. Mix well so that the oil is distributed throughout the flours.

3. When the yeast has foamed, add it to the flours. Mix well, then turn out onto a lightly floured surface and knead for 5 minutes. Add a little extra flour to the work surface so the dough does not stick.

4. Transfer dough to a lightly oiled bowl. Turn to coat the dough with oil on all sides. Cover with plastic wrap and let rise in a draft-free place till it doubles in size, about 45 minutes. (You know the dough has risen enough when the indentation left by your finger in the dough doesn't rise back at you.)

5. Punch down dough and turn out onto a lightly floured work surface and knead just enough to bring dough into a ball. Divide dough into 4 equal pieces. Work with 1 piece at a time, keeping the other pieces covered with plastic wrap.

6. Add fresh or dried herbs, kneading 1 kind of herb into each one-quarter piece of dough.

7. Roll out each dough quarter into a circle. Cut with a knife or pizza cutter into 8 triangle-shaped pieces, then cut triangles in half so you have 16 thin triangle-shaped pieces. Repeat with remaining dough quantities.

8. Roll up each triangle from the small end toward the large end. Roll the dough between your hands, then place dough on the work surface. Roll, using both hands and spreading your fingers as the breadstick gets longer to keep the width of each breadstick as even as possible.

9. Place on a lightly oiled cookie sheet. Bake for 25-30 minutes at 325°F.

Each serving (8 breadsticks) contains approximately 20 calories, 0.6 grams protein, 0.5 grams total fat, 0 mg cholesterol, 17 mg sodium.

POPPYSEED GINGER RICE ROLLED AND WRAPPED IN NORI SEAWEED

Serves 8

There is a technique to making these appetizers, so practice before promising to feed a house full of hungry friends! It's kind of like learning to make pancakes—the first couple may not be your best effort, but improvement is evident with each successive batch. Once you've mastered it, you'll come to appreciate how light and nutritious these Nori Rolls are—delicate in beauty, dramatic in presentation. Leftovers keep well for one or two days, and make a very special brown bag treat.

A tool you will need to buy to make this recipe is a bamboo sushi mat, which is available at natural foods stores and Oriental grocery shops. They are quite inexpensive. If you don't have a mat, simply roll up the seaweed, rice and veggies, like you would roll up a carpet.

1 cup short grain brown rice
2 1/2 cups water
2 TB poppy seeds
1/2 tsp Ume plum vinegar or apple cider vinegar
1 scallion, thinly sliced
1 tsp grated fresh ginger
1 small carrot, cut into very thin matchsticks
1/4 daikon radish, cut into very thin matchsticks
   (optional)
1 raw beet, cut into very thin matchsticks
1/4 unpeeled hothouse or peeled cucumber, cut into
   very thin matchsticks
4 sheets nori seaweed
1 TB rice vinegar or white wine vinegar
1 cup water

1. To cook rice, add rice and water to a saucepan. Bring water to a boil, reduce heat to low, and simmer for 35 minutes. (You want the resulting rice to be sticky, so pick up the lid during cooking and stir the rice—this is usually discouraged because it makes rice sticky instead of fluffy.)

2. Meanwhile, make the Dark Sesame Dipping Sauce (see recipe below). Set aside.

3. Add the poppy seeds, vinegar, scallions, and ginger to the rice when it is done. Stir to mix and let cool enough to handle.

4. Lay the nori, shiny side down, on a bamboo sushi mat.

5. Pour the rice vinegar and water into a bowl.

6. Cover the bottom 1/3 of the nori with rice, leaving a 1" margin at the edge closest to you. Wet your hands with the vinegar/water and press down the rice in a neat level rectangle.

7. Lay the cucumber matchsticks in the center of the rice so they span all the way across the long side of the rectangle. Add matchsticks of other vegetables alongside the cucumber matchsticks.

8. To roll, work by holding the bamboo mat, not the nori alone. Roll the mat over the rice. Do not roll up the mat with the nori—the mat is your guide, not part of the food! Squeeze and tighten and roll almost to the end of the nori. Wet the edge of the nori with the vinegar/water mixture to seal.

9. Slice each Nori Roll into 6-8 pieces using a very sharp knife that has been slightly moistened with a little of the vinegar/water mixture. Repeat as directed with the remaining ingredients.

10. Serve with the Dark Sesame Dipping Sauce.

Each serving contains approximately 103 calories, 2.4 grams protein, 1.5 grams total fat, 0 mg cholesterol, 20 mg sodium.

DARK SESAME DIPPING SAUCE

Makes 8 servings

This sauce is medium hot. To adjust the hotness, alter the amount of wasabi powder according to your taste. Add just enough water to make a thick paste before you add the other ingredients. Wasabi powder, Japanese horseradish, can be found at Oriental groceries or natural food stores.

---

1 TB wasabi powder
about 1 TB water, as needed
2 drops toasted sesame oil
3 TB rice vinegar
2 TB low sodium soy sauce
¹/₂ tsp grated fresh ginger

1. Make a paste out of the wasabi powder and water.

2. Add all other ingredients. Serve with the Nori Rolls.

Makes approximately ¹/₂ cup or 8 servings.

BLACK BEAN CHILI NACHOS | Serves 6

A blustery winter day, the Sunday paper strewn over the floor, football on the TV, and a platter of Black Bean Chili Nachos. Perfect!

2 cups Black Bean Chili (see recipe page 115)
24 corn tortillas
Mexican seasoning blend as needed (optional)
3 scallions, sliced into rounds
2 ozs reduced fat Cheddar cheese, grated
nonfat plain yogurt as needed
salsa of choice as needed

1. Preheat oven to 350°F. Make a batch of Black Bean Chili or defrost a batch and warm it on the stove or in the microwave.

2. Cut tortillas into eighths. Place tortilla triangles on ungreased cookie sheets. Sprinkle with Mexican Seasoning, if using. Bake for 10 minutes, then turn tortillas over—sprinkle with more Mexican Seasoning, if

using, and bake for 7-12 more minutes. The tortillas should be crisp, not chewy. Remove chips from oven.

3. Increase oven temperature to Broil.

4. Place ¹/₃ of the chips on an oven-proof dish or platter. Spoon on some Black Bean Chili, sprinkle with scallions, then with grated cheese. Continue layering as directed.

5. Place Nachos under the broiler for 2-3 minutes--or until the cheese melts.

6. Spoon a dollop of yogurt on top and serve immediately with salsa on the side for dipping.

Each serving contains approximately 228 calories, 10 grams protein, 6.5 grams total fat, 11 mg cholesterol, 123 mg sodium.

CHICKPEA PURÉE WITH PITA WEDGES | Serves 8

T his hearty appetizer can double as a lunch. Line a half piece of pita bread with lettuce leaves, spoon in the chickpea purée, add some tomato slices, and lunch is ready! This purée will last for about five days in the refrigerator.

1¹/₂ cups canned chickpeas (garbanzo beans),
*   drained and well-rinsed*
1 clove garlic, finely minced
¹/₄ cup fresh lemon juice
2 TB nonfat plain yogurt
2 TB sesame tahini
1 TB extra virgin olive oil
¹/₂ cup fresh parsley leaves
water as needed
¹/₄ tsp cayenne
¹/₂ tsp black pepper

You can substitute 1 cup of raw garbanzo beans for the canned. Soak overnight, drain and simmer for 2 hours in 4 cups of water. Add kombu seaweed for first hour of cooking to aid digestion of beans.

low sodium soy sauce or salt or VegeSal, as needed
3 scallions, sliced (for garnish)
8 slices of pita bread

1. Place the chickpeas, garlic, lemon juice, yogurt, tahini, olive oil, and parsley in a food processor or blender. Process till smooth. Add water if needed to reach a smooth consistency.

2. Add cayenne and black pepper. Taste and adjust seasonings. If desired, add soy sauce or salt to taste.

3. If you have the time, cover and refrigerate overnight for flavors to blend.

4. When ready to serve, sprinkle sliced scallions over the dip as garnish.

5. Cut pita bread into eighths. Toast under the broiler till warm, then serve.

Makes about 2 cups.

Each serving contains approximately 260 calories, 10 grams protein, 5.5 grams total fat, 0.6 mg cholesterol, 340 mg sodium (the sodium is derived from canned, salted garbanzos. If you rinse them well, subtract about 175 mg of sodium. If you use unsalted canned garbanzo beans or make them from scratch, subtract 290 mg of sodium).

TOFU GINGER BITS

Serves 12

I'm a big fan of tofu and am constantly amazed that people turn up their noses at it. Tofu changes character according to its environment and is tremendously versatile. I use it in lasagne in place of ricotta cheese and in brownies and coffeecake in place of eggs. I also use it in the more traditional manner in stir-frys and Japanese soups in place of meat or fish.

In the following recipe, I freeze, then thaw and cook cubes of tofu with lots of ginger and garlic. Freezing changes tofu's texture so that it resembles a firm-fleshed fish or chicken. Serve this dish at your next gathering and watch jaws drop when you tell guests, "No, it's not chicken . . . it's tofu!"

> To freeze tofu, open tub, drain water, and cut tofu into 8 equal portions. Double wrap and freeze for at least 8 hours.

1 pound fresh tofu, firm, frozen
2 TB grated fresh ginger
8 cloves garlic, finely minced
2 tsp extra virgin olive oil or sesame oil
1 TB low sodium soy sauce
1 TB raw sesame seeds

1. Thaw tofu by placing it in a pot of boiling water. Turn off heat and let the tofu thaw. This should take 10-15 minutes.

2. Cut tofu into ½" cubes.

3. Place all the ingredients except the sesame seeds in a skillet.

4. Cook on low heat, turning occasionally, until the liquid is absorbed and the tofu is browned. This is a slow process—be patient! It will take 20-30 minutes.

5. Transfer tofu to a serving dish and sprinkle with sesame seeds. Serve warm, or refrigerate and serve cold. Use toothpicks as skewers.

Each serving contains approximately 44 calories, 3.3 grams protein, 3 grams total fat, 0 mg cholesterol, 89 mg sodium.

SALADS

WINTER GREENS SALAD AND FRESH PEAR VINAIGRETTE WITH WALNUTS

Makes 8 dinner salads

This salad looks like an early winter scene, with the creamy white dressing contrasting the dark greens of the lettuce. You

may be accustomed to substituting olive oil for all oils.
In this recipe, however, its distinct taste would over-
whelm the subtle flavor of the pear. If you don't have
safflower, substitute sunflower, canola, or walnut oil.

GREENS
  8 cups winter lettuce, such as red leaf, spinach,
    Swiss chard

DRESSING
  1 ripe pear, peeled, de-seeded, and cut into quarters
  2 TB raspberry vinegar
  4 TB safflower oil
  1 TB honey

GARNISH
  3 TB walnuts
  2 TB pomegranate seeds (optional)

1. Wash greens well, spin dry, and tear into bite-size
pieces.

2. Meanwhile make the dressing. Combine the pear
quarters, raspberry vinegar, safflower oil, and honey in
a food processor or blender and process till creamy.
Refrigerate till needed.

3. To assemble salad, toss greens with dressing. Divide
among 8 salad plates. Sprinkle with walnuts and pomegranate seeds, if using. Serve immediately.

**Each serving contains approximately 116 calories, 1.8
grams protein, 8.8 grams total fat, 0 mg cholesterol,
25 mg sodium.**

CAESAR SALAD

Makes 4 large or 8 dinner salads

If garlic is your game, this salad's got your name! The egg
traditionally called for in Caesar
Salad is omitted and not missed if
you toss the ingredients into the
salad in the order specified below.

The croutons are fat-free and fabulous. The trick is to
love the bread you are starting with! My favorite breads
for croutons are a multi-grain sourdough made by
Alvarado Street Bakery of Sonoma County, California
and my Parisian Baguette (see recipe page 107). The
denser the bread, the longer it takes to dry out in the
oven. You may want to make four or five times as
many croutons as you need and freeze the leftovers for
another salad, another day.

CROUTONS
  2 slices whole grain or other bread of choice

SALAD AND DRESSING
  1 large head romaine lettuce
  2 TB capers, rinsed
  2 anchovies (optional)
  6-10 cloves garlic, finely minced
  3 TB fresh lemon juice
  1 TB Worcestershire sauce
  1 tsp black pepper
  1/4 tsp cayenne
  1 tsp grated lemon peel
  4 TB extra virgin olive oil or Olio Santo (see page
    10)
  1/2-3/4 cup freshly grated Parmesan cheese

1. To make croutons, cut 2 slices of bread into 1/2"
squares. Place on a cookie sheet and let dry out in a
250° F. oven for 30-60 minutes, depending on the bread.
Check every 20 minutes and stir. The croutons are done
when they are crunchy throughout.

2. Meanwhile, wash lettuce well, spin dry and refrigerate.

3. Prepare dressing in the wooden bowl you will serve
the salad in. Mince the capers and anchovies, if using.
Add the garlic, lemon juice, Worcestershire sauce,
black and cayenne peppers, and lemon peel.

4. When croutons are done, let cool.

5. When you are ready to serve the salad, transfer the
dressing from the large serving bowl to a small bowl
and reserve.

6. Tear the lettuce into bite-size pieces and place in the
large wooden serving bowl. Toss with the olive oil,
making certain that the oil coats each piece.

7. Add the reserved dressing and toss, then add the Parmesan cheese and toss.

8. Add the croutons and toss till they have absorbed some of the dressing. Serve immediately.

Each serving: 8 dinner salads, using ³/₄ cup Parmesan cheese, contains approximately 138 calories, 5.7 grams protein, 9.6 grams total fat, 7 mg cholesterol, 264 mg sodium.

DAILY SALAD WITH GINGER VINAIGRETTE
Makes 10 dinner salads

This healthful salad is my very favorite-- it's practically daily fare around our house. I use whatever dark lettuce is available and look best. Dark lettuce is full of chlorophyll, which I call "sunshine energy," fiber, calcium, and iron. Sprouts offer enzymes, vitamin C, and protein. Carrots and beets add color, as well as beta carotene and potassium. Raw onions fight heart disease by lowering total cholesterol. You don't have to stop here even though the ingredient list below does! Add some finely chopped broccoli or shredded cabbage for a little cancer-fighting action and some grated raw winter squash for a dash more beta carotene. The dressing is very flavorful and will convince the most health-o-phobic to ask for second helpings! Any leftover dressing will keep for about a month if well-covered in the refrigerator.

SALAD
>   *as needed: dark lettuce, such as romaine, red leaf, oak leaf, or a combination*
>   *as needed: sprouts, such as sunflower, buckwheat, radish, or a combination*
>   *1-2 carrots*
>   *1-2 raw beets*
>   *¹/₄-¹/₂ red onion*

DRESSING
>   *3 cloves garlic*
>   *1 shallot*
>   *¹/₂" piece ginger*
>   *³/₄ cup extra virgin olive oil*
>   *¹/₂ cup apple cider vinegar*
>   *3 TB Dijon-style mustard*
>   *¹/₄ cup water, wine or mixture of both*
>   *¹/₂ tsp dried tarragon*

1. Wash lettuce well, spin dry, and tear into bite-size pieces into a large salad bowl. Add sprouts—chop sunflower sprouts so they're easier to eat. (Sprouts are usually already rinsed so they don't need to be washed.)

2. Scrub the carrots and beets free of all dirt. Grate and add to salad bowl.

3. Slice onion and add to salad bowl.

4. To make the dressing, place the garlic, shallot, and ginger in the food processor or blender. Process till finely minced. Add oil, vinegar, water, mustard, and tarragon. Process again, scrape down sides of bowl, and transfer to a jar. Or, if making dressing by hand, mince garlic and shallot with a chef's knife. Grate the ginger with a hand-held grater till you have 1 tsp. Place in jar. Add all other ingredients and stir or shake to combine. Makes 1¹/₄ cups dressing.

Each 1 TB of dressing contains approximately 50 calories, 0.1 grams protein, 6.5 grams total fat, 0 mg cholesterol, 20 mg sodium. Three ounces of salad contains about 22 calories.

JAKE'S SALAD
Makes 4 salads

Jake's is a local restaurant in San Diego, right on the beach. You sit at tables in an enclosed patio with creaking wooden floors, and watch the waves, the birds, the people. It's the kind of place you take your parents to when they're in for the week. A place you'd meet girlfriends after a day at the beach, all sun-kissed and brown. Or, in the winter, a place you and your husband sneak off to at about 4:00 for a glass of wine, an artichoke, and the sunset. And then you stay on, enticed by the memory of their wonderful salad, a roasty tasting baked potato, and a piece of swordfish. Here's my version of Jake's fabulous dinner salad.

DRESSING
2 cloves garlic, finely minced
1/2 cup apple cider vinegar
2 TB Dijon-style mustard
3/4 cup canola oil
1/4 cup dry white wine
1/2 tsp salt or VegeSal
2 tsp dried tarragon
2 tsp pepper, preferably white pepper
1 tsp dried basil
1 bay leaf

LETTUCE
1 head red leaf lettuce
1 recipe Croutons (see Caesar Salad page 6)

1. To make dressing, place all the ingredients in a jar and mix well, or place all ingredients except the bay leaf in a food processor or blender and process till smooth. Add the bay leaf and refrigerate.

2. Wash lettuce well, spin dry, and tear into bite-size pieces.

3. When ready to eat, toss lettuce with the dressing. Add croutons and toss again. To make it authentically "Jake's," you need to drench it in dressing!

Makes 1 3/4 cup dressing.

Each 1 TB of dressing contains approximately 56 calories. 0.15 grams protein, 6 grams total fat, 0 mg cholesterol, 14 mg sodium.

GREENS TOSSED WITH CUMIN ORANGE VINAIGRETTE AND CANDIED PECANS
Makes 8 dinner salads

Tart, sweet, and hot are the sensations of this winter salad. The recipe makes about 1 cup of dressing, so you will have leftovers, which will keep for about a week if well-covered in the refrigerator.

SALAD
12 cups mixed salad greens, such as romaine, butter lettuce, Swiss chard
2 oranges
1/2 small red onion, thinly sliced into rings

DRESSING
1/2 cup extra virgin olive oil
1/4 cup apple cider vinegar
2 TB frozen orange juice concentrate
1/8 tsp dried oregano
1/2 tsp ground cumin
2 tsp dried basil
1/4 tsp cayenne
3 TB Dijon-style mustard
1/4 cup nonfat plain yogurt

CANDIED PECANS
1/2 cup raw pecans
2 tsp low sodium soy sauce
1 tsp maple syrup or honey
1/8 tsp cayenne

1. Preheat oven to 325°F.

2. To candy the pecans, place the nuts in a mixing bowl. Toss with the soy sauce, maple syrup, and cayenne. Turn into an ovenproof dish or cookie sheet and toast in the oven for 25-30 minutes, stirring once during cooking.

3. Wash lettuce well and spin dry, tear into bite-size pieces. Set aside.

4. To make the dressing, whisk together all the ingredients in a small bowl or jar. Refrigerate till ready to serve.

5. Using a sharp knife, peel the oranges. Make sure to remove all the bitter white pith. Slice the oranges crosswise, about 1/4" thick.

6. To assemble the salad, toss the lettuce with the orange and onion slices and about 1 cup of the dressing. Divide among 8 salad plates. Top with a few warm or cooled-to-room-temperature pecans and serve immediately.

Makes 1 1/4 cups; there will be a little left over.

Each serving (4.5 oz each) of salad contains approximately 83 calories.

Each 2 TB of dressing contains approximately 100 calories, 0.6 grams protein, 10 grams total fat, 0 mg cholesterol, 58 mg sodium.

QUINOA SALAD WITH SUNFLOWER SAVORY DRESSING
Makes 8 dinner salads

Besides being higher in protein, calcium, and iron than any other grain, quinoa (pronounced "keen-wa") has another plus that most cooks will really appreciate: it takes only 10 minutes to cook! These little pearls of wonder, harvested by hand, are covered with saponin, an extremely bitter resin-like substance that must be rinsed away before cooking. Use a fine mesh strainer to do this as the grains are tiny.

The beauty of this salad, besides its nutritional and time-saving merits, is that it is the vegetable, the salad,

and the starch for the meal, all in one dish. The salad dressing gets its creamy texture from sunflower seeds. Process them to a fine powder before adding any of the other ingredients. Make sure to use fresh sunflower seeds--they should not taste bitter or sharp--bought in a store with high turnover.

QUINOA SALAD

1 cup raw quinoa, well-rinsed
1 1/2 cups water
2 carrots
1 cup fresh or frozen peas
red leaf lettuce as needed
radicchio or curly endive (chicory leaf) lettuce as needed

DRESSING

1/4 cup raw sunflower seeds
2 cloves garlic
3 scallions
1/2 cup firmly packed fresh parsley
1/2 cup extra virgin olive oil
1/2 cup sherry vinegar
1 tsp ground cumin
1/4 tsp dried, ground summer savory (1/2 tsp if dried leaves)
1 tsp low sodium soy sauce
1/4 tsp black pepper
2-4 TB water

1. Bring water to a boil and add quinoa. Reduce heat to low, and simmer for 10 minutes.

2. Meanwhile, cut carrots in diagonal chunks, measure out peas, and clean lettuce, spin dry and tear into bite-size pieces.

3. After 10 minutes, check quinoa. If there is water in the pot and the grain is crunchy, put lid on and cook for 3 minutes more or till all the liquid is absorbed and the grain is fluffy.

4. Meanwhile, make the dressing. Place sunflower seeds in a food processor or blender and process to a fine powder.

5. Add garlic, scallions, and parsley. Process, scrape down sides, and process again.

6. Add the rest of the ingredients, pour them into a jar, and refrigerate till needed.

7. When the quinoa is done, transfer it to a bowl. Add carrots, peas, and 4 TB of the Sunflower Savory Dressing. Chill and serve salad cold, or keep warm or let it come to room temperature.

8. Toss lettuce leaves with 4 more TB of the dressing. Arrange on salad plates. Spoon Quinoa Salad on top.

The dressing makes 12 2 TB servings.

Each serving of the salad contains approximately 182 calories, 5.8 grams protein, 6.3 grams total fat, 0 mg cholesterol, 60 mg sodium.

Each 2 TB of dressing contains approximately 116 calories, 1.4 grams protein, 12 grams total fat, 0 mg cholesterol, 43 mg sodium.

OLIO SANTO   *Makes 1-quart Olio Santo*

My sister Mary gave me this recipe years ago, and I don't know what I'd do without it! You'll see it in many recipes in this book. While you're at it, you might as well make a few bottles at a time-you'll want one "aging" while you're using one bottle. Olio Santo also makes a great hostess gift. Buy decorative bottles, or recycle old wine bottles, to fill. Use the Olio Santo in applications where you can appreciate its special flavor, such as in simple salad dressings, in and on breads, or tossed with steamed vegetables. The garlic and herbs lend a subtle flavor to the oil, while the chiles add a slight snap-but don't worry, it's not red hot.

7-10 whole cloves of garlic, peeled
7-10 dried red chiles (chiles arbol)
2 sprigs fresh herbs with tiny leaves, such as oregano, marjoram, or thyme
1 quart extra virgin olive oil

1. Place the garlic, dried chiles and herbs in a bottle.

Please, do not omit the dried chiles in the recipe. Unfortunately, there have been a few cases of botulism poisoning when garlic alone is immersed in oil. Botulism is soil-borne, which is where garlic grows. If the garlic was tainted with botulism, the botulism would need an anaerobic environment in which to grow. This is provided when you cover the garlic with oil. Luckily, the acidic environment the dried chiles creates kills off any botulism. This is also why the chopped garlic in the jar found at the grocery store has citric acid in it. Please don't let this information scare you from making this incredible oil! Just make sure to include the dried chiles!

2. Pour in the olive oil.

3. Let sit for 3 weeks in a cool, dry, dark place, like the pantry, wine cellar, or cellar.

All oils have the same amount of fat, 14 grams per 1 TB.

SOUPS

SPLIT PEA SOUP   *Serves 12*

This warming winter soup is a cinch to make. If you're good with a chef's knife and can dice and slice easily, it should take 10 minutes to prepare. If you're still honing your knife skills, allow 15-20 minutes of preparation. Or use your food processor to chop and slice. Rather than cooking this stovetop as directed, you can use a crock pot for all-day cooking. Follow the instructions as below, only let the soup cook for 6-8 hours before adding the red wine and seasoning. What a wonderful treat to come home to!

2 cups dried split peas, rinsed
8 cups water

6" strip kombu seaweed (optional)
1 bay leaf
3 cloves garlic, finely minced
1 medium red onion, diced
3 stalks celery, diced
3 carrots, sliced
1 medium potato, diced (omit if freezing soup)
4 TB dry red wine
1/4 tsp dried thyme
1/4 tsp dried basil
1/4 tsp dried marjoram
1/8 tsp dried rosemary
1/8 tsp dried sage
low sodium soy sauce to taste
black pepper to taste

1. Place split peas, water, kombu, bay leaf, garlic, onion, celery, carrots, and potato in an 8-quart Dutch oven. Bring to a boil, reduce heat and cook, covered, for 45-60 minutes, or until split peas are not just soft, but mushy.

2. Add red wine and seasonings and cook for 15 minutes more. Serve hot.

Each serving (9 oz) contains approximately 147 calories, 9 grams protein, 0.5 grams total fat, 0 mg cholesterol, 89 mg sodium (1 TB low sodium soy sauce).

ADUKI BEAN AND MISO SOUP
Serves 12

Aduki beans are not widely known, but they are worth getting acquainted with. They are the most digestible of all beans, and since they are so small, they require no overnight soaking. Miso can be found at a natural foods store or Oriental grocery. It adds flavor to a dish, and in this case it takes the place of a bouillon cube or flavored stock. See the Glossary to Ingredients, page 139, for more information. This is a thick, substantial soup, perfect for cold nights.

2 cups dried aduki beans, rinsed
6" strip kombu seaweed (optional)
1 bay leaf
8 cups water
4 cloves garlic, finely minced
1 large yellow onion, diced
4 stalks celery, diced
2 cups (about 1 pound) butternut squash
1 small head cauliflower, cut into florets (optional)
2 TB red miso

1. Place beans, water, kombu, bay leaf, garlic, onion and celery in an 8-quart Dutch oven. Bring to a boil, reduce heat to low, cook covered for 1 hour.

2. Place whole butternut squash in a 350° F oven and let bake for 30 minutes. The squash will be half done. Peel and dice squash and add to pot of soup.

3. Remove and discard the kombu. Add cauliflower if using. Cook for 20-30 minutes.

4. Right before serving, ladle about 1 cup of the broth into a bowl. Stir in the miso making sure it is well dissolved. Pour back into the soup pot and stir well to mix. Serve hot.

Each serving (9 oz) contains approximately 139 calories, 8.5 grams protein, 0.5 grams total fat, 0 mg cholesterol, 117 mg sodium.

PASTA E FAGIOLI
Serves 12

I can still hear my mother singing "pasta va-zhoo-la, pasta va-zhoo-la!" This is my version of the traditional Italian pasta and bean soup.

2 cups dried white beans
4 cups water
6" strip kombu seaweed (optional)
1 bay leaf
1 dried whole red chile pepper or 1 tsp crushed red peppers
4 cloves garlic, finely minced

1 large yellow onion, diced
3 stalks celery, diced
3 cups chicken broth or Homemade Chicken Stock
(see recipe page 44)
1 28-oz can Italian plum tomatoes, drained of liquid
1 tsp dried basil
1/8 tsp dried sage
1/4 cup short pasta, such as little bow ties or elbows
salt or VegeSal to taste
black pepper to taste
1 TB extra virgin olive oil (optional)
4 TB grated fresh Reggiano Parmigiano (optional)
crushed red peppers as needed (optional)

1. Soak beans for at least 8 hours, then drain soaking water. Or quick soak by placing beans in a saucepan with enough water to cover plus 2". Bring to a boil, turn off the heat, and let sit covered, for 1½ hours. Drain water.

2. Cook the soaked beans in the 4 cups of fresh water with kombu and bay leaf for 1 hour. Remove and discard the kombu. Cook until the beans are tender, about ½ hour longer.

3. When done, add the chile pepper or crushed red peppers, garlic, onion, celery, chicken broth, tomatoes, basil, and sage. Simmer for 20-30 minutes.

4. Remove and discard bay leaf and chile pepper, if using. Puree two-thirds of the soup in a food processor or blender. Return to pot and stir well to mix.

5. Bring soup to a boil, add pasta, and cook for 10 minutes. Taste and season with salt and pepper.

6. Right before serving, stir in the olive oil, if using.

7. Serve hot. Serve with crushed red peppers and Reggiano, if desired.

Each serving (9 oz, without oil and cheese) contains approximately 157 calories, 9.5 grams protein, 0.86 grams total fat, 0.1 mg cholesterol, 215 mg sodium. With oil and cheese, add 17 calories, 0.7 grams protein, 1.6 grams total fat, 1.3 mg cholesterol and 31 mg sodium.

QUICK RED LENTIL CURRY SOUP   *Serves 8*

You know those times when you'd do anything not to have to go to the grocery store to put a dinner together? Well, this is your answer. You're likely to have all these ingredients on hand as they are all staples or long lasting vegetables. Red lentils cook in about 30 minutes compared to 45-60 minutes for brown lentils, so you can whip up this soup pretty quickly too.

1 yellow onion, diced
4 cloves garlic, finely minced
1 carrot, diced
2 tsp grated fresh ginger
2 tsp curry powder
1 cup dried red lentils, well rinsed
1 TB canola or sesame oil
5-6 cups water
3" strip kombu seaweed (optional)
1 bunch or 1 package spinach, well washed, stems
removed, and sliced into shreds or frozen
spinach (optional)
low sodium soy sauce to taste

1. In a large pot, sauté onion, garlic, carrots, ginger, and curry powder in the canola oil. Cook for about 5 minutes over medium heat.

2. Add lentils, water, and kombu and let cook for 25 minutes. Remove and discard kombu.

3. Add spinach, if using, cover, and cook till spinach is wilted, 5-10 minutes more. If not using spinach, let the soup continue to cook till the lentils are creamy, about 5 minutes more.

4. Season with soy sauce to taste. Serve immediately.

Each serving (9.3 oz, with spinach) contains approximately 120 calories, 8.4 grams protein, 2 grams total fat, 0 mg cholesterol, 92 mg sodium.

MINESTRONE DI ABRUZZI
Serves 8

There are periods of time when I make this soup once a week. I used to call it "Beans and Greens," but since it became such a favorite, I personalized its name (Abruzzi is the region of my Italian ancestry). This meal-in-a-bowl provides protein from the beans, starch from the potatoes and carrots, and greens from the Swiss chard. If you want to freeze it, replace the potatoes with elbow macaroni as potatoes become spongy when defrosted.

³/₄ cup dried navy beans (small white)
¹/₄ cup dried garbanzo beans
8 cups water
6" strip kombu seaweed (optional)
1 bay leaf
1 russet potato, diced or 3 smaller red potatoes, cut into rounds
1 medium red onion, diced
4 cloves garlic, finely minced
2 carrots, cut into matchsticks or sliced into rounds
4 stalks celery sliced on diagonal
1 TB extra virgin olive oil
1 tsp dried oregano
1 tsp dried basil
¹/₂ tsp dried thyme
4 cups chopped Swiss chard, well washed
1 14¹/₂ oz can tomatoes, drained or 6 Romas, peeled, seeded, and diced
2 TB red miso
crushed red peppers to taste (optional)

1. Soak beans at least 8 hours in three times as much water. Or, quick-soak by placing beans in a saucepan, with enough water to cover plus 2". Bring to a boil,

turn off heat, and let sit, covered, for 1¹/₂ hours. Drain water.

2. Cook the soaked beans in the 8 cups of fresh water in an 8-quart Dutch oven. Add kombu and bay leaf. Cook for 1 hour. Remove kombu and discard. Cook for 30-60 minutes more, or until the beans are tender.

3. When the beans are done, add the potatoes to the pot.

4. Sauté the onion, garlic, carrots, and celery in the olive oil in a sauté pan. When the onion is transparent, add the herbs to the sauté pan and cook for 1 minute more.

5. Add the onion mixture to the soup pot. Add Swiss chard and tomatoes.

6. Cover and let chard wilt, about 10 minutes.

7. When chard is wilted, ladle out 1 cup of broth into a bowl. Stir in the miso, making sure it is well dissolved. Pour back into the pot, stir, and season with crushed red peppers, if using. Serve hot.

Each serving contains approximately 188 calories, 8.66 grams protein, 2.6 grams total fat, 0 mg cholesterol, 226 mg sodium.

FISH

PAN SEARED SALMON SERVED WITH JULIENNE CARROTS AND LEEKS PLUS TANGERINE JUICE
Serves 6

Slowly cooking the leeks and carrots gives this dish an ever-so-slight sweetness. The leeks, which are less dense than the carrots but cook for the same amount of time, actually carmelize while cooking. The tangerine juice adds a tart/sweet finish. The recipe is also visually appealing--a beautiful composition of pastels that looks dramatic served on a dark colored plate.

2 leeks
2 carrots
1 TB extra virgin olive oil
2 pounds salmon steaks
3 tangerines, cut in half, visible seeds removed

1. Cut away the root end and the dark green parts of the leeks and discard. Slice the leek in half lengthwise and clean out any dirt from between the layers. Cut each half lengthwise in strips to form matchsticks about 4"-5" in length. Set aside.

2. Scrub the carrots, and cut off the tips and ends. Cut in 4"-5" lengths. Cut lengthwise in half, then into thinner strips. If they are too thick to look like matchsticks, slice them down the center again.

3. Add the olive oil, leeks, and carrots in a single layer to a sauté pan. Cover and turn the heat to low. Cook for 15 minutes, turning and stirring occasionally.

4. Meanwhile, wash and pat dry the salmon steaks. Remove and discard the skin. Heat a large, heavy non-stick skillet. When a drop of water sizzles on the surface, add the salmon steaks and cover. Cook for 4 minutes on the first side. Turn and cook for 1 minute on high, reduce heat to medium, and cook for 1-3 minutes, depending on how you like your salmon done.

5. To serve, arrange the leeks and carrots on each plate. Top with a salmon steak, and place a tangerine half to the side for guests to squeeze over the fish and vegetables.

Each serving contains approximately 256 calories, 31 grams protein, 7.8 grams total fat, 78.6 mg cholesterol, 121 mg sodium.

ORZO AND SAUTÉED SHRIMP WITH CURRIED TARRAGON SAUCE *Serves 6*

This dish illustrates the ease that proper timing can bring to cooking. If orchestrated well, this dish is quite simple to put together. Just chop and mea-sure out ingredients before you start the fires blazing.

3 cups chicken broth or
water
1 cup orzo (rice-shaped
pasta)
24 large shrimp, shelled and de-veined
1 TB extra virgin olive oil
1 tsp dried tarragon
¹/₂ tsp curry powder
4 cloves garlic, finely minced
3 scallions, sliced into rounds
2 TB fresh lemon juice
¹/₄ cup plus 2 TB dry white wine
4 TB fresh parsley, finely minced
¹/₄ tsp salt or VegeSal
¹/₄ tsp black pepper

1. Bring the chicken broth or water to a boil, add the orzo, let it come to a boil again, cover, and turn the heat to low. Cook for 10 minutes, or until all liquid is absorbed and the orzo is tender

2. Meanwhile, butterfly the shelled and de-veined shrimp by cutting half-way through the curved out side. You now have three surfaces on which to cook the shrimp.

3. Add the olive oil, tarragon, and curry powder to a non-stick skillet large enough to hold all the shrimp without crowding. Cook over low heat for about 2 minutes.

4. Increase heat to high, add the garlic, scallions, and shrimp, cut sides down, and cook for 1 minute.

5. Reduce heat to medium. Turn the shrimp and cook for 30 seconds on each of the other sides.

6. Add the lemon juice and white wine, reduce heat to low, and simmer for about 1¹/₂ minutes.

7. Add the parsley, salt, and pepper. Stir to distribute evenly.

8. Spoon orzo onto dinner plates. Add shrimp and top with sauce. Serve immediately.

Each serving contains approximately 204 calories, 22.5 grams protein, 3.8 grams total fat, 174 mg cholesterol, 486 mg sodium.

SPINACH FETTUCINE WITH PARSLEY CAPER SAUCE AND PAN SEARED SEA BASS
Serves 6

The sauce in this dish is uncooked. It's tossed with pasta and then spooned onto seared fish. It is all quite effortless to make. You can substitute salmon or shrimp for the sea bass, and cook them in the same manner. For a prettier presentation, use white fettucine noodles instead of the green spinach ones called for in the recipe.

SAUCE
   3 TB Olio Santo (see page 10) or extra virgin olive oil
   3 TB fresh lemon juice
   2 TB capers, rinsed
   ³/₄ tsp dried marjoram
   to taste black pepper
   ¹/₄ cup minced fresh parsley

FISH
   2 pounds fresh sea bass fillets

PASTA
   12 oz dried spinach fettucine noodles

1. Bring a large pot of water to a boil for the pasta.

2. Meanwhile, combine all the ingredients for the sauce in the bowl you'll toss the pasta in. Stir, then take out 2 TB of the sauce and set aside.

3. Wash the sea bass and pat dry.

4. Spray a large, heavy non-stick skillet with a little vegetable oil spray and heat the pan to high. When the pasta water is at a rolling boil, add the fettucine noodles, cover, and bring it back to a boil. Remove lid when it's boiling again.

5. As soon as a drop of water sizzles on the surface of the non-stick skillet, add the fish and cover immediately. Cook for 3 minutes on the first side. Turn and cook for 1 minute on high, reduce heat to medium, and cook for 1-3 more minutes, depending on how rare you like your fish.

6. When the pasta is done, drain it, and turn it out into the bowl with the sauce. Toss well.

7. Divide pasta among 6 plates. Top with the sea bass and 1 or 2 tsp of the reserved sauce. Serve immediately.

Each serving contains approximately 345 calories, 26 grams protein, 15 grams total fat, 81 mg cholesterol, 104 mg sodium.

POULTRY

CHICKEN PROVENÇAL WITH FORTY CLOVES OF SWEET GARLIC
Serves 8

You'll notice that the boneless, skinless, chicken breasts called for in this recipe are cooked for only 10 minutes. They will be perfectly done--moist and tender, so don't be tempted to cook them longer. Remember, they are not protected against drying out with a layer of skin, nor are they fortified with a structure of bones to lend flavor if they are in the oven for too long. This recipe is a re-make of a standard. With holiday shopping and all the demands of the season, this quick version is great to have. It's also much lower in fat than the traditional. Serve with a piece of crusty bread and a mixed green salad.

40 whole cloves of garlic, with their paper skins left on
¹/₂ cup dry white wine
8 skinless, boneless chicken breasts
¹/₂ cup flour (semolina, whole wheat pastry, millet,
*   rice, or other flour of choice)*
1 TB extra virgin olive oil
2 tsp Herbes de Provence or dried basil
1 bay leaf
³/₄ cup chicken broth
¹/₄ cup chopped fresh parsley

1. Add the unpeeled cloves of garlic to the white wine. Microwave for 4 minutes. (Alternately, simmer the wine and garlic together in a small saucepan for 15 minutes.)

2. Wash and pat dry chicken breasts. Dredge them in the flour and set aside.

3. Add the olive oil to a sauté pan large enough to hold all of the chicken breasts in a single layer.

4. Heat the oil and add the chicken breasts so they sizzle when added. Cook on the first side for 3 minutes. Turn and cook for 2 minutes on the other side. They should be lightly browned. Remove from pan and set aside.

5. Add the wine and garlic cloves to the sauté pan. Increase heat to high. Add the Herbes de Provence or dried basil and the bay leaf. Add the chicken breasts and turn so the herbs are evenly distributed. Cook for about 1 minute on high.

6. Add the chicken broth, bring to a boil, reduce heat, and simmer, covered, for 5 minutes.

7. Just before serving, sprinkle the parsley over the chicken breasts. Serve 1 piece of chicken plus 5 cloves of garlic per person. Squeeze the cloves of garlic with your fingers onto the chicken or piece of bread.

Each serving contains approximately 200 calories, 29 grams protein, 3.4 grams total fat, 73 mg cholesterol, 118 mg sodium.

PEANUT GLAZED CHICKEN BREASTS *Serves 6*

A piquant yet sweet peanut sauce carmelizes the chicken while baking.

---

4 shallots, finely minced
2 cloves garlic, finely minced
1 TB grated fresh ginger
¹/₂ tsp crushed red peppers
1 TB low sodium soy sauce
4 TB peanut butter
1 TB rice vinegar
4-6 TB sake or dry white wine or water
2 TB honey
6 half (2¹/₂ pounds) chicken breasts with bones, skinless

1. Preheat oven to 425°F (or Broil).

2. Sauté shallots, garlic, ginger, and crushed red peppers in the soy sauce for about 5 minutes.

3. Stir in the peanut butter, rice vinegar, sake, and honey. Cook over low heat for 5 minutes.

4. Coat chicken breasts with the sauce. Place on broiler pan (or on a wire rack set over a baking dish). Bake for 30 minutes. Cover with foil, if needed, and bake for 10 minutes more. (Or, broil for a total of 20-25 minutes. Check after 15 minutes and cover with foil if the sauce is becoming too brown.)

Each serving contains approximately 307 calories, 47 grams total protein, 7.9 grams total fat, 109 mg cholesterol, 281 mg sodium.

BAKED CHICKEN BREASTS VINAIGRETTE

Serves 4

This dish takes very little time to prepare. Marinate the chicken in the refrigerator before you go to work in the morning. When you get home, you'll have just enough time to toss together a simple salad and simmer some rice to accompany the chicken breasts.

1 clove garlic, finely minced
1 TB Dijon-style mustard
1 tsp extra virgin olive oil
¼ cup dry white wine
4 half skinless, boneless chicken breasts
2 pieces whole grain bread or bread of choice

1. Combine garlic, mustard, olive oil, and wine to make the marinade.

2. Wash and pat dry the chicken breasts. Place in a baking dish large enough to hold the chicken breasts in a single layer. Pour marinade over, turning once, and let chicken marinate for at least 1 hour, or overnight.

3. Preheat oven to 325°F.

4. Place bread in a food processor or blender and process to make crumbs.

5. Place the bread crumbs on a dinner plate. Dredge the marinated chicken breasts in the bread crumbs, coating on both sides. Discard marinade.

6. Place chicken in a lightly oiled baking dish or on the broiler rack and bake for 20-25 minutes. Serve immediately.

Each serving contains approximately 206 calories, 29.2 grams protein, 3.5 grams total fat, 68 mg cholesterol, 237 mg sodium.

CHICKEN BREAST, PARSNIP, RUTABAGA STEW WITH SAGE DUMPLINGS

Serves 6-8

This is comfort food at its best--a wholesome, simmering pot of chicken and vegetables with plump, aromatic biscuits bobbing in the stew.

STEW

5 cups chicken broth or Homemade Chicken Stock
(see page 44)
1 bay leaf
2 cloves garlic, finely minced
1 yellow onion, diced
2 stalks celery, diced
2 carrots, sliced into ½" thick rounds
2 parsnips, sliced into ½" thick rounds
1 rutabaga, peeled and diced
1/2 tsp salt or VegeSal
3½-4 pounds (about 6-8 half) chicken breasts, with
bones, skinless
½ bunch (about 1½ cups) kale or mustard greens or
Swiss chard (optional)
as needed paprika

DUMPLINGS

¾ cup whole wheat pastry flour or ¾ cups plus 1 TB
unbleached flour
1 tsp baking powder
1 tsp fresh sage or ¼ tsp dried sage
¼ tsp salt or VegeSal
¼ tsp black pepper
1 TB extra virgin olive oil
⅓ cup low-fat milk or soy milk or evaporated skim
milk

1. Place all the ingredients for the stew except the chicken and kale in an 8-quart Dutch oven and bring to a boil. When boiling, add the chicken, then reduce heat to low. Cook, covered, for 15 minutes.

2. Meanwhile, wash the kale and chop into bite-sized pieces. After 15 minutes, add the kale and cook, covered, for 15 minutes more.

3. To make the dumplings, place the flour, baking powder, sage, salt, and pepper in one bowl. Pour milk and oil into another bowl.

4. When the kale is wilted, pour the milk and oil mixture into the bowl of dry ingredients. Stir only enough to moisten the dry ingredients.

5. Using a teaspoon, spoon out 8 dumplings. Roll them in your palms into balls and add them to the pot. Try to get them into the broth and not on top of the chicken breast--they need to cook in the liquid. Cook, uncovered, for 10 minutes, then cover and cook for 5 minutes more. Serve in soup bowls, dishing out 1 breast, 1 dumpling, vegetables, and about $^{1}/_{2}$ cup of broth per serving. Sprinkle paprika on the chicken breasts for color.

Each serving contains approximately 228 calories, 31.5 grams protein, 4 grams total fat, 68.7 mg cholesterol, 542 mg sodium.

VEGETABLE MAIN DISHES

HOLIDAY LASAGNE   *Serves 8*

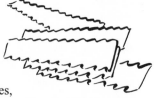

Every Christmas Eve our table is graced by at least one tray of lasagne. It pleases many palates, and can be accompanied by a variety of pasta dishes, fish entrées, salads, and vegetables. Each year the feast is a little different, yet reassuringly anchored by the presence of this light Holiday Lasagne. Note: It is not necessary to pre-cook the lasagne noodles before assembling. They will cook during baking.

1 recipe Liza's Spaghetti Sauce (see recipe below)
2 bunches spinach or Swiss chard, well washed or 2 packages frozen spinach
4 cloves garlic, finely minced
1 yellow onion, diced
1 TB extra virgin olive oil
pinch nutmeg
1 tsp grated lemon peel
2 cups fat-free or low fat ricotta cheese or low fat cottage cheese
$^{1}/_{2}$ cup freshly grated Parmesan cheese
8 ozs part-skim milk mozzarella cheese, shredded
8-12 lasagne noodles or Fresh Lasagne Noodles (see page 55)

1. Preheat oven to 350ºF. Make Liza's Spaghetti Sauce as directed below, or defrost a batch from the freezer. Bring sauce to a boil in a 3-4 quart saucepan, reduce heat to low, and simmer until needed.

2. Remove the stems and discolored leaves from the spinach or Swiss chard and discard. Chop into bite-size pieces.

3. In a large sauté pan, saute the garlic and onion in the olive oil for 5 minutes, or until the onion is transparent.

4. Add nutmeg, lemon peel, and spinach or Swiss chard. Cover and cook till the spinach is wilted, about 5 minutes.

5. Add the spinach mixture to a bowl. Stir in the ricotta or cottage cheese and the Parmesan cheese. Stir well to mix.

6. To assemble the lasagne, spoon a thin layer of Liza's Spaghetti Sauce in the bottom of a 9" x 13" baking dish. Cover this with enough lasagne noodles to cover the entire bottom of the pan. Cut noodles to size, if necessary.

7. Spread more sauce over the noodles, add half of the mozzarella cheese, more lasagne noodles, half of the spinach/cheese mixture, more lasagne noodles, sauce, the rest of the mozzarella cheese, lasagne noodles, and the remaining spinach/cheese mixture. Finish with the sauce and a sprinkling of Parmesan cheese.

8. Bake, covered with foil, for 25 minutes, then uncover and bake for 15 minutes more, or until bubbly. Let cool a bit, then cut into pieces and serve.

Each serving (using 2% cottage cheese) contains approximately 382 calories, 24.9 grams protein, 13.3 grams total fat, 23.7 mg cholesterol, 653 mg sodium.

LIZA'S SPAGHETTI SAUCE
Makes about 7 cups

When I was in kindergarten, I met Cristy. Every Friday evening throughout grammar school, I would spend the night at her house. It was understood that her mom would make spaghetti for dinner. I adored her sauce! It must have irritated my Italian mother to no end, but mom's sauce just couldn't compete with Cristy's Jewish mom's sauce! A few years ago I asked Cristy for the recipe. This is my version of Liza's incredible, versatile, tasty, and easy spaghetti sauce. I call for it in the Holiday Lasagne, a couple of pizza recipes, the Light Lasagne Rolls and Spaghetti and Meatballs. It freezes well, so double up when you make it.

5 cloves garlic, finely minced
2 medium yellow onions, diced
2 TB extra virgin olive oil
2 bay leaves
2 tsp dried oregano
1 tsp dried basil
4 TB dry red wine

4 TB chopped fresh parsley (optional)
2 28-oz cans crushed tomatoes with added purée

If you can't find crushed tomatoes with added purée, use 1 28-oz can whole tomatoes, drained of liquid and re-filled with purée to the top (approximately ¹/₂ of a 16-oz can of tomato purée).

1. In a 4-quart saucepan, sauté garlic and onions in olive oil for 5 minutes, or until onions are transparent.

2. Add all other ingredients. Bring to a boil, then reduce heat to low, and simmer for at least 45 minutes or preferably 2-3 hours to produce the tastiest, thickest sauce.

Each cup contains approximately 104 calories, 2.7 grams protein, 4.3 grams total fat, 0 mg cholesterol, 212 mg sodium.

PIZZA DOUGH
Serves 12

I've given you many options in this recipe. You can choose to use 2 or 4 TB of oil. Four tablespoons makes a chewier crust, but it also has twice as much fat. You can select extra virgin olive oil or the flavorful Olio Santo (see page 10). I suggest you use the Olio Santo only for pizzas with lightly flavored toppings so you can appreciate its contribution to the dough.

Should you use all unbleached flour or semolina flour? Half of each? Some whole wheat pastry flour? The semolina is chewier; the unbleached flour is lighter; the whole wheat pastry adds a nutty taste, as well as the bran and germ of the whole grain. All are good, it just depends on personal preference and your choice of light or heavier toppings. For a crispier crust, roll the dough out thinner and bake it a little longer.

1 package yeast
1 1/8 cups water
1 tsp honey or maple syrup or sugar
2-4 TB extra virgin olive oil or Olio Santo (see page 10)
3 cups unbleached flour or 1¹/₂ cups unbleached flour and 1¹/₂ cups semolina flour or 3 cups semolina flour or 1¹/₂ cups unbleached flour and 1¹/₄ cups whole wheat pastry flour
about ¹/₄ cup additional flour for kneading, as needed

1. Heat water to bath water temperature (105°-115° F.) Add yeast and sweetener and let sit for 5 minutes or till the yeast begins to foam. If it hasn't foamed within 5 minutes, that means your yeast is no good. Discard and begin again with a fresh package.

2. Place the flour in a medium-size bowl. Add oil and mix well so that the oil is distributed throughout the flour, and stir until the dough comes together into a ball.

3. When the yeast has foamed, add it to the flour. Mix well, then turn out onto a lightly floured surface. Dust hands with flour and knead for 5 minutes. To knead, first gather the dough into one lump. Then fold it over in half towards you. Lightly press down on the dough with the heels of your hands as you smear the seam of the fold back into the dough. Turn it a quarter and repeat. While kneading, add a little extra flour to the work surface so the dough does not stick. Knead till dough is smooth, elastic, and shiny.

4. Shape the dough into a ball and transfer to a lightly oiled bowl. Turn to coat the dough with oil on all sides.

5. Cover with plastic wrap or a damp towel and let rise in a draft-free place till it doubles in size, 45-60 minutes. You know the dough has risen enough when the indentation left by your finger in the dough doesn't rise back up at you.

If you can't bake the pizza dough within 2 hours after rising, punch the dough down again, re-oil the bowl to coat once more, cover the bowl lightly with plastic wrap, and refrigerate. The dough can be punched down a total of 4 times and kept refrigerated up to 36 hours before the yeast is exhausted and the dough is unusable. Let chilled dough come to room temperature before forming, topping, and baking.

If you wish to freeze the dough for future use, wrap the pieces tightly in plastic wrap, or seal in an airtight container, and freeze up to 4 months. Before using, thaw in refrigerator for 1 or 2 days or for a few hours at room temperature.

6. Punch down the dough on a lightly floured work surface and knead just enough to bring dough into a ball. Divide into 2, 4, 8 or 16 pieces to make either 2 15" pizzas, 4 8" pizzas, 8 4" pizzas, or 16 2" pizzettes.

7. Top as per instructions on individual pizza recipe.

8. For the 15" pizzas, roll out, then fit into a lightly oiled pizza pan. For all other size pizzas, form on work surface, transfer to lightly oiled cookie sheets, top, and bake. I suggest preheating the oven with a dark cookie sheet in the lowest rack in your oven. Put cookie sheet with pizzas on it on the rack above that. The dark cookie sheet absorbs and reflects the heat, somewhat like a pizza stone. If you have a pizza stone (the best way to bake pizzas), place it in the oven before preheating. Sprinkle cornmeal on the pizza stone to prevent pizzas from sticking. Form pizzas on the work surface and transfer to the pizza stone using a pizza peel.

9. Bake for 12-18 minutes. (See specific recipes for exact times.) If using a pizza stone, use the pizza peel to retrieve the pizza from the oven. Serve immediately.

Each serving (assumes dough is made with 3 TB olive oil, 2 cups unbleached flour, and 1 cup whole wheat pastry flour) contains 153 calories, 4 grams protein, 3.8 grams total fat, 0 mg cholesterol, 2 mg sodium.

PEPPERONCINI AND BLACK OLIVE PIZZA   `Serves 12`

Unbelievably flavorful! If you like a real bite to your pizza, substitute marinated jalapeños for the pepperoncinis.

---

1 recipe Pizza Dough (see previous recipe)
1/2 recipe Liza's Spaghetti Sauce (see page 19)
12 pepperoncinis, stems discarded, sliced into rounds
15-20 kalamata black olives, pitted, rinsed, and sliced
1 yellow onion, sliced into rounds
12 ozs part-skim milk mozzarella cheese, shredded

1. Make Pizza Dough (see previous recipe) and let rise.

2. Make Liza's Spaghetti Sauce (see page 19) or, defrost a batch and bring to a boil, then keep warm on stove.

3. Preheat oven to 500° F. Note instructions in Pizza Dough recipe about using cookie sheets or a pizza stone.

4. When the dough has risen, punch it down, form it into a ball, and divide the dough into 2, 4, 8, or 16 equal pieces.

5. Form into the size pizzas you want using a rolling pin. Spoon on the Spaghetti Sauce and spread it evenly over the surface of the pizza, leaving a margin around the outer edge with no sauce.

6. Add pepperoncinis, olives, and onion rounds. Sprinkle with shredded mozzarella cheese.

7. Bake for 12-15 minutes, or until bubbling.

Each serving (assuming 15" pizzas, 6 slices each, 12 7-oz servings) contains approximately 284 calories, 12.9 grams protein, 11.4 grams total fat, 15 mg cholesterol, 287 mg sodium.

CHICKEN, SHIITAKE MUSHROOMS, AND SUN-DRIED TOMATO PIZZA
Serves 12

I am always asked if my husband ever cooks. He actually does-- occasionally. Here is one of his best recipes. It's delicious!

---

1 recipe Pizza Dough (see page 19)
18-20 sun-dried tomatoes
¹/₄ cup sherry
boiling water as needed
4 half skinless, boneless chicken breasts
1 red onion, sliced into rounds
6-8 ounces (about 15) shiitake mushrooms, stems removed, sliced
1 TB extra virgin olive oil
¹/₄ tsp salt or VegeSal
12 ounces part-skim milk mozzarella cheese, shredded

1. Make Pizza Dough (see page 19) and let rise

2. Preheat oven to Broil.

3. Place the sun-dried tomatoes in a bowl. Pour in the sherry. Pour in enough boiling water to just cover the tomatoes. Let soak for 15-20 minutes, or until the tomatoes are soft.

4. Broil chicken breasts for 8 minutes. Remove from oven, let cool, then slice into strips. Reduce heat of oven to 500° F. Note instructions in Pizza Dough recipe about using cookie sheets or pizza stone.

5. Meanwhile, sauté the onions and shiitake mushrooms in olive oil till the onions are soft. If you need more liquid, add sherry.

6. When the sun-dried tomatoes are soft, purée them and the soaking liquid in a food processor or blender. Add salt to the purée.

7. When the dough has risen, punch it down, form it into a ball, and divide the dough into 2, 4, 8, or 16 equal pieces.

8. Form into the size pizzas you want using a rolling pin. Spoon on the sun-dried tomato puree and spread it evenly over the surface of the pizza, leaving a margin around the outer edge with no purée.

9. Arrange chicken strips evenly over surface of pizzas. Add mushroom/onion mixture evenly over surface of pizzas. Sprinkle with shredded mozzarella cheese.

10. Bake for 18 minutes, or till bubbling.

Each serving (assuming 2 15" pizzas, 6 slices each, 12 7 oz servings) contains approximately 327 calories, 21.7 grams protein, 10.8 grams total fat, 39 mg cholesterol, 229 mg sodium.

PASTAS

Pasta Marsala Serves 4

This is an excellent example of what cooking from a well-stocked pantry can be—easy, spontaneous, and delicious! No more after-theater grilled cheese sandwiches once you've tasted this!

³/₄ cup marsala wine
6-8 sun-dried tomatoes
1 tsp grated lemon peel
1 TB capers, rinsed
8 oz dried linguine, spaghetti, or angel hair pasta
2 TB extra virgin olive oil or Olio Santo (see page 10)
2 TB grated fresh Parmigano Reggiano

1. Heat marsala in saucepan or microwave until boiling.

2. Add sun-dried tomatoes and let sit for 30 minutes.

3. After the 30 minutes, pour the liquid from the soaking sun-dried tomatoes into a skillet and set aside. Add the garlic, lemon peel, and capers. Cook over medium high heat until liquid is reduced by one-third. Watch as this will happen quickly.

4. Slice sun-dried tomatoes and add to skillet.

5. Meanwhile, bring a large pot of water to a boil. Cook pasta in the boiling water for 10 minutes, or until al dente. Drain, and transfer to a serving bowl.

6. Toss pasta with olive oil or Olio Santo, then add the sun-dried tomato mixture and toss again. Serve with grated Reggiano.

Each serving contains approximately 330 calories, 11.4 grams protein, 8.6 grams total fat, 6 mg cholesterol, 141 mg sodium.

Healthy Fettucine Alfredo with Peas Serves 4

I enjoy this version of Fettucine Alfredo as a main dish and as a side dish to a fish or chicken entrée. It's not as heavy as the usual version, yet it's still creamy and rich. I use baby peas to break up the monotony of a single smooth texture. If you want to make this during the spring, snow peas cut in half lengthwise are great, too.

8 oz fettucine noodles
2 TB unsalted butter
¹/₂ cup evaporated skim milk
¹/₂ cup frozen baby peas
¹/₄ cup freshly grated Parmesan cheese

1. Bring a large pot of water to a boil. Cook pasta in the boiling water for 10 minutes, or until al dente.

2. Meanwhile, melt butter in a large sauté pan. Add evaporated skimmed milk and cook until thickened slightly, about 3 minutes.

3. Cook the peas in a small sauce pan or put the peas in a small collander and immerse them in the pasta water for 2-3 minutes while the pasta is cooking.

4. When the pasta is done, drain it and add it to the butter/milk mixture in the sauté pan. Toss. Sprinkle with Parmesan cheese, add the peas, and toss again. Serve immediately.

Each serving contains approximately 450 calories per serving, 9.8 grams protein, 7.7 grams total fat, 24 mg cholesterol, 202 mg sodium.

Spaghetti and Turkey Meatballs Serves 12

Can't you just visualize a steaming hot platter of spaghetti, thick red sauce, and a mountain of meatballs? And the aroma!

SAUCE

1 recipe Liza's Spaghetti Sauce (see page 19)

TURKEY MEATBALLS

3 TB dry red wine
3 TB boiling water
6 sun-dried tomatoes
¹/₄ medium yellow onion
2 cloves garlic
1 egg white
1¹/₂ TB balsamic vinegar
1¹/₂ pounds ground turkey
¹/₄ tsp salt or VegeSal

PASTA

1 pound dried spaghetti

1. Make Liza's Spaghetti Sauce and let simmer. Or, defrost a batch, bring to a boil, then let simmer.

2. For the turkey meatballs, pour the red wine into a medium-size mixing bowl. Pour in the hot water and add the sun-dried tomatoes. Let soak for 15-20 minutes.

3. Meanwhile, place the onion and garlic in a food processor or blender. Process until minced.

4. When the sun-dried tomatoes are soft, add them and half the soaking liquid to the mixture in the food processor. Process until the tomatoes are broken up and puréed.

5. Add the egg white and balsamic vinegar. Process until well mixed.

6. Place ground turkey in a large mixing bowl. Stir in the sun-dried tomato mixture. Add the salt. Mix again.

7. Form 24 meatballs. Add meatballs to a large non-stick skillet—don't crowd them. Cook them until they are done, about 15 minutes, turning so that all sides are lightly browned.

8. Meanwhile, bring a large pot of water to a boil. Cook pasta in boiling water for 10 minutes, or until al dente. Drain, and transfer to a serving platter or pasta bowl.

9. Toss with Liza's Spaghetti Sauce. Add the meatballs, then add more sauce, if needed. Serve immediately.

Each serving contains approximately 337 calories, 21 grams protein, 10 grams total fat, 44 mg cholesterol, 275 mg sodium.

VEGETABLE SIDE DISHES

HERBED TOMATOES, SWISS CHARD, AND POTATOES PARMIGIANA   *Serves 8*

Swiss chard is available all year round, and is especially appreciated in winter when other fresh greens are hard to come by.

³/₄ pound (1-2) potatoes
1 TB extra virgin olive oil
¹/₂ tsp crushed red peppers
4 cloves garlic, finely minced
¹/₂ tsp dried oregano
1 28-oz can whole Italian plum tomatoes
2 pounds Swiss chard, red or white
2-4 TB freshly grated Parmigiano Reggiano

1. Scrub potatoes and cut them into 1" cubes (leave skins on). Place in a steamer basket and steam for about 15-20 minutes, or until tender.

2. Add garlic, crushed red peppers, and olive oil to a large sauté pan and cook over low heat for 10 minutes. Do not turn the heat up to high.

3. Add oregano and canned tomatoes with liquid, breaking the tomatoes apart with a wooden spoon or your fingers as you go. Cook over medium-high heat until thickened, about 10 minutes.

4. Meanwhile, wash Swiss chard well. Cut off the main stems and discard. Chop the leaves into bite-size pieces.

5. Add chard and potatoes to the thickened tomato sauce. Cover and simmer for 10 minutes, stirring occasionally.

6. Right before serving, grate the cheese over the vegetables. Cover so the cheese will melt. Serve immediately.

Each serving (using 3 TB Reggiano total) contains approximately 4.8 grams protein, 2.8 grams total fat, 1.5 mg cholesterol, 442 mg sodium.

WHOLE GRAIN AND LENTIL "STUFFING" Serves 12

This stuffing offers a crunchy texture from the toasted pine nuts and whole grain croutons, and abundant flavor from the combinations of herbs and vegetables. This is a great prepare-ahead dish: early in the day you can make the croutons, toast the pine nuts, and cook the lentils. You can also chop the vegetables, and cover and refrigerate them until you're ready to put the casserole together.

---

5 pieces whole grain bread
¹/₄ cups pine nuts
¹/₂ cup raw lentils
1¹/₄ cups water
3" strip kombu seaweed (optional)
2 TB extra virgin olive oil
4 TB dry sherry
8 cloves garlic, finely minced
2 medium yellow onions, diced
4 stalks celery, diced
24 (about ¹/₂ pound) mushrooms, coarsely chopped
¹/₄ tsp dried sage
¹/₂ tsp dried marjoram
¹/₂ tsp dried basil
¹/₂ tsp dried summery savory
¹/₂ tsp celery seed
black pepper to taste
1 tsp grated lemon peel
1 cup chopped fresh parsley
1¹/₂ bunches spinach, cleaned and chopped
2-8 TB additional water, as needed
low sodium soy sauce to taste

1. Preheat oven to 200° F. Make croutons from the 5 pieces of bread. This will take up to 1 hour and can be done days in advance. Or, bring a batch of frozen croutons to room temperature—you'll need about 3 cups. Set aside. Increase the oven temperature to 325° F.

2. Toast pine nuts in the oven 10-12 minutes, or until light golden in color. Set aside.

3. Cook the lentils and kombu in 1¹/₄ cups water until done, about 45 minutes. Set aside.

4. Place olive oil, sherry, garlic, onion, celery, and mushrooms in a large sauté pan. Cook over medium-low heat for 10 minutes, being careful to preserve the juices the mushrooms will give up by keeping the heat low enough.

5. Add all dried seasonings and cook for 1 minute.

6. Add spinach and cover pan to wilt the spinach leaves, about 5-10 minutes.

7. Increase heat of oven to 375° F.

8. Add lemon peel, parsley, toasted pine nuts, croutons, lentils, and water, if needed. Stir well to mix. Taste and add soy sauce, if needed.

9. Turn out mixture into a covered casserole dish and bake for 20 minutes.

Each serving contains approximately 166 calories, 8.2 grams protein, 4.9 grams total fat, 0 mg cholesterol, 117 mg sodium.

ROGER COLE'S YUMMY YAMS Serves 8

This very simple recipe brightens up the naturally sweet flavor of yams and adds crunch to their smooth texture.

---

4 large (2 pounds) yams
¹/₂ cup walnuts, chopped
2 tsp grated fresh ginger

1. Preheat oven to 425° F. Bake yams until well done, about 60-75 minutes. They will drip, so place a pan with water in the oven below the yams for easier clean up.

2. Let the yams cool enough to handle, then scrape the flesh away from the skin into a bowl.

3. Add the walnuts and fresh ginger and mix well. Serve immediately.

Each serving contains approximately 122 calories, 2.7 grams protein, 4.1 grams total fat, 0 mg cholesterol, 6 mg sodium.

RICE AND STUFFED MUSHROOMS
Serves 6

Such little effort, and such a beautiful side dish!

1 cup raw brown rice, short or long grain
2 cups water
1 bay leaf
12 medium to large mushrooms
2 cloves garlic, finely minced
1/2 small red onion, chopped
1 TB extra virgin olive oil
1/4 cup dry white wine

1. Bring water to a rapid boil. Add rice and bay leaf, cover, and reduce heat to low. Cook for 30-35 minutes, or until the water is absorbed and the grains are tender.

2. Meanwhile, clean mushrooms with a wet paper towel. Snap out their stems and chop. Set mushroom caps aside.

3. Sauté garlic, red onion, and chopped mushroom stems in the olive oil on low heat. Cook until onions are transparent, about 10-15 minutes.

4. Add 2 TB of the white wine and cook until reduced to 1 TB.

5. Transfer one-quarter of the cooked rice to a mixing bowl. Add garlic mixture and all the liquid. Mix together well.

6. Spoon rice and garlic into the mushroom caps.

7. Add the remaining 2 TB wine to the sauté pan, then add filled mushroom caps, and cover. Simmer for 10-15 minutes.

8. Spoon the rice onto a platter. Using a slotted spoon, transfer the stuffed mushrooms to the platter. Drizzle any liquid left in the pan onto the rice. Serve immediately.

Each serving contains approximately 153 calories, 3.3 grams protein, 3 grams total fat, 0 mg cholesterol, 8 mg sodium.

SUBTLE PILAF
Serves 6

Kombu seaweed gives this pilaf an ocean fresh flavor. It's very faint—you can't quite put your finger on what it is, but it's very appealing. The pine nuts and parsley add to the fresh yet subtle flavor.

2 dried shiitake mushrooms or 4 fresh shiitake mushrooms
6" strip kombu seaweed
2 cups water
1 cup raw brown rice, short or long grain
1/4 cup pine nuts
1/4 cup fresh parsley, minced

1. Preheat oven to 325° F.

2. Place dried shiitake mushrooms, kombu, and water in a saucepan. Bring to a boil, reduce heat to low, and simmer for 15 minutes.

3. Remove shiitake mushrooms and let cool a bit so you can handle them. Cut off and discard the stems. Slice up the mushroom caps very thinly and add them back to the pot.

4. Pour in the rice, return water to a boil, lower heat, and cook, covered, for 30-35 minutes.

5. Meanwhile, toast the pine nuts in the oven for 10 minutes, or until lightly golden.

6. When rice is done, remove and discard kombu. Add pine nuts and parsley to the rice. Stir to mix well and serve immediately.

Each serving contains approximately 129 calories, 4.8 grams protein, 5.4 grams total fat, 0 mg cholesterol, 9 mg sodium.

SWEETS

SUGAR PUMPKIN AND GINGERSNAP TARTLETS
Serves 8-12

If you've ever wondered why pumpkin pies made with canned pumpkin are better than those made from scratch, it's because pumpkins are bred for different purposes. Canned pumpkin is made from sugar pumpkins and is as sweet as the name implies. A carving pumpkin is bred for its large size, not its flavor. Buy the smaller but tastier sugar pumpkin for these tartlets, or use canned—there's absolutely nothing else in the can but pumpkin!

PIE FILLING
2 cups (about a 3 pound pumpkin) baked sugar
*   pumpkin or 1 16-oz can pumpkin*
$1/2$ cup maple syrup
1 cup evaporated skim milk
2 egg whites
1 tsp ground cinnamon
$1/4$ tsp ground cloves
$1/4$ tsp ground ginger
$1/2$ tsp salt (optional)

CRUST
enough ginger snap cookies to equal $2^1/4$ cups crumbs
3 TB maple syrup
vegetable spray as needed

1. Preheat the oven to 350° F.

2. To bake a sugar pumpkin, poke holes all over with a sharp knife and place the whole pumpkin in the oven. Bake for 60-90 minutes or until very tender.

3. When done, let cool, then cut in half. Using a grapefruit spoon, remove and discard the seeds and strings. Scrape away 2 cups of the flesh and set aside. Or, use a 16-oz can of pumpkin.

> If you or your kids are allergic to dairy products, make these tartlets using 1 10.5-oz box of silken tofu, firm, and 1 tsp arrowroot instead of the evaporated skim milk and egg whites. Just purée it all and continue with Step 6.

4. To make the crust, process the ginger snap cookies to a powder in a food processor or blender. Add the maple syrup and process.

5. Lightly oil 8 4³/₄ tart pans with vegetable spray. Press about ¹/₄ cup of the cookie mixture into each tart pan. Press from the center to the edges and up the fluted sides. Place all the tart pans on a cookie sheet and bake for 15 minutes. Remove from oven and set aside to cool a bit. Increase oven temperature to 425° F.

6. Meanwhile, place the filling ingredients in a clean food processor or blender. Purée very well.

7. Spoon the filling into the pre-baked ginger snap crusts. Smooth out the tops and bake for 15 minutes. Reduce heat to 350° F and bake for 20 minutes more.

Makes 8 tartlets or 1 11" tart.

> If using an 11" tart pan, press all the cookie mixture into the pan. Pre-bake the crust at 350° F for 20-25 minutes. Increase heat to 425° F and bake the filled pie for 15 minutes, then reduce heat to 350° F and bake for 40-45 more minutes.

Each tartlet contains approximately 279 calories, 6.5 grams protein, 5 grams total fat, 3.8 mg cholesterol, 426 mg sodium.

Each slice of an 11" tart (12 slices) contains approximately 186 calories, 4.3 grams protein, 0.5 grams total fat, 2.6 mg cholesterol, 284 mg sodium.

APPLE STRUDEL   **Makes 12 slices**

I think the most difficult part about this dessert is slicing it up to serve without making a complete mess of the dinner table! For a few variations, you might want to plump the raisins in hot amaretto liqueur instead of water, and use toasted pecans instead of walnuts.

$^1/_2$ cup walnuts
$^1/_2$ cup raisins
$1^1/_2$ pounds apples, cored, peeled, and sliced to less
    than $^1/_8$ inch thick
$^1/_2$-$^3/_4$ cups brown sugar
$^3/_4$ tsp ground cinnamon
$^1/_8$ tsp ground cardamon (optional)
$^1/_4$ tsp ground ginger
10 sheets (14" x 18" each) phyllo dough
$1^1/_2$ cups (about 15 pairs of cookies) amaretti cookie
    crumbs
vegetable oil spray as needed

1. The day before you want to make this strudel, take the phyllo dough out of the freezer and place it in the refrigerator overnight. On the day, remove it from the refrigerator and leave it at room temperature for 1 hour. Or, take the dough straight from the freezer and leave it at room temperature for 3-4 hours. Do not unwrap the dough until you are ready to use it.

2. Preheat oven to 325° F.

3. Toast the walnuts in the oven for 12 minutes. Remove from oven and cool. Increase oven temperature to 375° F.

4. Pour enough hot water over the raisins to cover them. Let sit for 15 minutes to plump, then drain them well.

5. Chop the walnuts, then combine them in a large mixing bowl with the apple slices, sugar, raisins, and spices. Toss well to mix. Set aside.

6. Remove 10 sheets of phyllo from the package. Rewrap phyllo dough well and refrigerate for use within 7 days.

7. Cover your work surface with wax paper or parchment paper (make a squre about 20" x 20"). (This step is optional, but it does make the strudel easier to roll.)

8. Place 1 sheet of phyllo on top of the paper. Lightly spray it with a little vegetable spray. Sprinkle on $^1/_{10}$th of the cookie crumbs.

9. Place a second sheet of phyllo on the paper, overlapping the first sheet of phyllo, to create a 16" x 18" rectangle. Spray again and sprinkle on some more cookie crumbs.

For the brown sugar you can substitute the same amount of date sugar, which can be found at natural foods stores, farmer's markets, and gourmet stores. See the Glossary to Ingredients on page 139 for more information on date sugar.

10. Continue layering the strudel in the same way, using the remaining 8 sheets of phyllo. End with a layer of phyllo sprayed with oil.

11. Spoon the apple mixture along the length of the phyllo dough, leaving a 3" margin along the top edge and 2" margins at the sides.

12. Fold the long edge of the phyllo over the apple mixture and carefully roll up the phyllo jelly roll-fashion, tucking in the short sides as you roll. Press firmly but gently as you roll it up.

13. Lightly spray the tops and the sides of the roll with oil so that it will brown in the oven.

14. Place the strudel, seam side down, on an ungreased cookie sheet. Bake for 30-35 minutes.

15. Let cool for 20 minutes before slicing.

Each slice contains approximately 278 calories, 4.1 grams protein, 3.7 grams total fat, 1.7 mg cholesterol, 219 mg sodium.

HOT CHOCOLATE CUSTARD   *Serves 6*

I f you like hot chocolate on a cold winter morning, then you'll love this baked Hot Chocolate Custard on a cold winter evening! If you prefer, add $^1/_4$ tsp cinnamon to the milk in Step 2.

1½ cups low fat milk
2 TB + 1 tsp cocoa powder
2 eggs
¼ cup sugar
½ tsp vanilla

1. Preheat oven to 350° F.

2. Pour milk into a small saucepan. Sift the cocoa into the milk and whisk them until combined. Bring the mixture to a boil, then turn off heat and let sit.

3. In a mixing bowl, beat the eggs lightly. Add the sugar and vanilla and beat until thoroughly combined.

4. Pour the hot chocolate mixture into the egg mixture, whisking constantly.

5. Pour the custard through a strainer into a measuring cup or jug with a spout.

6. Place 6³⁄₄-cup custard cups or ramekins into a baking pan. Fill the ramekins two-thirds full with the custard. Add water to the baking pan to come halfway up the sides of the ramekins.

7. Bake for 35-40 minutes, or until the custards are just set but still slightly jiggly in the center.

8. Remove the ramekins from the water and set aside to cool.

9. Serve the custards at room temperature, or refrigerate them after they have cooled to room temperature and serve chilled.

Each serving contains approximately 92 calories, 4.5 grams protein, 3.3 grams total fat, 75 mg cholesterol, 55 mg sodium.

AMARETTI ALMOND TORTE — *Serves 8*

This elegant dessert is a single layer cake, doused with amaretto liqueur and topped with almonds and cookie crumbs. The buttermilk gives the cake so much

moisture that it resembles a coffee cake. Note: You can also bake this cake in 4 4" tart pans. Bake for 20-25 minutes.

CAKE
½ cup whole wheat pastry flour or ½ cup + 1 TB unbleached flour
½ cup unbleached flour
½ tsp baking powder
½ tsp baking soda
¼ tsp salt
½ cup maple syrup
1 egg white
½ cup buttermilk
½ tsp almond extract
¼ cup almond oil or canola oil
vegetable oil spray as needed

TOPPING
⅓ cup sliced almonds
2 pair amaretti cookies, crushed into crumbs

SYRUP
2 TB amaretto
2 TB maple syrup

1. Preheat oven to 350° F.

2. Place dry ingredients for cake in one bowl and wet ingredients for cake in another bowl. Combine the two mixtures, mixing until smooth.

3. Pour the batter into a lightly oiled (with vegetable oil spray) 8" springform pan.

4. Bake for 30 minutes, or until the center of the cake springs back when touched.

5. Set on a rack to cool for 5 minutes. Increase oven temperature to Broil.

6. Meanwhile, heat the amaretto in a saucepan, or in the microwave on high power for 1 minute to cook away the alcohol. (This step is optional.)

7. Poke holes all over the cake with a toothpick or wire cake tester. Brush amaretto all over the top of the cake with a pastry brush and let it soak in.

8. Cover the top of the cake with the sliced almonds and amaretti cookie crumbs.

VOLUME EQUIVALENTS

3 teaspoons ....1 tablespoon
2 tablespoons.................................1 fluid ounce
4 tablespoons ....$^1/_4$ cup
5 tablespoons plus 1 teaspoon ...$^1/_3$ cup
8 tablespoons ....$^1/_2$ cup
16 tablespoons ....1 cup
1 cup ....8 fluid ounces
2 cups..1 pint
4 cups..1 quart
4 quarts ....1 gallon
8 quarts ....1 peck (dry)
16 ounces ....1 pound

ONE CUP EQUIVALENTS

$^1/_2$ large onion, diced
4 oz chopped walnuts
5 oz pine nuts
3 stalks celery, diced
2 carrots, diced
1 large tomato, diced
$^3/_4$ pound honey

ONE POUND FOOD EQUIVALENTS

3 medium apples (3 cups sliced)
3 medium bananas ($2^1/_2$ cups sliced)
4 cups grated reduced fat Cheddar cheese
2 cups cottage cheese
$3^1/_4$ cups whole wheat pastry flour
$3^1/_4$ cups unbleached flour
$4^1/_2$ cups old fashioned oats
$2^1/_4$ cups short grain brown rice
2 cups dried navy (small white) beans
$1^1/_2$ cups maple syrup
$1^1/_3$ cups honey
$1^2/_3$ cups chopped walnuts
3 medium red potatoes ($2^1/_3$ cups sliced)
3 medium yams (3 cups sliced)
3 medium tomatoes

SUBSTITUTES

1 teaspoon baking powder *SUBSTITUTE*
   $^1/_2$ teaspoon cream of tartar plus $^1/_4$ teaspoon baking soda
1 cup buttermilk *SUBSTITUTE* 1 cup plain yogurt *OR* 1 tablespoon lemon juice or vinegar plus enough milk to make 1 cup (let stand 5 minutes before using)
1 tablespoon prepared mustard *SUBSTITUTE*
   $^1/_2$ teaspoon dry mustard plus 2 teaspoons vinegar

9. Pour maple syrup evenly over the surface of the cake on top of the almonds and cookie crumbs.

10. To brown the topping, place the cake on a rack in the oven about 6 inches from the heat source and broil until the topping is lightly browned. Watch the entire time the cake is under the broiler so you don't burn it.

11. Let cool for about 10 minutes, then loosen the sides of the cake pan. Slide a knife around the edges of the cake, then slowly release the springform sides. Slice and serve.

Each serving contains approximately 189 calories, 4.1 grams protein, 2.6 grams total fat, 0.6 mg cholesterol, 169 mg sodium.

SLICED PEARS IN PHYLLO PILLOWS
Serves 8

Crunchy on the outside, these phyllo pillows flake when cut open to reveal steaming hot pears in a maple cinnamon syrup. Serve with cold, creamy frozen yogurt.

---

12 sheets (14" x 18" each) phyllo dough
1 TB butter (optional)
1 tsp ground cinnamon
pinch nutmeg
8 pears, peeled, cored, and sliced
$^1/_2$ cup maple syrup
vegetable oil spray as needed
8 scoops vanilla frozen yogurt

1. The day before you want to make these phyllo pillows, take the phyllo dough out of the freezer and place it in the refrigerator overnight. The next day, remove it from the refrigerator and leave it at room temperature for an hour. Or take the dough straight from the freezer and leave it at room temperature for 3-4 hours. Do not unwrap the dough until you are ready to use it.

2. Preheat oven to 375° F.

3. In a large non-stick skillet, melt the butter, if using. Add cinnamon and nutmeg to the pan and cook over medium heat for 1 minute.

4. Increase the heat to high and add the pears. Toss to coat the pears in a cinnamon mixture.

5. Add the maple syrup, reduce heat to low and simmer for 5 minutes.

6. Remove the pan from the heat to cool.

7. Meanwhile, cut the sheets of phyllo dough into strips 13$^1/_2$" long and 4"-4$^1/_2$" wide.

8. For each phyllo "pillow," you will use 4 strips of dough. Keep strips you are not using covered. Work quickly. Take 1 strip of dough and lightly spray it with vegetable oil spray. Add second strip on top of first and spray it. Proceed as directed with the last 2 strips.

9. Place about $^1/_4$ cup of the pear mixture at the bottom right end of the 4-layered strip. Fold it, plus the section of dough it is placed on, up to the left. Continue to fold it up like a flag, lightly misting each section of dough between foldings. See illustration this page. Each completed phyllo pillow will be in the shape of a triangle.

10. Place each triangular pillow on an ungreased cookie sheet as soon as it is done. You will have 8 pillows. Spray tops of the pillows with oil to ensure they will brown.

11. Bake for 10-15 minutes, or until lightly browned.

12. Serve 1 pillow per person with a scoop of vanilla frozen yogurt on the side.

Each serving contains approximately 381 calories, 5.3 grams total fat, 13 mg cholesterol, 203 mg sodium.

CHRISTMAS COOKIES

In California, Christmastime is subtle. Sometimes the temperature is a little cooler than normal, and perhaps it'll rain occasionally, but most often it's sunny and 70°. Californians have to work hard for that Christmas "feeling!" I've found the best way to inspire the holiday spirit is to spend the afternoon baking

Christmas cookies. I prefer it to decorating the tree or caroling, and it's infinitely better than shopping! Here are some of my favorite cookie recipes.

ALMOND CRESCENT COOKIES

Makes about 6 dozen cookies

These melt-in-your-mouth delights are also good half-dipped in semi-sweet chocolate.

¹/₄ cup almonds
¹/₂ cup sweet butter, at room temperature
¹/₄ cup honey
1 tsp vanilla
¹/₂ tsp almond extract
1³/₄ cups oat flour

1. Grind the almonds to a powder in a food processor or blender. Set aside.

2. Cream the butter well with the ground almond "flour" in a bowl. Add the honey, vanilla, and almond extracts. Beat until well mixed.

3. Add the oat flour and mix well.

4. Divide the dough into 2 pieces. Cover with plastic wrap and roll each half into a log. The dough will be sticky so do your best. Refrigerate for at least 1 hour, or overnight. The dough will firm up, making it easier to roll it into a log.

5. Preheat oven to 350° F.

6. Take 1 log from the refrigerator. Unwrap it, then slice it into ¹/₂" slices. Cut each slice in half and form a crescent moon shape with it.

7. Place each crescent on a lightly oiled cookie sheet and bake for 10-12 minutes. Repeat with the second log.

You can buy oat flour at a natural foods store or make 1³/₄ cups oat flour by processing 2 cups of old-fashioned oats in the food processor to a powder, or "flour."

Each cookie contains approximately 26 calories, 0.5 grams protein, 1.6 grams total fat, 4 mg cholesterol, 11 mg sodium.

HONEY VANILLA SHORTBREADS

Makes 30 1¹/₂" cookies

The most basic of cookies, shortbreads can be refrigerated, rolled, and cut into Christmas shapes as described below, or shaped into balls and pressed flat with the tines of a fork.

¹/₂ cup sweet butter at room temperature
¹/₄ cup rice flour or whole wheat pastry flour or unbleached flour
¹/₄ cup honey
1 tsp vanilla
1 cup whole wheat pastry flour or 1 cup + 2 TB unbleached flour

1. Preheat oven to 325° F.

2. Cream the butter well with the rice flour in a bowl. Add honey and vanilla and beat until smooth.

3. Add whole wheat pastry flour and beat until smooth.

4. Divide dough into 4 equal pieces, wrap in plastic wrap, and refrigerate for at least 1 hour, or overnight.

5. Flour the dough and roll out each piece between 2 pieces of wax paper to about ¹/₈"-¹/₄" thick.

6. Cut out with cookie cutters and place shapes on ungreased cookie sheets. Bake for 12-15 minutes.

Each cookie contains approximately 52 calories, 3.2 grams total fat, 8.3 mg cholesterol, 27 mg sodium.

CHEWY PEANUT BUTTERIEST COOKIES

Makes 4 dozen cookies

Rather than the usual chalky texture, these peanut butter cookies are chewy. Be sure to choose a natural peanut butter—one where the oil separates from the peanut butter—for the healthiest, most peanutty cookies. Laura Scudder™ makes a good peanut butter, but you can't beat the fresh-ground kind at natural foods stores.

1/2 cup sweet butter, at room temperature
1 cup peanut butter or roasted almond butter
2/3 cup honey
1 egg white, lightly beaten
1 tsp vanilla
1 cup whole wheat pastry flour or 1 cup + 2 TB
*   unbleached flour*
1 tsp baking soda
1/4 tsp salt (optional)
semi-sweet chocolate chips as needed (optional)
jelly as needed (optional)

1. Preheat oven to 375° F.

2. Cream the butter and peanut butter together in one bowl. Add the honey, egg, and vanilla, and beat until smooth.

3. In another bowl, mix together the flour, baking soda, and salt, if using.

4. Add the dry ingredients to the peanut butter mixture and mix well.

5. Cover bowl and refrigerate dough for at least 1 hour or overnight.

6. When ready to bake, roll dough into 1" balls and place on ungreased cookie sheets. Flatten with fingers or with tines of a fork. Bake for 8-10 minutes.

Each cookie contains approximately 61 calories, 2. grams protein, 3.4 grams total fat, 0 mg cholesterol, 52 mg sodium.

Black and White Oatmeal Cookies

Makes 7 1/2 dozen cookies

I was stuck. I couldn't come up with an oatmeal cookie recipe that I was wild about. I tried

adding molasses, a little orange peel, pineapple juice, flaked coconut. I decreased the flour, increased the sweetener. They were good, but not IT. I should have known that all it would take was chocolate—dark and white. Finally, an oatmeal cookie I can get excited about!

2 whole eggs or 4 egg whites
1 cup maple syrup
1/2 cup + 2 TB canola oil
1 tsp vanilla
1 1/2 cups whole wheat pastry flour or 1 1/2 cups + 3
*   TB unbleached flour*
2 cups oats
1 tsp baking soda
1 tsp baking powder
1/4 tsp salt (optional)
10 oz semi-sweet or bittersweet chocolate bits
3 oz white chocolate, broken into small bits

1. Preheat oven to 375° F.

2. Beat together eggs, maple syrup, and canola oil.

3. Place dry ingredients in a medium-size bowl and stir to mix.

4. Add dry ingredients to the wet ingredients and mix well.

5. Stir in chocolate pieces.

6. Spoon onto lightly oiled cookie sheets or cookie sheets lined with parchment paper.

7. Bake for 12-15 minutes, or until golden.

Each cookie (using 4 egg whites) contains approximately 59 calories, 0.9 grams protein, 3.3 grams total fat, 5 mg cholesterol, 16 mg sodium.

SPRING

No matter what part of the country you live in, spring is always dramatic. Abundant blooms of color appear suddenly. Mere shadows of trees plump with greenery. And grocery store bins don't look so sad anymore. Every day new fruits and vegetables appear—tables appear—tender lettuce, fresh asparagus, new potatoes, baby carrots, the first trickles of the year's berries—warmly welcomed by eager hands pinching, pressing, carefully selecting their edible treasures to carry home.

SUGGESTED MENUS

EASTER BRUNCH
Spinach Mint Salad
Calzones with Roasted Red Pepper Sauce
Strawberry Phyllo Tarts

MOTHER'S DAY DINNER
Sopa di Verduras
Fresh Herb Marinated Swordfish and Salsa with
*   Green Olives and Basil*
Potato Tomato Gratin
Lemon Semolina Pound Cake with Fresh Berries

MEMORIAL DAY DINNER GROUP *
Aduki Bean and Vegetable Egg Rolls
Umeboshi Plum and Hot Mustard Dipping Sauces
Mushroom Won Tons in Japanese Broth
Napa Cabbage Salad with Sesame Ginger Dressing
Cool and Spicy Thai Linguine
Strawberry Banana Swirl

BABY OR WEDDING SHOWER
Herbed Bread Tea Sandwiches
Chicken Breasts with Cilantro Lemon Sauce
Beet Greens and Fresh Baby Carrots
Lemon Lavender Cookies
Fresh Berry and Kiwi Pastry Tart with Chambourd

DINNER I
Baby Lettuce with Cilantro Vinaigrette
Green Chile Pockets
Seasoned Purée of Tomato and Chicken Soup

DINNER II
Stuffed Grape Leaves
Greek Quesadillas
California Paella
*Fresh Fruit***

DINNER III
Spinach Salad with Orange Zest and Sun-Dried
*   Tomato and Chili Dressing*
Shredded Chicken and Spinach Tacos wth Goat
*   Cheese*
Blueberry Tofu Cheesecake

* This menu would be a lot of work to make on your own, so why not organize a Dinner Group? Each couple that gathers at your house will be responsible for making and bringing one of the dishes. Send recipes to the other couples at least a week in advance.

**Recipe not included

APPETIZERS AND BREADS

ADUKI BEAN AND VEGETABLE EGG ROLLS
Makes 20 egg rolls

What a wonderful way to enjoy spring's abundance of green vegetables! Once you've combined all the ingredients that will go into the egg rolls, taste it. It's a delicious, fat-free salad. I've chosen aduki beans as the protein component to these egg rolls (see the introduction to Adkui Bean and Miso Soup on page 11 for more of these flavorful beans.) If you prefer, substitute any other cooked protein, such as black beans, leftover chicken or fish, crab or lobster.

BEANS
1/2 cup dried aduki beans, rinsed
1 1/2 cups water
3" strip kombu seaweed (optional)

VEGETABLES
6 cups assorted greens, such as spinach, bok choy, escarole, Swiss chard, napa cabbage, cut into shreds
4 green onions, whites and fresh greens, sliced diagonally
1 1/2 cups grated carrots
5 TB minched shallots
2 cloves garlic, finely minced
1 cup mung bean sprouts
2 TB rice vinegar
2 TB low sodium soy sauce
1 tsp Ume plus vinegar or apple cider vinegar
2 TB sherry
20 egg roll wrappers

1. Place rinsed beans and kombu in a saucepan of water. Bring to a boil, reduce heat to low, and simmer, covered, for about 35-40 minutes, or until the beans are tender, but not mushy. Remove and discard kombu. Set beans aside.

2. Combine greens with green onions, carrots, shallots, garlic, bean sprouts, and aduki beans. Toss gently to mix.

3. Add the rice vinegar, soy sauce, vinegar, and sherry to greens mixture. Toss well but gently so that you do not break up the beans.

4. To assemble egg rolls: Take 1 wrapper and place it on a dry surface with a corner facing you. Place about 2 TB of filling in the center of the wrapper. Moisten each corner with a little water. Fold the bottom corner over the filling. Fold the 2 side corners over that, then roll toward last corner, which will seal the egg roll as it is rolled up. Continue with each wrapper until filling is gone. Cover and refrigerate rolls overnight, or cook immediately.

5. To cook, spray a non-stick griddle or skillet with vegetable oil spray. Heat to medium high. Add egg rolls. Cook on 1 side until it turns golden brown.

6. Turn egg rolls over to other side and cook until that side is golden brown.

7. Turn egg rolls on edge. You may need to press down to get them to stand on edge. When golden brown, turn to the other edge. Lightly spray with more oil as needed.

8. Serve hot or at room temperature with the Umeboshi Plum and Oriental Hot Mustard Dipping Sauces below.

Each Egg Roll contains approximately 45 calories, 2.7 grams protein, 0.2 grams total fat, 0 mg cholesterol, 119 mg sodium.

UMEBOSHI PLUM DIPPING SAUCE

1 TB fresh lemon juice
2 TB mirin
1 tsp umeboshi plum paste
1 TB rice vinegar
2 cloves garlic, very finely minced

Mirin should contain only sweet rice, salt, rice koji, and water. Rice koji is sometimes not mentioned on the label. Many brands sold in Oriental markets are not naturally brewed and are sweetened with sugar or corn syrup.

Umeboshi plum paste can be found in natural food stores and Oriental markets. A little goes a long way, so it's fortunate that it lasts indefinitely. It is very tart and salty if eaten alone. The fruit it is made from resembles an unripe apricot. In preparing the paste, fresh plums are packed into vats with crude salt and shiso leaves, which give the paste its red color and tangy flavor. Shiso is a natural preservative, which possesses over one thousand times the preserving ability of synthetic preservatives. The salt draws out the juices of the plums which turns to vinegar. The plums are then taken out of the vats to dry in the sun, then returned to the vats to absorb more of the plum vinegar during the night. The cycle is repeated for three or four days. The plum vinegar becomes more and more alkaline with age, and the plum flesh absorbs more and more of it over time. The alkalinity is medicinal and is said to help rid the body of lactic acid, aid in digestion, and strengthen the blood.

1. Combine all ingredients in a bowl. Mix to distribute unmeboshi plum paste well.

ORIENTAL HOT MUSTARD DIPPING SAUCE

2 tsp Oriental hot mustard
3 tsp water
2 tsp low sodium soy sauce

1. Stir well. Let sit for 2 minutes. Use sparingly as this is HOT!

GREEK QUESADILLAS `Serves 8`

The judicious use of feta cheese and an aromatic spinach purée adds a Mediterranean flair to these quesadillas.

6 cloves garlic, finely minced
1 large yellow onion, diced
1 tsp extra virgin olive oil

2 heads spinach
1/2 cup crumbled feta cheese, rinsed
8 flour tortillas, preferably whole wheat

1. Sauté garlic and onion in olive oil.

2. Wash spinach well and remove and discard stems and any discolored leaves. Chop into small pieces and add to garlic and onion mixture. Cook, uncovered, for 10 minutes, or until spinach is wilted. Purée in food processor.

3. Spoon 1/8 of the spinach mixture and 1 TB of the feta cheese onto one-half of each flour tortilla.

4. Fold tortilla over so spinach and cheese are covered. Heat a non-stick skillet to medium high and cook each tortilla until lightly browned on the outside and the feta is beginning to melt, about 5 minutes.

5. Cut each tortilla into thirds and serve.

Each serving contains approximately 115 calories, 5.2 grams protein, 4 grams total fat, 6 mg cholesterol, 228 mg sodium.

BABY SQUASH STUFFED WITH CORN SALSA `Serves 8`

If you can't find baby squash, substitute zucchini cut into 1½" chunks and hollowed out like a barrel.

16 baby pattypan squash
1 cup corn, fresh or frozen and defrosted
3 scallions, chopped
2 TB salsa of choice
4 oz reduced fat Monterey
  Jack cheese with
  jalapeños, grated

1. Preheat oven to 400° F.

2. Plunge squashes in a pot of boiling water for approximately

Variation: Use 1 diced tomatillo and/or 1/4 cup chopped fresh cilantro instead of the salsa.

2 minutes. Rinse in cold water and set aside to drain and cool.

3. Combine corn, scallions, salsa, and cheese in a bowl.

4. With a melon baller, scoop out the center of each squash, making sure you do not break through the bottom of the squash.

5. Spoon corn mixture into each squash. Bake on a cookie sheet for approximately 10 minutes, or until cheese is melted. Serve immediately.

Each serving contains approximately 81 calories, 5.7 grams protein, 3.6 grams total fat, 10 mg cholesterol, 116 mg sodium.

HERBED BREAD TEA SANDWICHES
Makes 36 sandwiches

April showers may bring May flowers but they also bring lots of other showers—baby and wedding showers, that is. I especially enjoy doing the "English Tea" theme, with tiny tarts, Lemon Lavender Cookies (see page 68), and heart-shaped sandwiches. This herbed bread has a soft texture, and is therefore easy to cut out with cookie cutters into any shape you desire. I cut out cucumbers in the same shape as the sandwiches, spread on a light cream cheese and herb mixture, and arrange them on a doily-covered plate. How elegant!

BREAD
1/2 cup buttermilk
1/2 cup water
2 TB maple syrup
1 package yeast
1 cup whole wheat flour
1 1/2 cups unbleached flour
2 TB extra virgin olive oil
2 TB minced fresh parsley
2 TB minced shallots
1 tsp salt or VegeSal

1 tsp dried tarragon or 1 TB minced fresh tarragon
1 tsp dried dill or 1 TB minced fresh dill

SANDWICH FILLING
1/2 cucumber
1/2 cup low-fat cream cheese, whipped
1/4 cup low-fat or no-fat cottage cheese or yogurt cheese
2 tsp dried dill or basil or 2 TB minced fresh dill or fresh basil
salt or VegeSal to taste
black pepper to taste
sprigs of fresh mint or fresh dill as needed (optional)

1. Heat the buttermilk and water together to bath water temperature (105°-115° F). Add the maple syrup and yeast. Stir and let sit for 5 minutes or until the mixture begins to foam. If it hasn't foamed within 5 minutes, that means your yeast is no good. Discard and begin again with a fresh package.

2. Place flours in a bowl. Add olive oil and mix well, using the back of a fork to break up the little pearls of oil and flour to smaller and smaller pieces.

3. Add the parsley, shallots, salt, and herbs to the flour mixture.

4. Pour in the buttermilk/yeast mixture and stir well to form into a loose dough.

5. Turn out onto a lightly floured surface and knead for 5 minutes. Add up to 1/4 cup more flour (either kind) to the work surface so the dough does not stick.

6. Transfer dough to a lightly oiled bowl. Turn to coat the dough with oil on all sides. Cover with plastic wrap or a wet towel and let rise in a draft-free place till double in size, 45-60 minutes.

7. When risen, preheat the oven to 375° F. Punch down the dough and knead it into a ball.

8. Form into 1 or 2 baguettes and place on a lightly oiled cookie sheet. Cover with plastic wrap or a damp towel and let rise another 30 minutes.

9. When risen, slash the tops so the bread won't break open while baking.

10. Bake for 17-20 minutes for 2 loaves, 20-25 minutes for 1 loaf.

> You'll have leftover bread from cutting out shapes. To make croutons, place bread scraps on a cookie sheet and dry out in a 200° F oven, about 45 minutes. Cut into unevenly shaped croutons. Or process bread scraps in a food processor to make bread crumbs.

11. Meanwhile, slice the cucumber into rounds. If it is a hothouse cucumber or an organic cucumber, you do not have to peel it before slicing. Cut out the cucumber rounds into desired shapes, or leave round, and set aside.

12. To make the filling, mix together the cream cheese and cottage cheese or yogurt cheese in a food processor or blender.

13. Stir in the dill or basil. Taste and season with salt and pepper.

14. When the bread is done, let the baguettes cool on a wire rack. When cool enough, slice the bread with a serrated knife into fairly thin slices. Cut the bread into desired shapes.

15. To assemble the sandwiches, spread the cream cheese mixture lightly on the slices of cut-out bread. Add the cut-out cucumber to each slice of bread. Garnish the tops of each open-face sandwich with a tiny mint leaf or dill sprig.

16. Arrange on a plate and serve. May be refrigerated for up to 2 hours before serving.

Makes about 3 dozen open-face cut-out sandwiches from 1 larger loaf, 48 oval-shape open-face sandwiches from 2 smaller loaves.

Each sandwich (using 1% cottage cheese in the filling) contains approximately 52 calories, 1.7 grams protein, 1.7 grams total fat, 2.6 mg cholesterol, 96 mg sodium.

The bread alone has 66 calories per oz, 1.9 grams protein, 1.4 grams fat, 0.2 mg cholesterol, 99 mg sodium.

LITTLE RANCH DRESSING AND DIP
Makes 1½ cups

Much fresher tasting than the bottled or packaged versions!

¼ cup nonfat plain yogurt
¾ cup buttermilk
1½ TB extra virgin olive oil or Olio Santo (see page 10)
1 TB apple cider vinegar
1 tsp honey
1 clove garlic, finely minced
2 scallions
2 TB fresh parsley
½ tsp dried marjoram
⅛ tsp dried dill
½ tsp salt or VegeSal (optional)
black pepper to taste

1. Place the yogurt in a coffee filter and let it drain for a few hours over a glass. The resulting "yogurt cheese" is thicker, and will result in a richer dressing than if you used the yogurt without draining some of the liquid, or whey, from it.

2. Combine the yogurt cheese, buttermilk, olive oil, vinegar, and honey in a small mixing bowl.

3. Place the garlic, scallions, and parsley in a food processor or blender and process till finely minced.

4. Add garlic mixture to yogurt cheese mixture. Add remaining ingredients, stir, and refrigerate for at least 1 hour, or overnight.

5. Serve as a salad dressing or a dip with raw vegetables, such as sugar snap peas, strips of bell peppers, celery, carrots, fennel slices, etc.

Each 1 TB contains approximately 16 calories, 1 mg protein, 0 grams total fat, 0 mg cholesterol, 25 mg sodium.

STUFFED GRAPE LEAVES

Serves 8-12

If you have a grapevine growing, or if you can find unsprayed grape leaves somewhere in your neighborhood, this dish would be even more rewarding to make. When using fresh rather than grape leaves from a jar, simply blanch them until tender, as instructed below, before filling.

24 (about ¹/₂ jar) grape leaves
2 cloves garlic, finely minced
1¹/₂ yellow onions, diced
2 TB extra virgin olive oil
3/4 cup raw long grain brown rice
1 cup boiling water
¹/₄ cup minced fresh parsley
1 TB minced fresh dill or 1 tsp dried dill
2 TB minced, fresh mint leaves
at least 1¹/₂ cups water
1 lemon

1. Rinse the grape leaves well under cold running water. Some batches of leaves are more pliable or tender than others. If they're too tough, you may want to blanch them. To do this, place them in a steamer basket and plunge them into a saucepan of boiling water for 1 minute, then immediately refresh them in a saucepan of cold water to stop the cooking process.

2. In a 3-4 quart saucepan, sauté the garlic and onions in the oil until the onion is clear, about 5 minutes.

3. Add the rice and cook, stirring, till the rice is lightly browned, about 5 minutes.

4. Slowly pour the boiling water over the rice. Bring it back to a boil, cook, covered, for 25 minutes, or until the rice absorbs all the liquid. The rice will be only half done at this point.

5. Add the fresh herbs to the rice and stir to mix. Let the mixture cool enough to handle it.

6. To stuff the leaves, place the shiny side of each grape leaf facing down on a work surface. Add 1 TB of the rice mixture to the center of each leaf.

7. Fold the side up over the rice mixture, covering the rice, then roll it up like a cigar.

8. Choose a saucepan to layer the grape leaves in. Find a plate or flat lid to a smaller saucepan to fit snugly inside the saucepan. Lay the stuffed leaves in the bottom of the saucepan, seam sides down, in even, tight rows. When one layer is completed, make a second layer on top of the first.

9. Lay the plate or lid directly on top of the stuffed grape leaves. (This will keep them in place so they don't bob around in the water while cooking.)

10. Add enough water to the saucepan to half cover the leaves—at least 1¹/₂ cups. Cut the lemon in half and squeeze its juice into the pan, too.

11. Cook, uncovered, at medium high heat until the liquid has been totally absorbed, 35-45 minutes. Check after 30 minutes to make sure the bottom of the pan isn't burning.

12. Serve hot, warm, or chilled.

Each serving (for 8) contains approximately 117 calories, 2.25 grams protein, 4 grams total fat, 0 mg cholesterol, 5 mg sodium.

SALADS

BABY LETTUCE WITH CILANTRO VINAIGRETTE

Makes 12 dinner salads

Spring gardening is often about thinning the vegetable garden—and most rewarding is thinning lettuce plants because you can eat what you pinch away! If you're not a gardener, you can find whole heads of baby lettuce at many grocery stores. Pick up a few different types: oak leaf, red leaf, romaine; and try a few kinds of "designer lettuce":

mizuna, maché, radicchio. Farmer's markets are another good place to find baby lettuce, often washed and all mixed up in a bag, with a few edible flowers thrown in for color. The dressing will keep in the refrigerator for about a month if well covered.

DRESSING

3 cloves garlic, finely minced
1 TB finely minced red onion
3 TB minced fresh cilantro
³/₄ cup extra virgin olive oil or avocado oil
¹/₂ cup fresh lemon juice
2 TB-¹/₄ cup wine, water, or mixture of both
2 TB Dijon-style mustard, with jalapenos, if desired

SALAD

12 cups baby lettuce
¹/₄ avocado per person (optional)

1. To make the dressing, combine all ingredients in a jar and shake to mix. Or, place in a food processor or blender and process until well mixed. Refrigerate while preparing the lettuce.

2. Wash lettuce and spin dry. Tear into bite-size pieces into a large salad bowl. Cut the avocado, if using, into chunks.

3. Toss the lettuce and avocado with the dressing. Serve immediately.

Makes about 1¹/₂ cups dressing.

Each salad with avocado contains approximately 215 calories, 1.95 grams protein, 21.5 grams total fat, 0 mg cholesterol, 41 mg sodium.

Each salad without avocado contains approximately 134 calories, 0.9 grams protein, 13.8 grams total fat, 0 mg cholesterol, 36 mg sodium.

SPINACH MINT SALAD   *Makes 6 dinner salads*

I like to try different types of mint when I make this salad. So far my favorite is pineapple mint. Its lightly flavored, pale green leaves are edged in white.

Bunches of all types of mint are available during the spring at most grocery stores, but why not grow your own? All mints grow like weeds, so I suggest you plant them in pots so they don't take over the garden.

1 recipe croutons (see Caesar Salad page 6)
1 bunch spinach
1 small red onion, thinly sliced
2 cloves garlic, finely minced
1 TB minced fresh mint
4 black or Greek olives, pitted and rinsed (optional)
3 TB champagne vinegar or white wine vinegar
3 TB extra virgin olive oil or Oli Santo (see page 10)
2 oz feta cheese, rinsed (optional)

1. Make croutons and set aside

2. Wash spinach well and remove and discard stems and any discolored leaves. Spin dry. Tear into bite-size pieces.

3. Toss spinach leaves with the onion, garlic, mint, olives, if using, vinegar, and olive oil in a large salad bowl.

4. If using feta cheese, crumble it into the salad bowl.

5. Add croutons. Toss thoroughly so each leaf is coated with the olive oil and vinegar.

Each salad with feta contains 143 calories, 5.2 grams protein, 10.3 grams total fat, 8 mg cholesterol, 259 mg sodium.

BUTTER LETTUCE SALAD WITH NO-OIL HERBED VINAIGRETTE   *Makes 6 dinner salads*

Butter lettuce is so soft and so creamy that it seems to melt in your mouth. The way the leaves are formed allows the dressing to catch in all the folds and so the salad seems that much more fla-

vorful. I think this is why iceberg lettuce lovers also like butter lettuce. The No-Oil Herbed Vinaigrette is loaded with flavor, and can be used as a template for other fat-free creations of your own. For instance, use lime peel in place of lemon peel and change the herbs to chili powder or cumin. Cottage or farmer's cheese adds body to the salad, without contributing much fat.

DRESSING
4 cloves garlic, finely minced
1 TB minced shallots
$^{1}/_{2}$ cup apple cider vinegar
2 TB fresh lemon juice
$^{3}/_{4}$ cup water
1 TB honey
2 TB Dijon-style mustard
$^{1}/_{2}$ tsp grated lemon peel
$^{1}/_{2}$ tsp dried oregano or dried thyme
salt or VegeSal to taste
black pepper to taste

SALAD
2 small heads butter lettuce
2 ripe tomatoes
$^{1}/_{4}$ cup low-fat cottage cheese or farmer's cheese, crumbled (optional)

1. To make the dressing, combine all ingredients in a jar and shake to mix. Or, place in a food processor or blender and process until well mixed. Refrigerate while preparing the salad.

2. Wash butter lettuce and spin dry. Tear into bite-size pieces into a large salad bowl.

3. Slice, quarter, or dice tomatoes and add to salad bowl.

4. If using the cottage or farmer's cheese, add this to the bowl.

5. Toss with the dressing, so the cheese is distributed well throughout the salad.

Makes 1$^{3}/_{4}$ cups dressing.

1 TB of salad dressing contains 7 calories.

The salad with dressing contains approximately 40 calories, 0 grams protein, 0.5 grams total fat, 0.6 mg cholesterol and 70 mg sodium.

SESAME MISO SALAD
Makes 8 dinner salads

The colors and shapes of the vegetables in this salad allow you to compose masterpieces on plates!

SALAD
8 cups mixed lettuce, such as romaine, butter lettuce, red leaf
$^{1}/_{2}$ cup fresh cilantro leaves
8 scallions, sliced into rounds on the diagonal
4 small carrots, sliced into rounds on the diagonal
24 yellow wax beans
1 small red bell pepper, very thinly sliced into strips

DRESSING
4 TB sesame oil (not toasted sesame oil)
2 TB yellow or white miso
3 TB rice vinegar
3 TB water or white wine
2 TB sesame seeds, toasted for 10 minutes at 325° F

1. Wash lettuce and spin dry. Place in large bowl and add cilantro leaves.

2. Steam beans for 7 minutes, or until al dente.

3. Make dressing. Combine all ingredients in a small bowl and whisk together. Toss half of the dressing with lettuce and cilantro leaves.

4. Arrange lettuce mixture on 8 salad plates.

5. Toss rest of dressing with sliced vegetables and add these to the plates of lettuce. Serve immediately.

Each serving contains approximately 40 calories, 2.2 grams protein, 1.3 grams total fat, 0 mg cholesterol, 140 mg sodium.

ESCAROLE SALAD WITH WARM MUSHROOM LEMON VINAIGRETTE

Makes 8 dinner salads

This is a salad of contrasts: warm dressing covering cool lettuce, the hardy escarole leaf next to tender leaves of butter lettuce, escarole's bitter flavor mellowed by the peppery sweetness of watercress. The dressing is adaptable enough to allow these contrasts to be appreciated.

LETTUCE
1 head escarole lettuce
2 heads butter lettuce
1 bunch watercress

DRESSING
8-10 shiitake mushrooms, stems discarded
24 mushrooms
3 cloves garlic, finely minced
1/2 tsp dried Italian herb blend or dried basil
1/4 tsp crushed red peppers
1/4 cup dry red wine
1 lemon, cut into 8 wedges
3 TB extra virgin olive oil or Olio Santo (see page 10)

1. Wash lettuce and watercress and spin dry. Tear into bite-size pieces and add to a large salad bowl.

2. Clean and slice mushroom tops and set aside.

3. When ready to serve, add mushrooms, garlic, herbs, crushed red peppers, and red wine to a sauté pan. Cook, covered, over medium heat until mushrooms are tender and you begin to smell their aroma, about 5 minutes.

4. Meanwhile, toss the lettuce and watercress with the olive oil. Toss very well, making sure each leaf is coated with the oil. Arrange on 8 salad plates.

5. When the mushrooms are done, spoon some onto each of the 8 plates atop the lettuce leaves, along with some of the mushroom juices.

6. Squeeze a wedge of lemon over each and serve immediately.

Each serving contains approximately 73 calories, 1 gram protein, 5.4 grams total fat, 0 mg choiesterol, 5 mg sodium.

SPINACH SALAD WITH ORANGE ZEST AND SUN-DRIED TOMATO AND CHILI DRESSING

Makes 8 dinner salads

This dressing is made by purée-ing sun-dried tomatoes along with their soaking water. Just a touch of orange juice concentrate is added for sweetness, then a dash of chili powder to finish. You can soak and purée the sun-dried tomatoes ahead of time and refrigerate them, covered, for about a week. This sun-dried tomato purée can also be used in recipes that call for regular tomato paste.

SALAD
1 bunch spinach
16 strips orange peel
2 tomatoes, sliced into rounds

DRESSING
8 sun-dried tomatoes
3/4 cup boiling water
1/2 cup extra virgin olive oil
1 tsp chili powder
1 clove garlic
2 TB orange juice concentrate
1/4 cup apple cider vinegar

low sodium soy sauce to taste
$^1/_4$ tsp black pepper

1. To make dressing, soak sun-dried tomatoes in the boiling water for 20-30 minutes. You want the tomatoes to be not only plumped, but soft.

2. Meanwhile, wash spinach well and remove and discard stems and any discolored leaves. Spin dry. Tear into bite-size pieces, and set aside.

3. When sun-dried tomatoes are ready, place them in a food processor or blender and process until they are liquified.

4. Add the remaining dressing ingredients and process until creamy. Pour into a jar and refrigerate to blend flavors.

5. When ready to serve, toss the spinach leaves with $^1/_2$ to $^3/_4$ cup of the dressing. Arrange on salad plates. Top each salad with 2 strips of orange peel and surround with tomato slices.

Makes $1^1/_4$ cup dressing.

Each 1 TB of dressing contains approximately 103 calories, 4.25 grams protein, 2 grams total fat, 0 mg cholesterol, 27.4 mg sodium.

LATE SPRING SALAD WITH CONCASSÉ OF CUCUMBER AND BASIL

Makes 8 dinner salads

Lettuce in shades of green to yellow is scattered over whole radicchio leaves, subtly striped in red, plum, and cream. Cubed vegetables in reds and deep greens top the salad. Glance at the finished salad—it looks like a Georgia O'Keeffe painting!

LETTUCE
2-3 heads of various lettuce, such as oak leaf, butter lettuce, frisée, romaine, or red leaf

1 handful kale flowers or other edible flowers (optional)
1 small head radicchio or red cabbage

CONCASSÉ
1 hothouse or other unwaxed cucumber
2 medium-size ripe tomatoes, diced
6 scallions, sliced into rounds
3 TB minced fresh basil
squeeze of fresh lemon juice
salt or VegeSal to taste
black pepper to taste

DRESSING
$^1/_4$ cup extra virgin olive oil
2 TB red wine vinegar
1 TB water
1 TB nonfat plain yogurt
1 TB white miso
$1^1/_2$ TB fresh basil, minced
salt or VegeSal to taste
black pepper to taste

1. Wash lettuce leaves well and spin dry. Tear into bite-size pieces except the radicchio or cabbage. Reserve 8 outer leaves of the radicchio or cabbage whole. Place all torn lettuces in a large salad bowl. Reserve the whole leaves in a plastic bag in the refrigerator.

2. To make the concassé, cut the cucumber in half lengthwise. Scrape out the seeds and discard. Dice cucumber and place in a medium-size mixing bowl. (If cucumber is waxed, peel first; otherwise, there is no need to peel.)

3. Add diced tomato, scallion rounds, and minced basil to the mixing bowl.

4. Squeeze on lemon. Season with salt and pepper. Adjust seasonings to your taste. You may refrigerate the concassé for up to 2 hours.

5. For dressing, whisk all ingredients together. Refrigerate until you are ready to use.

6. To assemble salad, arrange 2 whole radicchio or cabbage leaves on 8 salad plates.

7. Add equal amounts of torn lettuce to each plate.

8. Spoon on dressing. Add 2 TB of the concassé. Garnish with edible flowers, if using, and serve immediately.

Each serving contains approximately 95 calories, 2.3 grams protein, 7.2 grams total fat, 0 mg cholesterol, 145 mg sodium.

NAPA CABBAGE SALAD WITH SESAME-GINGER DRESSING
Makes 8 dinner salads

Napa cabbage is one of those "aliens in the produce section"—a curious looking vegetable no one seems to know what to do with. Well, this salad is one answer. The Napa cabbage, also known as Chinese cabbage, is a crinkly globe of leaves, pale green in color, with a delicate crunch to it. The Sesame Ginger Dressing has an Asian feel and accents this delicious salad.

DRESSING
1/2 cup sesame oil (not toasted) or canola oil
1/8 tsp toasted sesame oil
1/4 cup balsamic vinegar
2 TB fresh lime juice
2 1/2 tsp grated fresh ginger
2 cloves garlic, finely minced
1 tsp low sodium soy sauce
1/2 tsp honey

SALAD
1 head napa cabbage, cut into shreds
4 scallions, sliced diagonally and thinly
2 TB minced fresh mint
2 TB minced fresh cilantro

GARNISH
1/2 cup raw cashew pieces
8 leaves red cabbage

1. To make dressing, combine all ingredients in a jar and shake to mix. Or, place in a food processor or blender and process until well mixed. Refrigerate to blend flavors.

2. To prepare salad, combine cabbage shreds, scallions, and herbs in a large bowl.

3. To toast cashews, either add to a dry skillet and cook on high, watching carefully. Remove from heat when you smell the first aroma of toasting cashews, or (the safer option) place in a preheated 325° F oven for 12-15 minutes. Set aside to cool.

4. Choose 8 of the best red cabbage leaves. Look for the right size, a good cup shape, and leaves without tears. Set aside.

5. Toss dressing with salad. Arrange in the red cabbage cups. Sprinkle with the toasted cashews and serve immediately.

Each serving contains approximately 160 calories, 2 grams protein, 15 grams total fat, 0 mg cholesterol, 84 mg sodium.

SOUPS

SOPA DI VERDURAS
Serves 8

This garden greens soup is very nourishing—in fact this is a great soup if you're feeling under the weather. It's full of mineral-rich vegetables, cleansing garlic, and healing chicken broth. Very smooth in texture, the soup is made creamy from the purée of the vegetables, with no cream added.

4 cloves garlic, finely minced
1 average size leek, white part only, sliced
1 1/4 cups sliced carrots
1 stalk celery, sliced
2 average (8 oz) zucchini, sliced
1 TB extra virgin olive oil

¹/₂ cup fresh parsley
1 large (8 oz) tomato
1 bay leaf
4 cups chicken broth or Homemade Chicken Stock
  (see recipe below)
1 bunch spinach
¹/₂ tsp dried basil
¹/₈-¹/₄ tsp cayenne
¹/₄ tsp salt or VegeSal
paprika as needed for garnish

1. In a 3-4 quart saucepan sauté the garlic, leek, carrots, celery, and zucchini in the olive oil over medium-low heat for about 5 minutes.

2. Add parsley, tomato, bay leaf, and chicken broth, bring to a boil, then reduce heat to low. Cook, covered, for 30 minutes, or until carrots are soft.

3. Meanwhile, wash spinach well, and discard stems and discolored leaves. Add the spinach, basil, cayenne, and salt to the cooked vegetables. Bring to a boil, turn heat to low, and cook, covered, for 5-10 minutes, until spinach has wilted.

4. Remove bay leaf and purée soup in batches in a food processor or blender. Return to pan and season with salt, if needed.

5. Ladle soup into bowls and top with a sprinkle of paprika.

Each serving contains approximately 64 calories, 3.7 grams protein, 2.3 grams total fat, -.2 mg cholesterol, 276 mg sodium.

HOMEMADE CHICKEN STOCK | Makes 16 cups

Many cooks find their chicken stock too pale tasting. The reason is they are making their stock with a 3-pound chicken, rather than with 3 pounds of chicken bones. Big difference. Since flavor comes from the bones, and a 3-

pound chicken has at most 1 pound of bones, the resulting stock is pale and tasteless. Most butchers would be happy to save or order you chicken bones. You might also want to freeze the bones from breasts you de-bone yourself.

Note: The method I use to de-fat chicken stock is an overnight process. If you don't have the time for that, remove the fat that accumulates on the top using a turkey baster.

3 pounds chicken bones (backs, necks, wings)
16 cups water
2 medium yellow onions, roughly chopped (don't
  bother to peel)
2 medium carrots, sliced into rounds
2 stalks celery, sliced
4 cloves garlic, crushed (you can leave the paper
  skins on)
3 sprigs fresh thyme or ¹/₄ tsp dried thyme
6 sprigs fresh parsley
¹/₄ tsp black peppercorns
3 whole cloves
1 bay leaf

1. Place all ingredients into an 8-quart stock pot. Bring to a boil, reduce heat to low, cover, and simmer for 2 hours. Skim off the foam periodically.

2. Strain the vegetables and bones through a strainer, or colander. Refrigerate the broth for 8 hours, or overnight. The fat will rise to the surface and harden, allowing you to spoon it off easily. Use within 2 days, or freeze (it keeps for 3 months in the freezer).

Each serving (1 cup) contains approximately 38 calories, 4.3 grams protein, 0.5 grams total fat, 5 mg cholesterol, 24 mg sodium.

POTATO LEEK SOUP | Serves 6

Occasionally spring weather has more of the proverbial lion than lamb in it. Those are the nights when this substantial soup is especially welcome.

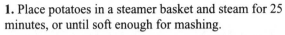

*3 russet potatoes, unpeeled and
    cut into quarters*
3 cloves garlic, finely minced
1 small yellow onion, sliced
*3 leeks, white part only, sliced
    into rounds*
1 TB extra virgin olive oil
12-15 mushrooms, sliced
*1 cup evaporated skim milk or
    low-fat milk or plain soy milk*
¹/₄ tsp nutmeg
¹/₂ tsp black pepper
¹/₄ tsp salt or VegeSal

1. Place potatoes in a steamer basket and steam for 25 minutes, or until soft enough for mashing.

2. In a 3-4 quart saucepan, sauté garlic, yellow onion, and leeks in olive oil.

3. When onions are limp, add sliced mushrooms and sauté for 5-10 more minutes. Keep on a low heat so the juices the mushrooms produce don't cook away.

4. When the potatoes are done, process ²/₃ of the potatoes with 1 cup of the potato water that was left in the pot from steaming. Process in a food processor or blender until smooth.

5. Add the milk and process again.

6. Chop the remaining steamed potatoes into smaller pieces. Return chopped potatoes and processed potato mixture to the sauté pan.

7. Heat, add seasonings, and adjust to taste.

Each serving (10 oz) contains approximately 207 calories, 6.9 grams protein, 2.7 grams total fat, 2 mg cholesterol, 159 mg sodium.

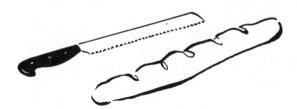

Mushroom Won Tons in Japanese Broth (Dashi)

Serves 8

This is a great soup even if it appears very complicated and foreign. To make it doesn't take any unusual skill, nor is it so exotic tasting that it appeals only to the most adventurous. You need to break it down into parts. The broth is the simplest of vegetable stocks. And the won tons are sautéed vegetables, wrapped in a cute little dough, steamed, then plopped into the soup just before serving. I have to admit, though, that I had trouble with steaming the won tons when I first made this recipe. They kept sticking to the steamer basket. What should I do? One day I was browsing in a book store and a cookbook fell off the shelf in front of me, opened to a page on won tons. "Line a steamer basket with lettuce leaves to prevent sticking," it said. Ask and you shall receive!

BROTH (DASHI)
4 dried shiitake mushrooms
4¹/₂ cups water
6" strip kombu seaweed
2 TB mellow red miso

WON TONS
¹/₂ pound (2 cups sliced) standard mushrooms
¹/₂ red onion, diced
4 cloves garlic, finely minced
2 medium jalapeño chiles, seeded and chopped
1 TB sesame oil or canola oil
1 TB brandy
4 oz fresh, firm tofu, cut into ¹/₄" dice (optional)
¹/₂ cup chopped fresh cilantro
low sodium soy sauce to taste
24 won ton wrappers
lettuce leaves as needed

TO FINISH

*16 snow peas, tips and ends removed, and sliced in
   half lengthwise*
16 sprigs fresh cilantro
1 tsp shredded fresh ginger

1. In a saucepan, soak dried shiitake mushrooms in the
4¹/₂ cups water for at least 3 hours. Alternately, soak for
just 20 minutes to impart their flavor to the dashi, but
you will not be able to use them in the won ton mixture
as described in Step 4.

2. Add kombu to the water after the soaking period.
Bring water to a boil, reduce heat to low, and simmer
for 15 minutes.

3. Remove kombu and discard.

4. Remove shiitake mushrooms from dashi, then cut off
and discard stems. Slice caps and set aside.

5. For the won tons, slice the mushrooms. If the mushrooms are very big, cut in half before slicing (remember, these have to fit in a little won ton wrapper).

6. Sauté mushrooms plus reserved sliced shiitake mushrooms, red onion, garlic, and chiles in the sesame oil
and brandy over medium heat for about 5 minutes.

7. Add cubed tofu, if using, Increase heat to medium-
high and cook until all liquid is gone, stirring frequently.

8. Add chopped cilantro and cook for 1 minute more.
Remove from heat and allow mixture to cool.

9. To assemble won tons: Place 1 won ton wrapper in
the palm of your hand, 1 corner facing you. Add 1 tsp
of the filling to the center of the wrapper. Moisten the 2
edges of the wrapper that are closest to the bottom of
your hand with a little water. Fold the wrapper in half,
forming a triangle shape. Press tightly to seal the entire
edge. Moisten the 2 tips of the long edge of the triangle
and press them together. As you finish the won tons,
place them on a dinner plate in a single layer. Cover and
refrigerate won tons overnight, or cook immediately.

10. To cook won tons, line a steamer basket with lettuce leaves or parchment paper. (This will prevent the
won tons from sticking to the pan.) Add won tons in a
single layer. Steam won tons over boiling water for 4
minutes.

11. Meanwhile, bring dashi back to a boil, then turn
heat immediately to simmer. Ladle out about ¹/₂ cup of
the hot broth and whisk in the 2
TB of red miso. Return to pan
when well mixed. Cover pan
and turn off heat.

12. Place 3 won tons in each of
8 shallow soup bowls. Ladle in
about ¹/₂ cup broth. Top with
snow peas, cilantro sprigs, and
a pinch of fresh ginger. Serve
immediately.

> Won Ton wrappers
> come in squares and
> circles. In this recipe,
> I give instructions
> using the square-
> shaped wrappers, but
> either shape will
> work.

**Each serving contains approximately 76 calories, 4.3
grams protein, 3.3 grams total fat, 0 mg cholesterol,
77 mg sodium.**

LENTIL VEGETABLE SOUP WITH GINGER Serves 8

Lentils are my favorite beans, and I
use them all year round. This colorful and wholesome lentil soup
takes advantage of many of spring's
new vegetables.

1 cup dried lentils
8 cups water
6" strip kombu seaweed (optional)
1 bay leaf
3 cloves garlic, finely minced
1 red onion, diced
2 stalks celery, diced
1 carrot, diced
1 yellow squash, diced
1 green zucchini, diced
¹/₂ cup corn, fresh or frozen
*1 cup spinach leaves, washed, stems removed, sliced
   into shreds*
2 TB fresh lemon juice
1 tsp ground cumin
1 tsp grated fresh ginger
1 TB low sodium soy sauce
¹/₄ cup chopped fresh parsley

1. Combine lentils, water, kombu, bay leaf, garlic, onion, celery, and carrots in an 8-quart Dutch oven. Bring to a boil, reduce heat to low, cover, and simmer for 1 hour.

2. Remove kombu and discard and check lentils. Cook until soft, about 15 minutes more.

3. Add remaining ingredients except parsley. Cook for 5 minutes more.

4. Add parsley and cook for 5 minutes more. Adjust seasonings to taste. Serve immediately.

Each serving (10 oz) contains approximately 124 calories, 8.9 grams protein, 0.5 grams total fat, 0 mg cholesterol, 104 mg sodium.

SEASONED PURÉE OF TOMATO AND CHICKEN SOUP
Serves 6

This recipe calls for a quick stock made with chicken breasts and aromatic vegetables. It is then combined with a Mexican version of my Classic Marinara Sauce (see page 96) for a flavorful and different chicken soup. To add more spice, use a minced serrano chile or two.

CHICKEN AND STOCK

2 half chicken breasts, with bones, without skin
2 carrots, sliced into rounds
1 yellow onion, diced
4 cloves garlic, finely minced
2 stalks celery
1 bay leaf
6 cups water

TOMATO PURÉE

4 cloves garlic, finely minced
1 TB extra virgin olive oil

1 14-oz can whole tomatoes plus juices
1 tsp ground cumin
$^1/_2$ tsp dried oregano
$^1/_2$ tsp ground coriander
$^1/_8$ tsp cayenne
salt or VegeSal to taste
black pepper to taste
$^1/_4$ cup minced fresh cilantro or fresh parsley

1. To make the stock, combine the chicken, carrots, onion, garlic, celery, bay leaf, and water in a 3-4 quart saucepan. Bring to a boil, then reduce the heat to low and simmer for 30 minutes.

2. Meanwhile, in a sauté pan, sauté the garlic in the olive oil over low heat for 5 minutes. Let this cook slowly—do not turn the heat up—so that the garlic sweetens and flavors the purée.

3. After the garlic has turned a light golden color, add the whole tomatoes, breaking them up with your hands or a wooden spoon.

4. Add all the seasonings except the cilantro. Cook for 10 minutes over high heat to thicken the sauce. Add the cilantro and cook for 2 minutes more. Turn off heat.

5. When the chicken is done, remove the chicken breasts from the stock and let cool. When cool enough to handle, remove the meat from the bones and tear into bite-size pieces. Discard the bones.

6. Remove bay leaf from the stock. In a food processor or blender, purée about 1 cup of the stock and the vegetables. Return purée to the saucepan with the remaining stock.

7. Add the chicken pieces and the Tomato Purée. Stir, taste, and adjust seasonings. Heat for 1 minute, then serve immediately.

Each serving (15 oz) contains approximately 103 calories, 10.6 grams protein, 3.1 grams total fat, 23 mg cholesterol, 250 mg sodium.

FISH

FRESH HERB MARINATED SWORDFISH `Serves 6`

I am often asked for a fast, after-work recipe that is suitable for guests. Broiled fish is the answer. I've added a few special touches to this recipe that take little time, yet add the character that marks this "company fare."

2 pounds swordfish
olive oil spray or olive oil with garlic spray as needed
4 TB dry sherry
4 cloves garlic, finely minced
1 bunch fresh cilantro or basil, finely chopped

1. Preheat oven to Broil

2. Wash fish, pat dry, and spray with oil.

3. Sprinkle with sherry, then distribute minced garlic and cilantro evenly over tops of fish.

4. Cover and marinate in the refrigerator for about 30 minutes, if you have the time. Otherwise, proceed immediately to the next step.

5. Place fish on a broiler rack and broil for 7-10 minutes. Turn once halfway through. (If you have a convection oven you don't need to turn the fish.)

6. Serve immediately with the following Salsa Verde with Green Olives and Basil.

Each serving contains approximately 226 calories, 38.6 grams protein, 5.3 grams total fat, 0 mg cholesterol, 105 mg sodium.

SALSA VERDE WITH GREEN OLIVES AND BASIL `Serves 6`

A dd this snappy salsa to the swordfish recipe above or toss it with pasta and a few clams.

12 green olives, rinsed and finely minced
2 TB minced shallots
2 cloves garlic, finely minced
¹/₄ cup minced fresh Italian parsley
¹/₄ cup fresh basil leaves, finely minced
1 tsp extra virgin olive oil or Olio Santo (see page 10)

1. Combine all ingredients, stir, and serve with Fresh Herb Marinated Swordfish.

Makes about 1¹/₄ cups.

Each serving contains approximately 13 calories, 0.3 grams protein, 2 grams total fat, 0 mg cholesterol, 80 mg sodium.

SAMBUCA SHRIMP, VEGETABLES, AND PASTA IN FENNEL FLAVORED BROTH `Serves 6`

F ennel, tarragon, and sambuca liqueur all have a black licorice flavor, but once they are cooked, the sharpness of the licorice gives way to a sweet, nutty taste. It blends beautifully with shrimp. There will be lots of broth, so serve this in a deep dish or shallow bowl, with plenty of bread to soak up the juices.

BROTH
1 large fennel bulb, diced, plus tops and greens, chopped
1 medium yellow onion, diced
1 head garlic, broken up and peeled
24 medium shrimp shells
2 cups water

VEGETABLES, SHRIMP, AND PASTA

24 medium shrimp
¹/₂ medium red onion
5 roma tomatoes, peeled, seeded, diced
8 oz dried pasta
1 large fennel bulb, diced, plus tops and greens, chopped
6 cloves garlic
2 TB sambuca liqueur
¹/₄ tsp cayenne
1 tsp low sodium soy sauce
1 tsp dried tarragon
2 cups (¹/₄ pound) haricot verts beans or other green beans, sliced in half lengthwise
1/4 cup chopped fresh parsley
2 TB extra virgin olive oil or Olio Santo (see page 10)

1. To make the broth, place diced fennel bulb, plus chopped tops and greens from both fennel bulbs, diced onion, garlic cloves, and shrimp shells (only!) in the 2 cups of water. Bring to a boil, reduce heat to low, and "sweat" the flavor out of the vegetables and shrimp shells and into the water. Cook for 30 minutes, occasionally pushing the vegetables down into water.

2. Bring a large pot of water to a boil.

3. Clean and de-vein the shrimp.

4. Cut the onion into quarters, then slice the quarters crosswise (as opposed to lengthwise), making "C's" of them. Set aside.

5. To peel and seed the tomatoes, slice a small cross into the bottom of each tomato. Drop each into the pot of boiling water for 10 seconds. Remove and rinse with cold water. You will use this same pot of water to cook the pasta in Step 8.

6. Remove skin, starting with where you made the cross. Cut in half and squeeze out the seeds. Chop into cubes and set aside.

7. When the broth is done, strain through a large sieve or colander and discard the vegetables. Reserve the broth. Keep hot.

8. Cook the pasta in the boiling water for 10 minutes, or until al dente.

9. At the same time, sauté the fennel, onions, garlic, and tarragon in the sambuca over medium-high heat for

2 minutes. Pour in the boiling broth. Add shrimp and beans, cover and cook for 3 minutes.

10. When pasta is done, drain well and toss with oil and raw tomatoes. Add broth/vegetable mixture. Serve immediately.

Each serving contains approximately 210 calories, 7.5 grams protein, 5.3 grams total fat, 14 mg cholesterol, 38 mg sodium.

SALMON AND DILL WITH LEEKS, ASPARAGUS, AND BABY SQUASH, BAKED IN PARCHMENT PAPER `Serves 6`

When cooking with parchment paper, in essence you are creating a casserole dish out of paper. The food is cooked by the steam trapped in the sealed paper. It's great for company because it makes such a lovely presentation—origami with food in it! Also, you can assemble the packets ahead of time, place them on cookie sheets, and refrigerate them until you're ready to cook. Since the packets themselves are rather large, I usually serve the rest of the meal on a separate plate—salad and rice or potatoes. I do garnish the "packet plate" with fresh herbs, tomato slices, or edible flowers.

---

2 pounds salmon
2 4" sprigs fresh dill
2 cloves garlic, finely minced
2 small leeks, white parts only, sliced
24 asparagus, wood parts broken off and discarded
6 baby sunburst squash or other squash, sliced
24 yellow wax beans, ends trimmed, sliced lengthwise
6 tsp dry white wine
1 tsp extra virgin olive oil or Olio Santo (see page 10)

1. Preheat oven to 400° F.

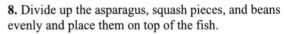

2. Wash and pat dry fish, remove skin, and cut into 1¹/₂" chunks. Set aside.

3. Arrange vegetables in separate piles or bowls so you can put the packets together like an assembly line.

4. Take out 6 pieces of parchment paper. Or, cut from a roll into pieces about 16" x 12". You can make the packets to cook the fish and vegetables in one of two ways: Either fold each piece of parchment paper in half so it measures 8" x 12" (approximately). Cut it out as if making a valentine. The finished piece, when opened, should be heart shaped. Fill by adding ingredients to the middle of one half of the heart. Fold the other half of the paper over the pile of ingredients. Seal by making overlapping folds all the way around, until you come to the tip of the package. Twist to close.
Or fold each piece of parchment paper in half so it measures 8" x 12" (approximately). Do not cut into any shape, just leave as a rectangle. Fill by adding ingredients to the middle of one-half of the rectangle. To seal, fold each of the 3 open, straight sides.

If you have difficulty sealing the packets, "glue" the edges before folding with a mixture of egg white and water. Brush on with a pastry brush, then fold to seal.

5. To assemble, add equal amounts of salmon chunks to the middle of one-half of each of the parchment packets.

6. Break up the sprigs of dill into smaller sprigs and place 1 piece on each chunk of fish in each packet.

7. Sprinkle with the garlic, then arrange the sliced leeks evenly over the fish.

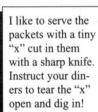

I like to serve the packets with a tiny "x" cut in them with a sharp knife. Instruct your diners to tear the "x" open and dig in!

8. Divide up the asparagus, squash pieces, and beans evenly and place them on top of the fish.

9. Add 1 tsp of wine to the top of each mound of fish and vegetables and sprinkle a few drops of oil over each.

10. Seal as described in Step 4.

11. Place packets on cookie sheets and bake for 15-18 minutes.

12. Serve 1 packet per person.

Each serving contains approximately 220 calories, 22.3 grams protein, 11.2 grams total fat, 66 mg cholesterol, 55 mg sodium.

POULTRY

CHICKEN BREASTS WITH CILANTRO LEMON SAUCE   *Serves 8*

This variation on basil pesto is also excellent on fish and tossed with linguine and peas.

SAUCE

4 cloves garlic, finely minced
2 tsp grated lemon peel
2 cups loosely packed fresh cilantro
¹/₂ cup loosely packed fresh parsley
¹/₄ cup chicken stock or white wine
¹/₄ cup fresh lemon juice
3 TB extra virgin olive oil
4 TB walnuts, chopped, or fresh breadcrumbs
4 TB freshly grated Parmesan cheese

CHICKEN

8 half skinless, boneless chicken breasts
1 large red onion, sliced into rounds

2 TB fresh lemon juice
$^1/_4$ cup chopped fresh parsley
1 bay leaf
2 cups chicken broth

1. Place garlic, lemon peel, cilantro, parsley, chicken stock or white wine, lemon juice, olive oil, walnuts, and Parmesan cheese in a food processor or blender and purée into a smooth sauce. Set aside.

2. Place the chicken breasts in a single layer in a large skillet. Top with the onion slices, lemon juice, parsley, and bay leaf. Pour chicken broth over the chicken. You need just enough so the chicken breasts are immersed. Bring to a boil, reduce heat to medium-low, and cook, covered, for 10 minutes, or until the chicken is done and no longer pink in the middle.

3. Using a slotted spoon, remove the chicken from the broth and arrange on serving plates. Top with onions from the pan, then add the sauce.

Each serving contains approximately 222 calories, 29.1 grams protein, 9.2 grams total fat, 68 mg cholesterol, 202 mg sodium.

CHICKEN, GRILLED ONION, AND FETA SALAD **Serves 4**

You can use an indoor grill, stovetop cast iron ridged grill, the broiler, or an outdoor barbecue to prepare the ingredients for this meal-size salad.

DRESSING
$^1/_2$ cup extra virgin olive oil
2 TB balsamic vinegar
3 TB fresh lemon juice
2 TB water, wine, or combination
1 TB Teriyaki sauce
2 tsp Dijon-style mustard
$^1/_2$ tsp dried tarragon

$^1/_4$ tsp salt or VegeSal
pinch cayenne

CHICKEN
1 red bell pepper
1 large red onion
4 half boneless, skinless chicken breasts
8 cups bite-size pieces of lettuce and greens, such as romaine, red leaf, oak leaf, Swiss chard, spinach, and radicchio
$^1/_2$ cup crumbled feta, rinsed
2 ripe tomatoes, cut into eighths

1. Prepare your grill and/or preheat the oven to Broil.

2. To make the dressing, combine all ingredients and whisk until well mixed. Refrigerate until needed.

3. Roast bell pepper by cutting in half lengthwise. Remove stems, seeds, and veins, and discard. Place, cut side down, on a lightly oiled cookie sheet and broil for 15-20 minutes, or until blackened. Place charred peppers in a bowl. Cover with a plate so the pepper steams in its own heat for 15 minutes to loosen the skin. When cool, peel away blackened skin and discard. Or, if using an outdoor grill, cut pepper halves into quarters. Grill on the skin side until blackened. Follow remaining instructions for peeling pepper. If using an indoor ridged grill for the chicken and onion, I suggest broiling the pepper. It's faster.

4. Cut peeled red pepper into strips and set aside.

5. Slice onion into $^1/_4$" thick slices. Grill or broil until soft, turning once. Separate into rings and set aside.

6. Grill or broil chicken for 5 minutes on the first side and 4 minutes on the second side. (If broiling in a convection oven, you don't need to turn the chicken.) When done, cut into strips.

7. To assemble the salad, toss the lettuce and greens with some of the dressing. (There will be leftover dressing.) Arrange on 4 dinner plates. Sprinkle feta on top of each. Add pepper strips, tomatoes, and grilled onion rings. Top with chicken strips and serve immediately.

Each serving of salad contains approximately 279 calories, 46.2 grams protein, 5.9 grams total fat, 114 mg cholesterol, 105 mg sodium.

Each serving (2 TB) of dressing contains approximately 62 calories, 0.1 grams protein, 6.8 grams total fat, 0 mg cholesterol, 85 mg sodium.

SHREDDED CHICKEN AND SPINACH TACOS WITH GOAT CHEESE
Serves 8

When I told my husband I was making these somewhat unconventional tacos for dinner, he thought it was blasphemy. Don's a die-hard Mexican food man, and any variation to him is shameful. One tentative nibble later, he declared it passable. After his third taco, it was clear he liked it. When he actually requested "those goat cheese tacos" for dinner one night, I knew I had a convert!

CHICKEN

4 half (about 2 pounds total) chicken breasts, with bones, skinless
1 large yellow onion, cut into quarters
1/2 tsp dried thyme
1 bay leaf
5 cups water
1 red onion, diced
4 cloves garlic, finely minced
4 jalapeño chiles, minced (optional)
1 TB extra virgin olive oil
4 medium-size ripe tomatoes or 1 28-oz can whole tomatoes, drained

TORTILLAS AND TOPPINGS

1 bunch spinach
8 corn tortillas
4 TB crumbled goat cheese or crumbled feta cheese, rinsed
4 scallions, sliced into rounds

1 recipe Fresh Salsa (see page 89) or salsa of choice, as needed

1. Place chicken breasts, onion quarters, thyme, and bay leaf in a pot filled with 5 cups of water.

2. Bring to a boil, cover, reduce heat to low and simmer for 15 minutes.

3. When done, remove chicken and set aside to cool. Reserve about 3/4 cup of the cooking water.

4. Remove chicken meat from bones. Shred, or tear apart, and set aside. Discard bones.

5. Sauté onion, garlic, and chiles in the olive oil for 5 minutes until the onion is transparent.

6. Dice or crush the tomatoes with your hands or a wooden spoon and add them to the sauté pan. Add 1/2 cup of the reserved cooking liquid from the chicken pot. Reduce heat to low and simmer for 10 minutes, until the sauce thickens.

7. Add shredded chicken and stir. Simmer for 5 minutes. Cover pan to keep hot.

8. Meanwhile, prepare the spinach. Wash well, and remove and discard stems and discolored leaves. Tear spinach leaves into bite-size pieces.

9. Heat about 1/4 cup of the reserved chicken cooking water in another sauté pan. Add spinach and cook, covered, for about 5 minutes, or until the spinach is wilted.

10. To heat tortillas, spray a non-stick skillet or pancake griddle with vegetable oil spray. Heat pan and cook tortillas for about 1 minute on each side, or until soft. (Alternately, cook longer, until golden and crisp and assemble these as tostadas, piling all the ingredients on top of a flat tortilla.)

11. To serve, place some chicken with sauce in the middle of a tortilla. Add cheese, then wilted spinach. Top with scallions and salsa. These are soft shell tacos, so either let them fall open, or pin them together with a toothpick.

Each serving contains approximately 221 calories, 20.2 grams protein, 5.9 grams total fat, 40 mg cholesterol, 186 mg sodium.

QUICK CHICKEN FAJITAS

Serves 8

Fast, easy and delicious!

4 half skinless, boneless chicken breasts
1 cup salsa of choice
4 cloves garlic, finely minced
1 TB canola oil
1 yellow onion, cut into strips
2 Poblano (hot) or Anaheim (mild) chiles, seeded, de-veined, and diced
black pepper to taste
8 flour tortillas, preferably whole wheat flour

1. Cut raw chicken breasts into strips of equal size. Add to a bowl of salsa and marinate for at least 1 hour, or overnight.

2. If you have a cast iron skillet, use it to sauté the garlic in oil over low heat. Otherwise, use any other good quality, heavy skillet.

3. Increase the heat to high. Using a slotted spoon or tongs, remove the chicken strips from the marinade and place in skillet. Discard remaining marinade.

4. When chicken has turned from pink to white, add onions, chiles, and black pepper and stir-fry mixture over high heat until cooked but not dried out. The onion strips will still be white, not transparent, so they will have a little crunch to them.

> Roll up tortillas and use them to "push" the chicken and vegetables onto your fork. Take a bite of the chicken, then of the tortilla. Or, you can also spoon the chicken mixture into the tortillas and eat them as tacos.

5. Meanwhile, warm the flour tortillas, 1 at a time, in a non-stick skillet. Or wrap all 8 tortillas in a damp paper towel and heat in the microwave for 1 minute on full power. Check and cook longer if needed.

6. Transfer chicken mixture to serving plates and serve tortillas on the side.

Each serving contains approximately 218 calories, 17.4 grams protein, 5.6 grams total fat, 34 mg cholesterol, 190 mg sodium.

VEGETABLE MAIN DISHES

CRANBERRY BEANS WITH MUSHROOMS AND SAGE, ON A BED OF DANDELION GREENS

Serves 8

Cranberry beans are also known as Fagioli della Regina, or The Queen's Beans! They are a lovely mottled rose color when raw, but cook up looking just like pinto beans. They are much creamier than pintos though, and have a richer flavor. Look for 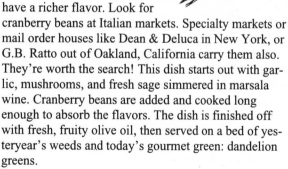 cranberry beans at Italian markets. Specialty markets or mail order houses like Dean & Deluca in New York, or G.B. Ratto out of Oakland, California carry them also. They're worth the search! This dish starts out with garlic, mushrooms, and fresh sage simmered in marsala wine. Cranberry beans are added and cooked long enough to absorb the flavors. The dish is finished off with fresh, fruity olive oil, then served on a bed of yesteryear's weeds and today's gourmet green: dandelion greens.

1¹/₂ cups dried cranberry beans or pinto beans
4 cups water
2 bay leaves
6" strip kombu seaweed (optional)
salt or VegeSal as needed
4 cloves garlic, finely minced
¹/₂ tsp dried sage or 1¹/₂ TB minced fresh sage

12 mushrooms, sliced
8 shiitake mushrooms, stems discarded, tops sliced
3 TB marsala wine
1 TB extra virgin olive oil
1-2 bunches dandelion greens or arugula or shredded radicchio

1. Soak beans for at least 8 hours, then drain soaking water. Or, quick soak by placing beans in a saucepan of water. Bring to a boil, turn off the heat, and let sit, covered, for 1½ hours. Drain water.

2. Add 4 cups of fresh water to soaked beans, then add the bay leaves and kombu seaweed. Bring to a boil, reduce heat to low, and cook covered, for about 1 hour, or until beans are tender.

3. Remove kombu seaweed and bay leaves and discard. Taste the beans and season with salt.

4. Meanwhile, in a sauté pan, sauté the garlic, sage, and mushrooms in the marsala wine over medium heat for 5 minutes.

5. Add the beans to the sauté pan mixture. Stir, taste, and adjust seasonings, adding more marsala or salt, if needed.

6. Remove from heat and let cook for about 10 minutes. Just before serving, stir in the olive oil.

7. Serve warm or at room temperature on a bed of dandelion greens, arugula, or shredded radicchio leaves.

Each serving contains approximately 116 calories, 5.5 grams protein, 2.5 grams total fat, 0 mg cholesterol, 138 mg sodium.

LIGHT LASAGNE ROLLS | Serves 8

L asagne is thought of as a heavy, filling dish. This version, however, is extremely light and perfect for the warmer days of spring. Tofu does

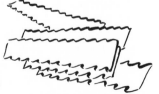

the trick! There is nothing you can substitute for it and achieve this wonderful light quality. Cottage cheese and ricotta make the usual, heavier version. If this is your first venture with tofu, buy the type of tofu in the tub. Cut the tub open and drain out the water. Rinse it, then crumble it into the food processor or blender per the instructions below. This is a wonderful luncheon dish served with any of the suggested sauces. I bet you a nickel at least one of your guests will ask you for the recipe!

---

*Liza's Spaghetti Sauce (see page 19) or Classic
   Marinara (see page 96) or Spring Marinara (see
   page 60), as needed*
½ bunch Swiss chard or spinach
1 medium yellow onion, diced
3 cloves garlic, finely minced
1 TB extra virgin olive oil
8 oz fresh tofu, firm
pinch nutmeg
1 tsp grated lemon peel
4 ozs part-skim milk mozzarella cheese or mozzarel-
   la-style soy cheese, shredded
16 Fresh Lasagne Noodles (see recipe below) or
   lasagne noodles, cooked and drained or store-
   bought fresh lasagne noodles, uncooked

1. Preheat oven to 350° F. Make sauce of choice or defrost a batch and heat in a saucepan.

2. Wash Swiss chard or spinach well and remove and discard stems and discolored leaves. Chop into bite-size pieces.

3. In a large sauté pan, sauté the onion and garlic in the olive oil for 5 minutes, until the onion is transparent.

4. Add chard or spinach. Cover and steam for 10 minutes until wilted.

5. Meanwhile, place the tofu in a food processor or blender and blend until creamy in texture. Add the nutmeg, lemon peel, and shredded cheese. Add the sautéed onion mixture, being careful not to add too much liquid from the pan into the food processor. Set aside.

6. Make the Fresh Lasagne Noodles or boil dried noodles and set aside or open the package of storebought fresh noodles.

7. To assemble the rolls, spread tofu mixture along the length of a lasagne noodle, and then top with a little sauce. Roll and place, seam side down, in a baking sheet that has been coated with sauce. Repeat with each lasagne roll.

8. Top each roll with extra sauce and bake, covered, for 15 minutes. Uncover and bake 20 minutes more. Serve 2 rolls per person. Add extra sauce, if desired.

Each serving contains approximately 286 calories, 12.5 grams protein, 10.4 grams total fat, 8 mg cholesterol, 388 mg sodium.

FRESH PASTA FOR LASAGNE NOODLES   *Makes 16 noodles*

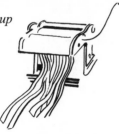

2 cups semolina flour or 1 cup
    unbleached flour and 1
    cup semolina flour
1 tsp extra virgin olive oil
    (optional)
1 egg white
water as needed

1. Blend the flours in a bowl and make a well in the center. Add the olive oil and egg white and mix with a fork.

2. Gradually mix in up to a ¹/₂ cup water until the dough can be pressed together into a solid ball.

3. Transfer the dough to a lightly floured surface and knead it for a few minutes. The dough should come cleanly away from the surface. If it is too wet, incorporate flour 1 TB at a time until the dough is no longer sticky. If the dough is dry and crumbly incorporate water until it is pliable.

4. Knead the dough about 3 minutes or until smooth and elastic.

5. Wrap the dough in a towel and let it rest for 15 minutes before rolling it out.

6. Divide the dough into 4 equal pieces. Work with 1 piece at a time, keeping the other pieces in the towel.

7. Flatten the first piece and lightly flour both sides. Set the knob of the pasta machine's rollers for the widest setting. Pass the dough through the feeder, cranking the rollers with one hand and catching the dough with the other.

8. On a lightly floured surface, fold the piece into thirds and press down to flatten it. Run it lengthwise through the machine once more. Repeat the process 2 more times, folding the dough into thirds each time.

9. Adjust the control to the next smaller setting, and feed the entire sheet through the machine, without folding. Repeat, narrowing the setting each time, until the desired thickness is achieved—usually to the second to last setting. Flour the dough as necessary to prevent it from sticking. Continue with remaining pieces of dough.

10. Let noodles dry slightly on a drying rack or laid flat over towels. While still moist, assemble lasagne rolls (see recipe above).

Each lasagne noodle contains approximately 25 calories, 1.5 grams protein, 0.5 grams total fat, 0 mg cholesterol, 4 mg sodium.

CALZONE WITH ROASTED RED PEPPER SAUCE   *Serves 8*

Calzones, stuffed pizzas, can be made with all sorts of appealing combinations, but this is my favorite. It is light because the calzone shell is very thin, and rich tasting because of the savory flavor of the sauce and the creamy texture of the cheese.

CHEESE AND DOUGH

1 Calzone Dough recipe (see recipe below)
4 oz part-skim milk mozzarella, shredded (optional)
¹/₂ cup freshly grated Parmesan cheese

ROASTED RED PEPPER SAUCE

4 red bell peppers
1 large yellow onion, diced
4 cloves garlic, finely minced
1 TB extra virgin olive oil
$^1/_8$ tsp dried marjoram
$^1/_4$ cup water
salt or VegeSal to taste

VEGETABLE FILLING

4 cups diced zucchini, crookneck squash, and/or
summer squash

1. Preheat the oven to Broil. Make calzone dough and set aside to rise.

2. To make sauce, roast red bell peppers by cutting each in half lengthwise. Remove stem, seeds, and veins and discard. Place cut side down, on a lightly oiled cookie sheet and broil for 15-20 minutes or until blackened. Place charred peppers in a bowl. Cover with a plate so the peppers steam in their own heat for about 15 minutes to loosen their skin. When cooled, peel away blackened skin and discard, saving any juices in the bowl. Reduce heat of oven to 500° F.

3. Place the peppers in a food processor or blender and process until smooth.

4. Meanwhile, sauté onion and garlic in olive oil for 5 minutes, or until the onions turn clear. Add marjoram and cook for 2 minutes more.

5. Place the onion mixture in a food processor with the roasted peppers and blend into a smooth sauce. Add water. Taste and add salt, if needed. Set sauce aside in a large mixing bowl.

6. Place vegetables in a steamer basket and steam for 2 minutes, or until al dente. When done, add to sauce and stir to mix.

7. When calzone dough is ready, divide into 8 equal pieces. Roll out each piece until flat and cut out a 6" circle using a sandwich plate as guide.

8. Place dough circles on lightly oiled cookie sheets. Fill half with vegetable/sauce mixture. Add 1 TB mozzarella and 1 TB Parmesan cheese.

9. Fold other half over and pinch edges around to seal. They should look like turnovers. Repeat with each calzone.

10. Bake at 500° F for 12 minutes. Serve immediately. Spoon on extra sauce, if desired.

Each serving contains approximately 264 calories, 14.6 grams protein, 10.3 grams total fat, 19 mg cholesterol, 308 mg sodium.

CALZONE DOUGH

Makes enough for 8 calzones

I f you want to make this dough the night before, see the notes on page 19 in the recipe for Pizza Dough on refrigerating and freezing dough.

$^3/_4$ cup water
1 package yeast
pinch honey or other sweetener of choice
1 cup whole wheat pastry flour or 1 cup + 2 TB
unbleached flour
1 cup unbleached flour
1 TB extra virgin olive oil

1. Heat water to bath water temperature (105°-115° F). Add yeast and sweetener and let sit for 5 minutes, or until the mixture begins to foam. If it hasn't foamed within 5 minutes, that means your yeast is no good. Discard and begin again with a fresh package.

2. Meanwhile, place the flours in a medium-size bowl. Add olive oil. Mix well so that the oil is distributed throughout the flours.

3. When the yeast has foamed, add it to the flours. Mix well, then turn out onto a lightly floured surface. Dust hands with flour and knead for 5 minutes. To knead, press down on the dough with the heels of your hands and push it away from you, then partially fold it back over itself. Turn it a quarter and repeat the procedure. While kneading, very gradually add a little extra flour to the work surface to keep the dough from sticking. Knead until dough is smooth, elastic, and shiny.

4. Shape the dough into a ball and transfer to a lightly oiled bowl. Turn to coat the dough with oil on all sides. Cover with plastic wrap or a damp towel and let rise in a draft-free place until double in size, about 45 minutes. You know the dough has risen enough when the indentation left by your finger in the dough doesn't rise back up at you.

5. Punch dough down and shape as indicated above in Calzone recipe.

Each serving contains approximately 126 calories, 3.9 grams protein, 2.2 grams total fat, 0 mg cholesterol, 2 mg sodium.

SPRING VEGETABLE ENCHILADAS
Serves 6

You know how at the end of the week you have an odd assortment of vegetables left and you're not quite sure what to do with them? Around here, it's typical that we have a half a zucchini, 3 asparagus, a quarter head of cauliflower, leftover steamed broccoli, and a small handful of almost-gone green beans. Well, these enchiladas will make wonderful use of all of them. Dice them up and wrap a tortilla around them! Kids barely even notice they're eating veggies! I call for Mexican Hot Sauce to top the enchiladas, but you can also use Fresh Salsa (see page 89), your favorite store bought salsa, or Tomatillo Sauce (see page 92).

---

3 cups diced assorted vegetables, such as cauliflower, broccoli, carrots, zucchini, asparagus, etc.
12 corn tortillas
1 recipe Mexican Hot Sauce (see recipe below) or Tomatillo Sauce (see recipe page 92)
6 ozs reduced fat Monterey Jack cheese or soy cheese, grated
Fresh Salsa (see page 89) or salsa of choice as needed

1. Make Mexican Hot Sauce and let simmer or defrost a batch and bring to a boil, then let simmer. Preheat oven to 350° F.

2. Dice vegetables in fairly small pieces—they have to be rolled up into a little tortilla.

3. Bring the water in your steamer pot to a boil. Place the vegetables in the steamer basket and steam for 3 minutes. Set aside to cool.

4. To make tortillas pliable enough to roll, save on oil, and flavor the tortilla, cook them in a non-stick skillet, using 1 TB of the Mexican Hot Sauce per tortilla to lubricate the pan.

5. When you are ready to assemble the enchiladas, spoon 1/2 cup of the Mexican Hot Sauce into the bottom of a 9" x 13" baking pan and spread evenly to coat.

6. Place about 2 TB of vegetables in a strip down the middle of each tortilla.

7. Sprinkle with 1 TB of cheese.

8. Place, seam side down, in a baking pan in a single layer. When all are assembled, spoon remaining sauce over top.

9. Bake for 15-20 minutes, or until heated through and bubbling.

10. Serve with salsa on the side, if desired.

Each serving (2 enchiladas) contains approximately 340 calories, 15.4 grams protein, 11.6 grams total fat, 19 mg cholesterol, 217 mg sodium.

MEXICAN HOT SAUCE
Makes 5 cups

This is an indispensable sauce. I always have a batch in the freezer, frozen in 8-ounce containers. Not only can you make enchiladas with it, but you can stir it into rice, top an omelette with it, toss it with pasta, mix it with black beans, jazz up a quesadilla, add it to veggies and rice, stuff peppers with it, dress up a tuna melt, stir it into boring canned soup—anything! I make it with ¹/₂ tsp cayenne and it's fairly hot. If you or your kids can't take it, use less, or omit the cayenne altogether.

---

1 medium red onion, diced
3 cloves garlic, finely minced
1 tsp ground cumin
¹/₄ tsp ground coriander
¹/₄-¹/₂ tsp cayenne
¹/₂ tsp chili powder
¹/₄ tsp black pepper
1 TB extra virgin olive oil
2 16-oz cans tomato purée
1 TB dry red wine

1. Sauté onion, garlic, and spices in the olive oil for 5 minutes, or until the onion is transparent.

2. Add remaining ingredients. Bring to a boil, then reduce heat to low and simmer for at least 45 minutes or up to 2 hours.

Each serving (1 cup) contains approximately 117 calories, 4 grams protein, 3.2 grams total fat, 0 mg cholesterol, 38 mg sodium.

CALIFORNIA PAELLA   `Serves 8`

Only a Californian would make a vegetarian paella! Slivered almonds take the place of any meat or seafood. And since it's already pretty "California," heck, why not add chiles and cilantro! An avocado wouldn't hurt either, come to think of it.

¹/₄ cup slivered raw almonds
2 large red onions, diced
5 cloves garlic, finely minced
2 TB extra virgin olive oil
1 tsp (0.2 grams) saffron threads
2³/₄ cups boiling water
1¹/₂ cups raw short grain brown rice
2 cups green or yellow beans, cut into 1" pieces
1 large red bell pepper, cut into strips
1 Anaheim (mild) or Poblano (hot) chile, seeded, de-
   veined, and cut into strips
6 roma tomatoes, quartered
1¹/₂ tsp black pepper
¹/₂ cup fresh cilantro leaves, chopped

1. Preheat oven to 325° F.

2. Toast almonds in the oven for 15 minutes, or until golden. Set aside. Turn oven off.

3. In a large sauté pan or paella pan, sauté onion and garlic in the olive oil for 5 minutes.

4. Dissolve the saffron in the boiling water.

5. Add the rice to the sauté pan and stir-fry for a few minutes. Add the boiling saffron water. Bring it back to a boil, reduce heat to low, and cook, covered, for 50 minutes.

6. After 35 minutes, add the almonds and beans. Cook for 5 minutes.

7. Add the red pepper and chile strips and cook for 10 minutes.

8. Add the tomatoes and black pepper to the cooked rice. Cover the pan and remove it from the heat. Let it sit for 15 minutes.

9. After lifting the lid, if there is still too much liquid in the pan, place it in the oven. Heat oven to 325° F for 5 minutes, then turn oven off. When ready to serve, stir in the fresh cilantro.

Each serving contains approximately 226 calories, 5.5 grams protein, 6.6 grams total fat, 0 mg cholesterol, 17 mg sodium.

PASTAS

COOL AND SPICY THAI LINGUINE `Serves 4`

There are so many different flavors in this pasta dish! It's cool from the mint and lime and spicy from the jalapeño. Yet it's also fresh from the sprouts and savory from the peanuts. I like to break the linguine noodles in half before cooking. When the dish is done you can't tell the difference between linguine and the same shaped but much differently textured mung bean sprouts. Soft or crunchy? You won't know until you taste it!

PASTA AND GARNISH
8 oz linguine
4 TB roasted peanuts, finely chopped

SAUCE
4 cloves garlic, finely minced
1 TB sesame oil (not toasted) or canola oil
3 TB dry sherry
1/2 cup canned tomato sauce
3 TB fresh lime juice
1 tsp grated lime peel
1/2 tsp Tabasco

VEGETABLES
3 scallions, sliced into rounds
1 jalapeño chile, finely minced
4 TB minced fresh mint
2 cups mung bean sprouts

1. Bring a large pot of water to a boil. Before cooking pasta, break it in half. Cook pasta in the boiling water for 10 minutes, or until al dente.

2. Meanwhile, in a small skillet, sauté garlic in the sesame oil over medium heat for 1 minute. Add the remaining sauce ingredients and simmer for 5 minutes.

3. Drain the pasta well and toss with the sauce.

4. Add scallions, chile, mint, and sprouts. Toss, garnish with the peanuts, and serve.

Each serving contains approximately 232 calories, 8.5 grams protein, 6 grams total fat, 0 mg cholesterol, 202 mg sodium.

PASTA PRIMAVERA `Serves 6`

This is my version of spring's favorite pasta dish! Add other vegetables if you have them around, such as peas, snow peas, wild mushrooms, asparagus tips, artichoke hearts, or squash blossoms. Just make sure you use some mushrooms in the dish, as their juices compose most of the sauce. In making this recipe, there are three steps that need to occur at about the same time, so clean and chop all the vegetables before you put even one thing in the sauté pan.

4 cloves garlic, finely minced
2 shallots, finely minced
1 TB extra virgin olive oil
3 TB dry white wine
4 large mushrooms, sliced
2 carrots, cut into matchsticks
1/2 cup broccoli, cut into florets
2 zucchini, sliced into matchsticks
1 yellow crookneck squash, sliced into matchsticks
8 oz dried spaghetti or linguine or fettucine
1 small red bell pepper, cut into thin strips
1/4 cup chopped fresh parsley
freshly grated Parmigiano Reggiano as needed

1. Bring a large pot of water to a boil for the pasta. Bring the water in your steamer pot to a boil.

2. Meanwhile, in a large sauté pan, sauté garlic and shallots in the olive oil and wine for about 5 minutes. Add mushrooms and sauté on low heat until they give up their juices, about 5-7 minutes, then turn heat off.

3. Place the carrots and broccoli in the steamer basket and steam for about 2¹/₂ minutes. Add the zucchini and squash and steam for about 1¹/₂ minutes. Set aside. They will not be completely cooked at this point.

4. Cook the pasta in the boiling water for 10 minutes, or until al dente.

5. Meanwhile, add the bell pepper strips to the mushroom mixture and cook over low to medium heat for 3 minutes. Do not cook away the juices.

6. Add the pre-steamed vegetables to the sauté pan and cook for 3 minutes more.

7. Drain the pasta well, and add it to a large serving bowl.

8. Add the sautéed vegetables, parsley, and Parmesan cheese to the pasta. Toss well and serve immediately.

Each serving (using ¹/₃ cup of parmigiano) contains approximately 222 calories, 8.8 grams protein, 5.3 grams total fat, 4 mg cholesterol, 111 mg sodium.

SPRING MARINARA `Serves 4`

I made this dish in the first cooking class I taught. The group of six students were friends from my Toastmasters club, all professional women. About an hour into class, the talk turned to guys, guys, guys—and it got wild! I think their reports of such fun helped my business grow as quickly as it did! I do know they learned something about cooking, however, because they all talk about "craving that Carrot Marinara," as they call this dish, and whipping it up at least twice a month.

4 cloves garlic, finely minced
2 medium yellow onions, diced
1 TB extra virgin olive oil
2 carrots, sliced
1 TB dried basil

3 TB dry white wine
¹/₄ cup water
1 28-oz can crushed tomatoes
*   with added purée*
8 oz dried spaghetti

> If you can't find crushed tomatoes with added purée, use 1 28-oz can whole tomatoes, drained of liquid and re-filled with purée to the top (approximately ¹/₂ of a 16-oz can of tomato purée).

1. Bring a large pot of water to a boil.

2. In a 3-4 quart saucepan, sauté garlic and onions in olive oil for 5 minutes, or until the onions are clear.

3. Add the carrots, basil, and wine. Simmer, covered, over medium-low heat for 20 minutes, or until the carrots are tender.

4. Cook the pasta in the boiling water for 10 minutes, or until al dente.

5. Place the carrot mixture in a food processor or blender and process until smooth, adding a little extra water as needed, up to ¹/₄ cup.

6. Pour the tomatoes into a saucepan. Add the carrot mixture. Stir well and heat until bubbly.

7. Drain the pasta well and transfer to a serving bowl. Add the sauce and toss.

Each serving contains approximately 397 calories, 15.1 grams protein, 8.3 grams total fat, 6 mg cholesterol, 189 mg sodium.

VEGETABLE SIDE DISHES

GREEN CHILE POCKETS `Serves 8`

Pockets made of chiles are stuffed with asparagus and cheese, then baked to a soft, creamy perfection.

¹/₂ recipe Mexican Hot Sauce (see page 58)
16 fresh Anaheim chiles or 16 whole green chiles
from a can
80 (2 bunches) asparagus, woody part broken off
and discarded
4 oz reduced fat sharp Cheddar cheese, grated
5 black olives, pitted, rinsed, and sliced (optional)

1. Preheat oven to Broil, if using fresh chiles; preheat to 350° F. if using canned chiles. Make Mexican Hot Sauce or defrost a batch, bring to a boil, then turn to simmer.

2. If using fresh chiles, cut a slit in them by slicing from the top down to the tip. De-seed and de-vein them, trying to keep the top on. Broil the chiles until blackened, turning to evenly cook. Place charred chiles in a bowl. Cover with a plate so they can steam in their own heat for 10 minutes to loosen their skin. When cooled, peel away blackened skin and discard. Reduce oven temperature to 350° F. Or, if using canned chiles, rinse and cut a slit in them by slicing from top to tip. Proceed as directed.

3. Meanwhile, place asparagus in a steamer basket and steam for about 3 minutes or until al dente.

4. Fill each chile "pocket" with 5 asparagus spears and about 1 TB of the grated Cheddar cheese.

5. Spoon Mexican Hot Sauce over the bottom of an 8" x 13" baking pan. Place filled chiles on top of the sauce. Spoon sauce over the top of the chiles. Sprinkle black olives over top, and a little more cheese.

6. Bake for 15 minutes and serve 2 stuffed chiles per person as a side dish or appetizer.

Each serving contains approximately 129 calories, 7.4 grams protein, 5.1 total fat, 12 mg cholesterol, 120 mg sodium.

BEET GREENS AND FRESH BABY CARROTS
Serves 6

Fresh carrots and garlic are cooked slowly until they melt and become a sort of "sauce" for the naturally sweet beet greens. If the carrots aren't

fresh and full of moisture, the dish won't work. If you can't pull them straight out of your own garden, make sure you buy carrots with fresh looking greens to assure their recent harvest.

---

2 TB pine nuts
2 cloves garlic, finely sliced
2 4-inch baby carrots, very thinly sliced
1 TB extra virgin olive oil
2 bunches beets, with greens attached
1 TB fresh lemon juice

1. To toast pine nuts, either add pine nuts to a dry skillet. Turn heat to high and watch very carefully. As soon as you smell the aroma of nuts toasting, remove them from the heat. Or preheat oven to 325° F. and toast for 10 minutes, or until lightly golden.

2. In a sauté pan, sauté garlic and carrots in olive oil over very low heat for 10-15 minutes, or until the garlic is light golden. Be patient—do not turn the heat up.

3. Meanwhile, cut the beet greens from the beets. Store beets in the refrigerator for another use. Wash the beet greens very well. Cut off any thick stems and discard. Chop into bite-size pieces.

4. When the garlic is light golden and the carrots have begun to "melt," add the beet greens. Water will still be on the leaves, which will help to wilt the beet greens. Cook, covered, for 10-12 minutes.

5. When done, squeeze lemon juice over greens and toss well. Add toasted pine nuts and toss again. Serve immediately.

Each serving contains approximately 108 calories, 4.6 grams protein, 4.9 grams total fat, 0 mg cholesterol, 302 mg sodium.

MUSTARD GREENS IN BROTH

Serves 6

I think by this time you've noticed that I am a nut about greens! This is one of the best ways I know to cook the bitter greens. They become soft and sweet while simmering in rich broth.

2 bunches mustard greens
2 cloves garlic, finely minced
1 small yellow onion, diced
1 TB extra virgin olive oil
1 cup chicken broth or Homemade Chicken Stock (see page 44) or Japanese Broth (Dashi) (see page 45)

1. Wash greens well. Do not dry them. Cut into bite-size pieces and set aside.

2. In a sauté pan, sauté the garlic and onion in the olive oil over medium heat for 5 minutes.

3. Add the broth and bring to a boil.

4. Add greens to the sauté pan. Reduce heat and simmer, covered for 25 minutes, or until the greens are tender. Serve immediately.

Each serving contains approximately 71 calories, 4.9 grams protein, 2.8 grams total fat, 0.1 mg cholesterol, 124 mg sodium.

POTATO AND TOMATO GRATIN

Serves 8

The heat of the oven blends and strengthens the flavors in this layered vegetable casserole, as it softens their texture. For a variation, you might like

to substitute a little grated Gruyere cheese for the olives.

4 medium size potatoes
1 large red onion, sliced into rounds
3 cloves garlic, finely minced
1 TB extra virgin olive oil
2 TB dry white wine
¹/₄ tsp dried thyme
¹/₂ tsp dried marjoram
4 medium size ripe tomatoes, sliced into rounds
10-12 black olives, pitted, rinsed, and sliced

1. Preheat oven to 400°F.

2. Slice the unpeeled potatoes into ¹/₄" rounds. Place in the steamer basket and steam for 20-25 minutes, or until they are soft.

3. Sauté the onion and garlic in the olive oil and wine for 5 minutes, or until the onion becomes transparent.

4. Add herbs and cook for 2 minutes more.

5. Cover the bottom of a gratin dish or casserole with half the onion mixture, then 1 layer of tomato slices, 1 layer of potato slices, a sprinkle of chopped olives, tomato slices, potato slices, olives, and so on. End with the other half of the onion mixture.

6. Bake, covered, for 20 minutes, then uncover and bake for 25 minutes more, or until the potatoes are done.

Each serving contains approximately 151 calories, 3.1 grams protein, 3.4 grams total fat, 0 mg cholesterol, 62 mg sodium.

ASIAN RICE SALAD

Serves 8

Lots of flavors, lots of colors. This salad is also good made with lentils in place of the rice. The recipe makes 1 cup of dressing, so there will be leftovers for tomorrow night's green salad.

RICE SALAD

2¹/₄ cup water
1 cup raw long grain brown rice
¹/₄ cup raw slivered almonds
2 tsp low sodium soy sauce
¹/₄ cup minced fresh cilantro
¹/₂ cup fresh peas or frozen and defrosted
2 scallions, sliced into rounds
3 cups mung bean sprouts

DRESSING

¹/₂ cup canola oil
¹/₄ cup red wine vinegar
2 TB water
1¹/₂ tsp toasted sesame oil
2 TB capers, rinsed
1 TB minced fresh mint leaves
1 tsp low sodium soy sauce
¹/₈ tsp cayenne

1. Preheat oven to 325° F.

2. Add the 2¹/₄ cups of water to a 3-4 quart saucepan and bring it to a boil. Add the rice, reduce heat to low, and simmer, covered, for 35 minutes, or until the rice is done and fluffy.

3. Meanwhile, toast the almonds in the oven for 12 minutes, or until light golden. Remove and set aside.

4. Stir the soy sauce into the cooked rice. Set aside to cool.

5. To make the dressing, place all ingredients in a food processor or blender and process till pureed.

6. Turn the rice out into a serving bowl. Mix in the almonds, cilantro, peas, scallions, and sprouts.

7. Toss with ¹/₄ cup of the dressing. Serve as is, or on a bed of lettuce. Serve warm or at room temperature.

Each serving (rice, vegetables, plus a total of ¹/₄ cup dressing) contains approximately 161 calories, 4.3 grams protein, 6.4 grams total fat, 0 mg cholesterol, 76 mg sodium.

Each 1 TB of leftover dressing contains approximately 66 calories, 0 grams protein, 7.2 grams total fat, 0 mg cholesterol, 21 mg sodium.

BRAISED FENNEL   `Serves 4`

As with all root vegetables, cut the stalks or greens off as soon as you bring the fennel home from the grocery store. Otherwise, energy will be robbed from the bulb to produce leaves in the tops. Topless fennel should last for a month in your refrigerator. Peel away any browned outer layers before using.

2 bulbs fennel
¹/₄ cup water
¹/₄ cup dry white wine
¹/₄ tsp black pepper
¹/₄ cup freshly grated Parmigiano Reggiano

1. Preheat oven to 400° F.

2. Cut bulbs of fennel lengthwise into ¹/₄" slices.

3. Add fennel slices, water, and wine to a sauté pan. Simmer, covered, over low heat for 20 minutes.

4. When fennel has cooked for 20 minutes, transfer to an ovenproof dish (or not if your sauté pan is ovenproof). Sprinkle the fennel with the cheese and bake for 15 minutes, or until lightly browned on top.

Each serving contains approximately 47 calories, 2.6 grams protein, 1.6 grams total fat, 4 mg cholesterol, 144 mg sodium.

SWEETS

LEMON SEMOLINA POUND CAKE WITH FRESH BERRIES

Serves 12

In the old days, a recipe for Pound Cake was easy to remember. A pound of eggs, a pound of butter, a pound of sugar, and a pound of flour made what must have been the largest and fattiest cake ever! The most common modern pound cake has been slimmed down to a mere 14 TB of butter and various combinations of the other ingredients.

My version calls for only 4 TB of butter, yet the result is full flavored and well-textured. You can make it in a loaf pan, or a 6-cup capacity Nordic Ware black bundt pan. The bundt pan most of us have, however, is a 12-cup capacity. Don't use that, or the pound cake will look like an "Inch Cake!" Do buy the smaller bundt pan, if you can. Use it not only for this pound cake, but for your banana and pumpkin breads, too. It's the perfect size to make loaf bread recipes in.

CAKE
3 egg whites
1/2 cup maple syrup
1 1/2 tsp vanilla
1/2 cup nonfat plain yogurt
1/4 cup semolina flour
1/4 cup sweet butter, at room temperature
1 3/4 cup unbleached flour
1 TB grated lemon peel
3/4 tsp baking powder
1/4 tsp baking soda
1/4 tsp salt

If semolina flour is unavailable, use more unbleached flour (for a total of 2 cups flour). Cream the butter with 1/4 cup unbleached flour in Step 4.

SYRUP
2 TB fresh lemon juice
2 TB maple syrup

GARNISH
1 pint strawberries, raspberries, or other berries of choice

1. Preheat oven to 350° F.

2. To make the cake, in a mixing bowl, combine egg whites, maple syrup, vanilla, and yogurt. Set aside.

3. In another bowl, combine unbleached flour, lemon peel, baking powder, baking soda, and salt. Stir well to mix and set aside.

4. In a large mixing bowl, cream together the semolina flour and the room-temperature butter. Mix on low speed for 30 seconds to blend well.

5. Add half the egg mixture to the flour mixture and mix on low speed until well incorporated. Increase speed to medium and beat for 30 seconds. Add the rest of the egg mixture and beat for 30 seconds.

6. Scrape down the sides of the bowl and gradually add the dry ingredients in two batches, beating well after each addition.

7. Lightly spray an 8" x 4" x 2 1/2" (4-cup capacity) loaf pan or a 6-cup capacity bundt pan with vegetable oil spray. Pour in the batter and smooth the top.

8. In a conventional oven, bake the pound cake for 70 minutes in a loaf pan, 50 minutes in black bundt pan. In a convection oven, bake for 65 minutes in a loaf pan, 45-50 minutes in a black bundt pan.

9. Right before the cake is done, combine the lemon juice and maple syrup in a small saucepan or in the microwave. Heat, stir, and remove from heat.

10. When the cake is done, remove it from the oven and set it on a wire rack. Poke the top of the cake all over with a wire cake tester or toothpick. Brush with half the syrup and let it soak in for 10 minutes. Remove from pan and invert. Brush syrup on the other side of the cake, plus sides, and let it soak in for another few minutes.

11. Serve warm or at room temperature. Garnish with strawberries, raspberries, or other seasonal fruit of choice.

Each serving contains approximately 165 calories, 3.9 grams protein, 3.7 grams total fat, 9.3 mg cholesterol, 55 mg sodium.

Fresh Berry and Kiwi Pastry Tart with Chambourd

Serves 12

Berries are first available in late spring, and since I can never wait to cook with them, most of my berry recipes are in the spring section. Summer is plentiful in berries, as is the first part of autumn here in California, so these recipes are appropriate most of the year. Use the types and amounts of berries in this recipe as a guide, not law—any combination of berries and pastry works! Chambourd is a raspberry liqueur, which adds a depth of flavor to the berries. Amaretto would be good, too, adding a sweet almond touch. The easiest way I know to make pastry crusts is with the food processor, so directions for that method follow. Or, you may cut the butter into the flour with forks or a pastry cutter. (See instructions in the recipe for Apple Pie, page 131.) Either method works, it's just a matter of personal preference.

TART CRUST
1 cup unbleached flour
1 cup whole wheat pastry flour or 1 cup + 2 TB
*   unbleached flour*
1 pinch salt
10 TB sweet butter, frozen
2 TB maple syrup
3-4 TB ice cold water

BERRY FILLING
1 pint fresh blackberries
1 pint fresh raspberries
2 pints fresh strawberries
2 kiwis

GLAZE
$^1/_3$ cup strawberry jelly or jam
2 TB maple syrup
1 TB chambourd liquer

1. To make the crust, place the flour(s) and salt in the food processor. Process to mix.

2. Cut the butter into $^1/_2$" dice and add to the flour mixture. Pulse about a dozen times or until the butter is broken up and well distributed throughout the dry ingredients.

3. Add the maple syrup and pulse a few times to mix.

4. Add 3 TB of water. Pulse a few times to mix, then pinch the dough together with your fingers. If it needs a little more liquid to come together into a dough, add $^1/_2$ TB more of water, check, and add $^1/_2$ TB more if needed, until dough comes together.

5. Flatten the dough and wrap it in plastic wrap. Refrigerate for about 1 hour. Preheat oven to 375°F.

6. When ready, roll the dough out to fit an 11" tart pan. (I like to roll out the dough between 2 pieces of parchment paper, lightly floured. It doesn't stick as much as wax paper does, and it makes it easier to manipulate the dough than rolling it out without the aid of paper "forms.")

7. Remove 1 sheet of parchment paper and fit the dough into the tart pan, paper side up. Remove the other sheet of paper and fit the dough into the pan. Cut away the excess around the edges by rolling the top edges of the tart pan with the rolling pan. The top edge of the dough should be even with the top rim of the pan.

8. Line the pastry with 1 sheet of parchment paper or foil. Fill with pastry weights or dried beans. (The weights or beans keep the dough from puffing up and bubbling when baking.) Bake for 15-18 minutes. Remove weights or beans and parchment paper and bake for 7-10 minutes more or until golden in color. Remove from oven and let cool.

9. Meanwhile, wash the berries and hull and halve the strawberries. (I cut the strawberries in half, and leave the blackberries and raspberries whole.) Peel and slice or quarter the kiwis.

10. To make the glaze, heat the strawberry jelly or jam and maple syrup in a small saucepan over low heat. Stir well. Let the jelly melt to a liquid, then cook for about

2 minutes. If you used jam, strain through a sieve. Stir in chambourd. Set glaze aside.

11. Lightly brush the cooled crust with a little of the strawberry glaze.

12. Arrange the berries as you like. (I start with the strawberries lining the outside edge, then kiwi quarters, then a 2" strip of mixed raspberries and blackberries, more strawberries, kiwis, then another strip of the mixed berries. Any artful presentation—including free form throw it all in at once—is fine, as long as the surface is pretty even.)

13. Brush the remaining glaze over the fruit. Serve immediately, or refrigerate for 1-3 hours and serve.

Each serving contains 247 calories, 3.3 grams protein, 10.3 grams total fat, 26 mg cholesterol, 134 mg sodium.

STRAWBERRY BANANA SWIRL
Serves 4

The frozen banana purée swirled throughout gives this dessert a creamy and more satisfying texture than sorbet alone.

---

1 banana, peeled and frozen
1-2 TB honey or maple syrup
1 pint strawberry sorbet
$^1/_2$ pint fresh strawberries (optional)

1. Place banana and honey in food processor or blender and process until smooth.

2. Place sorbet in a mixing bowl and stir until soft, making "soup."

3. Lightly stir in banana mixture so that it is not well mixed, but swirled throughout.

4. Re-freeze or serve immediately. Spoon into serving dishes or wine glasses. Add fresh strawberries just before serving, if desired. (Don't freeze the strawberries because they become too hard.)

Each serving contains approximately 122 calories, 0.9 grams protein, 0.4 grams total fat, 0 mg cholesterol, 7 mg sodium.

STRAWBERRY PHYLLO TARTS
Makes 8 tarts

Rather than slathering butter on each sheet of phyllo, just spritz it with a little oil from a can of vegetable oil spray. You'll have perfect results with much less fat. Remember to remove the phyllo dough from the freezer the night before you plan to make these tarts, and place it in the refrigerator. One hour before you want to assemble the tarts, remove the phyllo from the refrigerator and let it come to room temperature. Unwrap the package and take out the sheets you'll need. Re-wrap the unused portion of dough and refrigerate for use within the next 7 days.

$^1/_4$ cup whole raw almonds
2 pints fresh strawberries
$^1/_4$ cup honey
2 TB fresh lemon juice
$^1/_2$ tsp grated orange peel
1 TB arrowroot or cornstarch
4 sheets (14" x 18" each) phyllo dough
vegetable oil spray as needed

1. Preheat oven to 325° F. Toast almonds in oven for 15 minutes. Cool and chop into small pieces. Increase oven temperature to 400° F. Wash strawberries and remove stems. Pat dry. Cut into quarters and set aside.

2. Mix together honey, lemon juice, and orange peel. Add arrowroot or cornstarch and stir. Add to strawberries and toss to mix.

3. Take out 8 custard dishes or ramekins. Cut or slice sheets of phyllo to the width of your individual ramekins, about $2^1/_2$" x 5" long. Keep all but the strip you're working with on top of wax paper and under a damp towel. This will keep them from drying out.

4. Spray the first strip of phyllo with vegetable oil spray and drape it down the side and over the outside edge of the first ramekin. (You want to line the sides only of each ramekin, not the bottoms as it will become too soggy on the bottom.) Leave enough phyllo draped over the side to wrap up and form the top of the tarts. Use 6 to 8 strips in this manner for each ramekin, overlapping to make "star points." See illustration on previous page.

5. Sprinkle a layer of toasted, chopped almonds on the bottom of each ramekin. Spoon the strawberry filling over the almonds. Wrap phyllo up and over the fruit into a free form "top knot."

6. Bake for 7-10 minutes. Let cool and serve warm or at room temperature.

Each tart contains approximately 190 calories, 4.3 grams protein, 2.9 grams total fat, 0 mg cholesterol, 326 mg sodium.

BLUEBERRY TOFU CHEESECAKE `Serves 8`

It's usually the men around the table that groan at the mention of tofu! And it's the real men who actually try it! In one class when I was making this cheesecake, there was one male student and seven women. He absolutely refused to take a bite of it! While everyone else in the class was mmmming and aahhhing, he began to get a little curious. He finally agreed to the teeniest little nibble. He liked it! He ate two pieces of it. What a guy—not only a real man, but a real cool man!

CRUST
*enough whole wheat honey graham crackers to
    equal 1 cup crumbs, about 1 package from 1 box*
1/4 cup maple syrup

FILLING
2 10.5 oz packages Mori Nu silken tofu, firm
1 tsp grated lemon peel
1 TB roasted almond butter
1/4 cup + 2 TB maple syrup
1 tsp vanilla
2 TB arrowroot or cornstarch

FRUIT TOPPING
12 oz fresh or frozen blueberries, defrosted
1/2 tsp grated lemon peel
1 TB maple syrup
2 TB arrowroot or cornstarch

1. Preheat oven to 350° F.

2. To make the crust, process the graham crackers to fine crumbs in a food processor or blender. Add the maple syrup. Pat into the bottom of a lightly oiled 8" springform pan.

3. To make the filling, add all the filling ingredients to a cleaned food processor or blender and process until smooth. (Make sure to scrape down the sides and process very well so there are not lumps.)

4. Pour the filling into the springform pan. Bake for 45 minutes.

5. When done, put the cake immediately into the refrigerator for 45-60 minutes to set.

6. Once set, add the topping. To prepare, add the fruit, lemon peel, and maple syrup to a small saucepan. Bring to a boil. Add arrowroot or cornstarch, stirring until well incorporated. When the mixture thickens slightly, remove it from the heat.

7. Remove cake from refrigerator. Spoon on the topping, smoothing it as you go. Return cake to refrigerator for another 45-60 minutes.

8. When ready to serve, carefully remove the sides from the springform pan. Slice and serve.

Each serving contains approximately 236 calories, 8.5 grams protein, 5.2 grams total fat, 0 mg cholesterol, 90 mg sodium.

One serving of traditional cheesecake contains approximately 654 calories, 12.7 grams protein, 42 grams total fat, 177 mg cholesterol, 331 mg sodium.

LEMON LAVENDER COOKIES   *Makes 5 dozen cookies*

L avender is a beautiful plant with grey-green foliage and purple tips which are its flowers. Lavender's aroma is like a sweet rosemary with a touch of rose. Many people grow lavender because of its drought tolerance as well as its beauty. If you don't have lavender growing, you could substitute rose geranium leaves in this recipe. I know I am asking for two plants that are a bit esoteric, but perhaps you'll consider planting one or both of them. They are both virtually maintenance-free, and add color and fragrance to the garden. Those of you who do have these plants already growing will appreciate a recipe that calls for them.

¹/₂ cup sweet butter, at room temperature
1¹/₂ cups unbleached flour
³/₄ cup maple syrup
2 egg whites
¹/₂ tsp rose flower water (optional)
1 TB minced lavender leaves
1 tsp grated lemon peel
1 tsp baking soda
¹/₄ tsp salt (optional)

1. Preheat oven to 350° F.

2. Cream butter with flour in a bowl.

3. Add maple syrup and egg whites and beat for 2 minutes.

4. Add rose flower water, if using, minced lavender leaves, and grated lemon peel and beat until well incorporated.

5. Add baking soda and salt and stir well to mix.

6. Spoon mixture onto lightly oiled cookie sheets. Use a tsp measure from a set of measuring spoons for crisp, silver dollar-size cookies. Use a TB measure for large "cake-like" cookies.

7. Bake for 12 minutes.

Makes 5 dozen silver dollar-size cookies.

Each cookie contains approximately 36 calories, 0.5 grams protein, 1.5 grams total fat, 4 mg cholesterol, 38 mg sodium.

SUMMER

lobe-shaped tomatoes and eggplants, sweet peaches and plums, plump squash and corn, the tapered leaves of greens and many-scented herbs. This is summer's glorious culinary offering—an assortment of shapes, colors, and flavors that create some of the year's most luscious meals. Meals that are easier to put together than any other season's because of the variety and versatility of its abundant produce. Cooking becomes a game of mix and match—what else can be done with zucchini and tomatoes? Maybe cook them with rice instead, or use cilantro even when the recipe calls for basil. Play with these recipes, and enjoy!

SUGGESTED MENUS

FATHER'S DAY BARBECUE
Garden Turkey Burgers
Red Pepper and Pepperoncini Relish
Red Wine and Caper Mustard
New Potato Salad with Chives and Basil
Bing Cherry Tart with Almond Pastry Crust

GRADUATION
Gazpacho
*Tacos del Mar with Cornmeal and Pumpkin Seed
    Coating*
Light Tartar Sauce
Nectarine Blueberry Summer Bake

FOURTH OF JULY
Italian Greens with Balsamic Vinaigrette
Chard-Stuffed Tomatoes
Grilled Sea Bass on a Bed of Corn Relish
Fresh Watermelon Slices*

LABOR DAY PICNIC
Italian "Fried" Chicken
Tuscan Summer Bean Salad
Three Cabbage Cole Slaw
Plum Tart with Almond Pastry Crust

DINNER I
Salsa Stuffed Artichokes
Halibut Baked with Pasilla-Mole and Marsala
Subtle Pilaf (see page 25)

DINNER II
Chard with Cumin and Lime
Marinated Mexican Chicken with Fresh Salsa
Fresh Corn-on-the-Cob*
Strawberry Orange Frozen Yogurt

DINNER III
*Lesa and Sally's Garden Salad Dressing with
    Romaine, Sprouts, and Grated Carrots*
*Pasta with Grilled Chicken, Roasted Peppers,
    Garlic, and Tomatoes and Peanut Ginger Sauce*
Banana Walnut Frozen Yogurt

DINNER IV
Roasted Chile and Fresh Corn Chowder
*Seasoned Black Bean Tostadas with Summer Squash
    and Tomatillo Salsa*
*Raspberry Cabernet Sauce over Vanilla Frozen
    Yogurt*

DINNER V
Zucchini Cashew Cream Soup
*Breast of Chicken Stuffed with Basil, Tomatoes, and
    Watercress*
Individual Eggplant Parmigiana
Fresh Fruit*

* Recipe not included.

APPETIZERS AND BREADS

ANTIPASTI PLATTER

Think of the vegetables and herbs of summer—tomatoes, eggplants, zucchini, bell peppers, cherry tomatoes, basil, and parsley—and you think of Italian food. All the recipes I have created for the appetizers of summer are Italian. You could make a number of them for an antipasti platter, or just one to start the meal.

SALSA-STUFFED ARTICHOKES

Serves 4

The salsa in each artichoke serves as a fresh, no-fat dipping sauce.

4 artichokes
4 cups water

SALSA
4 shallots, finely minced
4 cloves garlic, finely minced
1 medium yellow onion, diced
5 medium-size tomatoes, diced
4 TB chopped fresh parsley
1 TB chopped fresh marjoram or basil or mint

1. Cut off the pointed tops of the artichoke with a serrated-edged bread knife and clip the thorns from the rest of the leaves with kitchen shears. Chop off the stem so the artichoke will stand upright.

2. Place artichokes and water in a large pot. Bring to a boil, reduce heat to low, and cook, covered for 20-25 minutes.

3. Meanwhile, combine stuffing ingredients in a bowl.

4. Remove partially cooked artichokes from the pot and refresh with cold running water. (The artichokes will "blossom" or open up which will facilitate stuffing.)

5. Drain artichokes well, pull out the top-most leaves, and spoon out the "choke" or hairy core and discard. (A grapefruit spoon works well.) Be careful not to scoop out the heart.

6. Spoon a little less than one-quarter of stuffing mixture into the center cavities of each artichoke. Spoon remainder between the leaves.

7. Place stuffed artichokes back in the pot. Reduce amount of water to cover just the bottom 1"-2" of the artichokes. Bring to a boil, reduce heat to low, and simmer for 20-25 minutes or until tender but not mushy.

8. Serve hot, cold, or at room temperature.

Each serving contains approximately 120 calories, 5.6 grams protein, 0.4 grams total fat, 0 mg cholesterol, 96 mg sodium.

GRILLED JAPANESE EGGPLANTS AND ZUCCHINI

Serves 12

Unless you have one of those great instant-ignite outdoor grills, it's a lot easier to grill vegetables stovetop than to get out the briquettes and lighter fluid, wait for the coals to turn white, clean off the grill, pray the vegetables don't fall in, and then cook the vegetables until done before they incinerate! Instead, I use a non-stick skillet on the stove—not a grill—so that you can put a lid over it all and allow the vegetables to steam as they cook at a high heat.

1 recipe Classic Marinara Sauce (see page 96)
8 Japanese eggplants
8 zucchini

1. Prepare the Classic Marinara Sauce and let simmer.

2. Slice vegetables lengthwise to about $1/4$" thick.

3. Spray a non-stick skillet with a little vegetable oil spray and heat over medium high heat. When the oil is hot, place the eggplants in the skillet in a single layer. Reduce heat to medium.

4. Cook covered, for 4 minutes per side, or until tender. When done, drain on paper towels. Continue in batches until all the eggplants are cooked.

5. Spray a little more oil in the skillet and cook the zucchinis in the same manner. Depending on their size, they should cook in about 3 minutes per side. Drain on paper towels.

6. Arrange vegetables on a platter and serve warm or at room temperature with Classic Marinara Sauce as a dipping sauce.

Each serving contains approximately 78 calories, 2.9 grams protein, 2.7 grams total fat, 0 mg cholesterol, 60 mg sodium.

CRUSHED RED PEPPER AND ROSEMARY BAGUETTE

Serves 16

This flavorful bread has a nice soft texture. If using fresh rosemary, mince it well before adding. Or, crush dried rosemary in your hands or with a mortar and pestle. You don't want to bite into a piece of bread with a needle of rosemary poking you!

2 cups water
1 package yeast
2 cups unbleached flour
2 cups whole wheat flour
1 cup oat flour
1 TB fresh rosemary or 1 tsp dried rosemary
1 tsp salt or VegeSal
1 tsp crushed red pepper

2 TB extra virgin olive oil or Olio Santo (see page 10) cornmeal as needed

> To make oat flour, place 1¼ cups old fashioned-oats in a food processor or blender. Process until you have a fine powder, or flour.

1. Heat water to bath water temperature (105°-115° F.) Add yeast and let sit for 5 minutes, or until the mixture begins to foam. If it hasn't foamed within 5 minutes, that means your yeast is no good. Discard and begin again with a fresh package.

2. Meanwhile, place flours in a large bowl. Add fresh or dried rosemary, crushed red peppers, salt, and oil. Mix well. Use the back of a fork to press the flour-coated oil into smaller and smaller pieces so it is distributed throughout the dough.

3. When the yeast has foamed, add it to the flours.

4. Turn out dough onto a lightly floured—with the cornmeal—surface. Knead the dough for 5 minutes. To knead, fold the dough in half towards you, push the dough away from you with the heel of your hands, and turn the dough one-quarter of a turn. Repeat this procedure over and over again. Add a little extra cornmeal to the work surface when needed to keep the dough from sticking.

5. Transfer dough to a lightly oiled bowl. Turn to coat the dough with oil on all sides. Cover with plastic wrap, and let rise in a draft-free place for 45 minutes, or until double in size. (Check by poking the dough with your finger. If the indent remains, and doesn't pop back up at you, it has risen enough.)

6. Preheat the oven to 500° F.

7. Punch down the dough. Divide it into 4 equal pieces. Knead each piece about 1 minute to press out any air bubbles, and form each into a long baguette by rolling with both hands, fingers splayed.

8. Place on a cookie sheet that has either been lightly oiled or sprinkled with cornmeal. Space the 4 baguettes out enough so that when they rise more in the oven they will not touch.

9. Make diagonal slashes (about ¼" deep) on the top surface of each baguette.

10. Bake for 20-25 minutes.

Makes 4 baguettes.

Each serving (4 slices) contains approximatley 152 calories, 4.7 grams protein, 2.8 grams total fat, 0 mg cholesterol, 135 mg sodium.

EGGPLANT SPREAD ON RADICCHIO

Serves 12

This spread is also great on slices of Crushed Red Pepper and Rosemary Baguette. It can serve as a dip too—try it with carrots, cherry tomatoes, fennel, and bell pepper strips. Or, fill roasted mushroom caps with a dab and sprinkle on minced parsley for color.

1 small (1 pound) eggplant
3 cloves garlic
1 medium red onion
1 TB extra virgin olive oil
1 large red bell pepper
1¹/₂ tsp capers, rinsed
2 TB chopped fresh parsley
¹/₄ tsp black pepper
radicchio leaves or endive leaves as needed

1. Preheat oven to Broil.

2. Slice eggplant into 1" slices. Cut away skin and dice. Place in a steamer basket and steam for 10 minutes, or until tender.

3. Meanwhile, sauté onion and garlic in the olive oil for about 5 minutes.

4. Roast the red bell pepper by cutting it in half lengthwise. Remove stem, seeds, and veins. Place, cut side down, on a lightly oiled cookie sheet and broil for 15-20 minutes, or until blackened. Place charred pepper in a bowl. Cover with a plate so the pepper steams in its own heat for about 15 mintues, to loosen its skin. When cooled, peel away blackened skin and discard.

5. When eggplant is done, place in a food processor or blender. Add onion mixture, roasted pepper, capers, parsley, and black pepper. Process, making sure to scrape down the sides of the bowl.

6. Peel the leaves from a head of radicchio. Spoon a little dip in the center of each or leave the leaves stacked or fanned out, and let your guests dip them into the eggplant spread. Serve hot, cold, or at room temperature.

Makes about 4 cups.

Each serving contains approximately 25 calories, 0.5 mg protein, 1.3 grams total fat, 0 mg cholesterol, 2 mg sodium.

OLIVATA

Makes about 1¹/₂ cups

This recipe is a little sinful, so go easy with this seasoned purée of olives. It will keep for about 3 weeks in the refrigerator.

1 clove garlic
6 oz black olives, pitted and rinsed
8 oz Greek olives, pitted and rinsed
2 TB extra virgin olive oil or water
1 TB fresh lemon juice
¹/₂ tsp minced fresh rosemary or ¹/₄ tsp
  dried rosemary
³/₄ tsp minced fresh oregano or ¹/₄ tsp dried oregano
pinch black pepper

1. Combine all ingredients in a food processor or blender and process until well blended.

2. Chill for at least 1 hour.

3. Serve with bread, crackers, or bread sticks.

Each serving (2 TB) made with olive oil contains approximately 52 calories, 0.3 grams protein, 6.6 grams total fat, 0 mg cholesterol, 372 mg sodium.

BRUSCHETTA Serves 12

You can use store bought bread for this, or make the Parisian Baguette (see page 107). Serve it with plenty of napkins—it's messy and so delicious that you tend to gobble it!

24 slices baguette-shaped bread
¼ cup Olio Santo (see page 10) or
    extra virgin olive oil
4 large ripe tomatoes
4 TB fresh oregano, minced
2 cups fresh basil leaves, torn into small pieces
black pepper to taste
salt or VegeSal to taste

1. Preheat oven to 425°F.

2. Brush one side only of each slice of bread with Olio Santo. Place on a cookie sheet, brushed side up, and set aside.

3. Bring a large pot of water to a boil. Immerse the tomatoes for 10 seconds, rinse in cold water, and peel away the skin.

4. Cut tomatoes in half and squeeze out the seeds. Dice the tomatoes and place them in a large bowl.

5. Add the fresh herbs, black pepper, and salt to the tomatoes and mix well.

6. When ready to serve, toast the bread slices in the oven until lightly browned. Turn bread over and lightly brown the dry side.

7. Serve the bowl of tomatoes with a platter of the toasted bread. Top bread with the tomato mixture.

Each serving contains approximately 205 calories, 6.1 grams protein, 5.3 grams total fat, 0 mg cholesterol, 320 mg sodium.

CHERRY TOMATOES STUFFED WITH MOZZARELLA AND SUN-DRIED TOMATOES Makes 40 stuffed tomatoes

These succulent tomatoes are a little labor intensive, but once you pop one in your mouth, you'll know why you're going to all this trouble.

8 sun-dried tomatoes
40 cherry tomatoes
8 oz part-skim milk mozzarella
4 cloves garlic, finely minced
2 TB shallots, finely minced
¼ cup chopped fresh basil leaves

1. Preheat oven to 400°F. Soak the sun-dried tomatoes in enough boiling water to cover.

2. Slice off the tops of the cherry tomatoes, and using a melon baller or grapefruit spoon, scoop out and discard the pulp and seeds.

3. Slice the mozzarella cheese into ¼" slices, then into ¼" dice, or as small as you can get.

4. Drain the sun-dried tomatoes and discard the water. With kitchen shears, cut the sun-dried tomatoes into the size of the mozzarella dice.

5. Combine the mozzarella, garlic, shallots, sun-dried tomatoes, and basil. Toss well to mix.

6. Spoon into the cherry tomatoes and place on a cookie sheet.

7. Bake for 5-7 minutes, or until the cheese has begun to melt. Serve immediately.

Each stuffed tomato contains approximately 21 calories, 1.7 grams protein, 1 gram total fat, 3 mg cholesterol, 29 mg sodium.

CAPONATA

Eggplant is my favorite summer vegetable. Here is one of many recipes for it. (If eggplant's not your favorite, you could substitute zucchini—just don't cook it as long.) I've seen many a traditional Caponata with a layer of olive oil floating on the top. I find that very unappealing. This version is full-flavored without extra oil. I like Caponata served with warm bread, or as a salad served on a bed of lettuce leaves.

1 small (1 pound) eggplant
5 cloves garlic, finely minced
1 red onion, diced
1 green bell pepper, diced
1 TB extra virgin olive oil
2-4 TB dry red wine
1/4 tsp dried basil
1/8 tsp dried oregano
2 TB capers, rinsed
10 black olives pitted, rinsed, and sliced into quarters lengthwise
6 roma tomatoes, diced
1/4 cup chopped fresh parsley

1. Peel and cube the eggplant.

2. Sauté the cubed eggplant, diced onion, garlic, and bell pepper in the olive oil. Cook over low heat, adding red wine, 1 TB at a time, as needed for moisture. Cook for 20 minutes, or until the eggplant is done.

3. Add the basil, oregano, capers, and black olives. Cook for 2 minutes.

4. Add the tomatoes and parsley and cook for 5 minutes more.

5. Serve hot, warm, or cold.

Each serving contains approximately 42 calories, 1.4 grams protein, 1.1 grams total fat, 0 mg cholesterol, 47 mg sodium.

PESTO PIZZETTES

You just can't beat pesto sauce on pizza. It's the best! These are made cookie-size and are perfect for appetizers. I prefer making this size pizza because it's a lot easier to transport them to and from the oven. Form the dough, place them on cookie sheets, top, and bake. I like to make these with yellow pear-shaped cherry tomatoes—they look like the famous green eggs (no ham)!

1 recipe Pizza Dough (see page 19)
4 cloves garlic
1/4 cup extra virgin olive oil
2 cups loosely packed fresh basil
1/2 cup fresh parsley
2 TB walnuts or pine nuts or toasted bread crumbs
1/4 cup freshly grated Parmesan cheese
9 cherry tomatoes, preferably yellow pear-shaped
6 oz part-skim milk mozzarella cheese

1. Make pizza dough and set aside to rise.

2. Meanwhile, make the pesto sauce. Place the garlic, oil, basil, parsley, nuts and Parmesan cheese in a food processor or blender and process until smooth.

3. Cut the cherry tomatoes in half. Shred the mozzarella cheese. Set aside. Preheat oven to 500° F.

4. When pizza dough has risen, form into 16 pizzettes.

5. Spoon pesto on pizzette dough, leaving a small margin around the edge with no pesto on it.

6. Add a cherry tomato half to the center of each, then sprinkle with mozzarella cheese.

7. Bake for 8-12 minutes.

Each pizzette contains approximately 191 calories, 9 grams protein, 6.8 grams total fat, 7 mg cholesterol, 79 mg sodium.

GRILLED BASIL DUMPLINGS AND ROASTED RED PEPPER SAUCE
Makes about 40 dumplings

During the hot months of summer, appetizers often compose the entire evening's meal. These dumplings would be perfect—nutritious, tasty, and satisfying.

SAUCE
1 recipe Roasted Red Pepper Sauce (see page 56)

FILLING
4 cloves garlic
2 cups fresh basil leaves
¹/₂ cup fresh parsley
¹/₄ cup pine nuts
2 TB fresh lemon juice
8 oz fat-free ricotta cheese
¹/₂ tsp salt or VegeSal

DUMPLINGS
40 won ton wrappers
water as needed

1. Make the Roasted Red Pepper Sauce and set aside. Wash food processor bowl or blender jar.

2. Place the garlic, basil, parsley, and pine nuts in a food processor or blender. Process until the garlic and the fresh herbs are finely minced.

3. Add the lemon juice and ricotta cheese and process until smooth.

4. Place 1 tsp of the filling in the center of one-half of a won ton wrapper. Moisten the edges of the wrapper with water. Seal tightly. When done, place them in a single layer on a plate lined with wax paper until ready to cook, or cook immediately.

5. Heat a non-stick griddle or skillet and spray with vegetable oil spray. (The more oil you use, the less dough-y the dumplings will taste. Too much oil, however, and they will taste too greasy.) Cook the filled dumplings for about 2 minutes, spray the uncooked side with oil, turn, and cook for 2 minutes more, or until lightly browned on the second side.

The filled but uncooked dumplings can be refrigerated, covered, overnight and cooked the following day. Or, you can freeze them. Bring them to room temperature before cooking.

6. Serve cooked dumplings on a bed of Roasted Red Pepper Sauce.

Each dumpling with sauce contains approximately 41 calories, 2 grams protein, 1.2 grams total fat, 0.3 mg cholesterol, 117 mg sodium.

SALADS

WATERCRESS SALAD WITH KALAMATA DRESSING
Makes 8 dinner salads

Why is it that olive oil has such a noble health standing, yet olives themselves don't? Eight olives (only one per person) replace some of the olive oil that would be called for in this dressing, and add tons of rich, Mediterranean flavor. I find it delicious and healthful!

SALAD
2 bunches watercress
2 heads butter lettuce
¹/₂ large red bell pepper
¹/₂ small red onion

DRESSING
> *4 TB Olio Santo (see page 10) or extra virgin olive oil*
> *8 Kalamata olives, pitted and rinsed*
> *3 TB red wine vinegar*
> *1-2 TB dry white wine or water*
> *¹/₄ tsp black pepper*

1. Wash the watercress and lettuce well. Remove the major stems from the watercress and discard. Spin dry. Tear into bite-size pieces.

2. Cut the bell pepper into strips and the onion into rounds. Add to watercress and lettuce. Set aside until ready to toss with the dressing.

3. To make the dressing, place all ingredients in a food processor or blender and process until mixed, making sure that the olives are completely broken up.

4. Toss the dressing with the salad and serve.

Each serving contains approximately 80 calories, 0.8 grams protein, 7.6 grams total fat, 0 mg cholesterol, 29 mg sodium.

ITALIAN GREENS SALAD WITH BALSAMIC VINAIGRETTE
Makes 8 dinner salads

In a traditional vinaigrette, three parts of oil are used for every one part of vinegar. Today, health-conscious cooks use at most two parts oil to one part vinegar. But with balsamic vinegar, you can get away with using only one part oil to one part vinegar—or even all vinegar! This is because of balsamic vinegar's powerful, yet sweet taste.

SALAD
> *1 head romaine lettuce*
> *1 small head radicchio*

> *¹/₂ head red leaf lettuce*
> *1 bunch arugula*

DRESSING
> *¹/₄ cup extra virgin olive oil*
> *¹/₄ cup balsamic vinegar*
> *2 tsp Dijon-style mustard*
> *salt or VegeSal to taste*
> *pinch cayenne*

1. Wash lettuces well, spin dry, and tear into bite-size pieces.

2. To make dressing, place all the ingredients in a bowl and whisk to blend. Toss with greens and serve.

Each serving contains approximately 77 calories, 1.4 grams protein, 7 grams total fat, 0 mg cholesterol, 58 mg sodium.

TUSCAN SUMMER BEAN SALAD
Serves 8

I made this salad up for my friend Lisa's baby shower last June. It was a very elegant shower—all white linen, china, and silver. Although beans are a humble food, these beans were an appropriate addition to the dressy event. (By the way, it was a boy—Jacob John Cole!)

> *1 cup dried navy beans (small white)*
> *3" strip kombu seaweed (optional)*
> *³/₄ medium red onion, quartered, then sliced into "C's"*
> *4 cloves garlic, left whole with paper skin on*
> *2 medium tomatoes*
> *3 TB minced fresh basil or 1 TB dried basil*
> *³/₄ tsp minced fresh thyme or ¹/₄ tsp dried thyme*
> *¹/₂ tsp minced fresh oregano or pinch dried oregano*
> *1 TB Olio Santo (see page 10) or extra virgin olive oil*
> *1-2 TB fresh lemon juice*

salt or VegeSal to taste
black pepper to taste

1. Soak beans as in Minestrone di Abruzzi (see recipe page 13).

2. Drain beans, return to a large saucepan and cover with fresh water, plus 1" more.

3. Add kombu, if using, cover, and bring to a boil. Reduce heat to low and cook for 1-1½ hours, or until beans are tender, but still hold their shape.

4. Preheat oven to Broil.

5. Place onion "C's" and garlic cloves on a cookie sheet and broil until the onion is slightly browned but not crisped, and the garlic is soft. This should take 10-15 minutes.

6. Cut out the stems of the tomatoes, cut in half around the centers, and place, cut sides down, on the same cookie sheet you used to broil the onions and garlic. (The moisture from the tomatoes will actually help clean the pan!) Broil for 9 minutes, until skins pop up and are slightly browned.

7. When the beans are done, drain any extra water and turn out into a serving bowl. Add the onions. Peel the garlic, chop, and add to bowl with beans. With a pair of cook's tongs, remove the browned skins from the tomatoes, squeeze out most of the seeds, and add the tomatoes to the bowl too. They should be very soft.

8. Chop the fresh herbs and add to bowl. Add the Olio Santo. Toss well.

9. Add 1 TB of the lemon juice, salt, and black pepper. Toss, then taste and adjust seasonings.

10. Serve warm or chilled.

Each serving contains approximately 64 calories, 2.7 grams protein, 1.9 grams total fat, 0 mg cholesterol, 39 mg sodium.

NEW POTATO SALAD WITH CHIVES AND BASIL `Serves 8`

There are so many varieties of potatoes available now and any type is appropriate for this recipe. Try Yellow Finn or Yukon Gold, both of which have golden, butter-colored flesh. Ruby Crescents, Caribes, Cherries Jubilee, and All-Blues have flesh ranging from blue to tan to creamy white, and skins from red to purple. Along with potatoes you'll find three kinds of onions in this recipe—chives, shallots, and red onions—for a layering of flavor. Add the herbs and lemon, and you have a very fresh, and colorful, potato salad!

---

2 pounds new potatoes of any sort
4 TB finely minced shallots
4 TB finely minced red onions
3 TB finely minced chives
2 tsp grated lemon peel
2 tsp fresh lemon juice
2 TB extra virgin olive oil or Olio Santo (see recipe page 10)
2 TB minced fresh basil or 2 tsp dried basil
½ tsp minced fresh rosemary or ⅛ tsp dried rosemary
salt or VegeSal to taste
black pepper to taste
2 bunches arugula (optional)

1. Scrub potatoes, but do not peel them. Cut them into ¾" square pieces.

2. Place potatoes in steamer basket and steam for 20-25 minutes, or until fork tender. (For potatoes, it's better to be a tad overdone than underdone.)

3. Mix together all other ingredients, except the arugula, in a large mixing bowl.

4. When potatoes are done, add to the mixing bowl and toss, being careful not to break up the potatoes.

5. Serve warm or cooled, on a bed of arugula, if using.

Each serving contains approximately 170 calories, 4.1 grams protein, 3.7 grams total fat, 0 mg cholesterol, 99 mg sodium.

CELERY LEAF AND CUCUMBER SALAD WITH YOGURT DRESSING
Makes 8 dinner salads

Come summertime, the celery has gone nuts! It's easy to use up the stalks, but what to do with the leaves? Here's a salad that showcases celery's hardy leaves, with a creamy, lightly-flavored dressing.

SALAD
8 cups mix of oak leaf, romaine, frisée, or other lettuce of choice
1/2 cup celery leaves, chopped
1 cucumber, seeded and diced
16 yellow pear-shaped cherry tomatoes
4 beets, preferably yellow or pink, grated

DRESSING
1/2 cup walnut oil or canola oil
1/3 cup rice vinegar
1/4 tsp dried marjoram
1/8 tsp celery seeds
1 TB minced shallots
3 TB nonfat plain yogurt
salt or VegeSal to taste
black pepper to taste

1. Wash greens well, spin dry, and tear into bite-size pieces. Add greens and other vegetables to a large salad bowl.

2. To make the dressing, place ingredients in a bowl and whisk to blend.

3. When ready to serve, toss dressing with greens and vegetables. Serve immediately.

Each salad contains approximately 32 calories, 1.8 grams protein, 0.3 grams total fat, 0 mg cholesterol, 22 mg sodium.

Each 1 TB of dressing contains approximately 83 calories, 0.3 grams protein, 7 grams total fat, 0 mg cholesterol, 48 mg sodium.

THREE CABBAGE COLE SLAW
Serves 8

Everybody's reaction to this simple cole slaw has been the same: "This is incredible! What is it that makes it so good?" It's the white miso, a pineapple-y, nutty tasting flavoring that is my secret ingredient in many recipes in this book.

4 cups combination of shredded cabbages (red, Napa, green, bok choy, or others)
1 TB white miso (try Westbrae brand)
1 TB white wine vinegar
2 TB safflower or canola oil

1. Place shredded cabbage in a large mixing bowl and set aside.

2. To make the dressing, place the miso, vinegar, and safflower oil in a bowl and whisk to blend.

3. When ready to serve, toss dressing with the cabbages. Serve immediately.

Each serving contains approximately 28 calories, 0.8 grams protein, 1.9 grams total fat, 0 mg cholesterol, 74 mg sodium.

Slice cabbage into shreds with a chef's knife or with the 4 mm slicing—not grating—blade of your food processor.

LESA AND SALLY'S GARDEN SALAD DRESSING

Makes about 2¹/₄ cups

I used to have this great little apartment in La Jolla, and my best friend Sally just about lived there with me. She only went home to sleep. Every night after work—in my days as a stockbroker—I would head straight to Sally's aerobics class. Afterwards, we'd come home to my apartment, via the grocery store, and make dinner together. One day, Sally bought me my first food processor. It was great, but was it ever noisy! We'd make this dressing almost every summer night, and I know the neighbors knew when it was dinner time. What a racket!

1 clove garlic
¹/₂ medium size green or red bell pepper
¹/₄ cucumber
3 ripe tomatoes, quartered
¹/₄ cup fresh cilantro or fresh parsley
¹/₄ cup apple cider vinegar
1 tsp low sodium soy sauce

1. Place the garlic, bell pepper, and cucumber in a food processor or blender and liquify.

2. Add all other ingredients and process until smooth. Taste and adjust with more vinegar and/or soy sauce, if needed.

3. Serve over any kind of lettuce, or use as a dip for vegetables or crackers.

Each serving (2 TB) contains approximately 6 calories, 0.2 grams protein, 0 grams total fat, 0 mg cholesterol, 13 mg sodium.

SOUPS

GAZPACHO

Serves 8

You've got to have ripe, healthy, robust tomatoes for this soup—pale, sad, mealy ones never do. Farmer's markets, roadside stands, and natural foods stores that sell organic produce are likely places for good tomatoes. If your only option is the regular grocery store, choose the more flavorful roma tomatoes. They're smaller than other types though, so buy a few more romas to compensate.

SOUP

2 cloves garlic
¹/₂ cucumber
1 small red onion
¹/₂ medium green or yellow bell pepper
7 medium-size ripe tomatoes
3 TB Olio Santo (see page 10) or extra virgin olive oil
3 TB champagne vinegar or white wine vinegar
1 bunch fresh cilantro
¹/₂ tsp Tabasco
¹/₂ tsp black pepper
1 tsp low sodium soy sauce

GARNISH

2 medium-size ripe tomatoes, diced
¹/₄ cucumber, diced
¹/₂ medium-size green or yellow bell pepper, diced
2 scallions, sliced into rounds

1. To make the soup, place garlic, cucumber, onion, and bell pepper in a food processor or blender and process for 30 seconds.

2. Cut tomatoes into quarters and add them to the food processor. Process another 30 seconds.

3. Add oil, vinegar, cilantro, Tabasco, pepper, and soy sauce. Process until smooth.

4. Refrigerate for about 2 hours.

5. Just before serving, prepare the vegetables for garnish. Place them in separate bowls so diners can choose how much of which vegetables they wish to use for garnish.

Each serving (7.4 oz) contains approximately 86 calories, 1.8 grams protein, 5.5 grams total fat, 0 mg cholesterol, 42 mg sodium.

ZUCCHINI CASHEW CREAM SOUP
Serves 8

Potatoes and zucchini are cooked down until they begin to disintegrate and make a thick, chunky broth. More zucchini is added for texture, and a cream made of ground cashews and water is added for richness. Cashew cream is actually less fatty than real cream, is high in nutrients, and adds an interesting flavor to this soup.

3½ cups canned chicken broth or Homemade
*   Chicken Stock (see page 44)*
1-2 (to make 3 cups diced) potatoes, diced
4 zucchini, dice 2 and slice 2 into rounds
1 large yellow onion, diced
3 cloves garlic, finely minced
2 TB chopped fresh parsley
1½ tsp dried basil
⅛-¼ tsp cayenne
¾ cup raw cashews
½ cup water
low sodium soy sauce to taste

For a vegetarian option, substitute 3½ cups water and 3½ tsp Bernard Jensen's Broth Powder for the chicken broth. Find the broth powder in natural food stores.

1. Place chicken stock, potatoes, diced zucchini, onion, and garlic in a 3-4 quart saucepan. Bring to a boil, lower heat, and simmer, covered, for 45 minutes, or until the potatoes and zucchini begin to break up.

2. Add the sliced zucchini, parsley, basil, and cayenne and cook for about 10 minutes, or until zucchini is tender.

3. Meanwhile, make cashew cream by grinding raw cashews in a food processor or blender to a powder. With the machine running, add ½ cup water to make the "cream."

4. Add cashew cream to soup. Stir and heat thoroughly. Add soy sauce to taste and serve immediately.

Each serving (10.5 oz) made with cashew cream contains approximately 148 calories, 5.6 grams protein, 6.4 grams total fat, 0 mg cholesterol, 233 mg sodium.

Each serving (11 oz) made with cream contains approximately 227 calories, 6.1 grams protein, 14.8 grams total fat, 31 mg cholesterol, 241 mg sodium.

ROASTED CHILE AND FRESH CORN CHOWDER
Serves 8

In this recipe, unhusked corn is soaked in water, then oven roasted so it steams in its own jacket. Then it is husked, the kernels cut from the cob, and puréed with a roasted chile and milk steeped with bay leaves. Although it's hard to improve upon simply prepared corn-on-the-cob, try this thick chowder as an occasional change of pace this summer.

---

6 ears of corn, unhusked
1 Poblano (hot) or Anaheim (mild) chile
1 medium yellow onion, diced
2 tsp extra virgin olive oil
1 tsp black pepper
pinch cayenne
1 cup beer or water
3½-4 cups evaporated skim milk or low fat milk
2 bay leaves

1. Preheat oven to Broil. Place unhusked corn in a sink full of water to soak for 20 minutes.

2. Cut the chile in half lengthwise. Remove the seeds and stem. Place, cut side down, on a lightly oiled cookie sheet and broil for 10 minutes, or until the chile is blackened. Place charred chile in a bowl. Cover with a plate so the chile steams in its own heat for 15 minutes to loosen its skin. When cooked, peel away blackened skin and discard.

3. Reduce oven temperature to 400° F.

4. Drain corn and place immediately in the oven on oven racks. Cook for 20 minutes, turning once or twice. (If you have an old oven with open gas flames, take care that the corn husks don't come in contact with the flames.)

5. When done, let the corn cool, then husk it, and cut the corn off the cobs. Set aside.

6. In a 3-4 quart saucepan, sauté the onion in the olive oil for 5 minutes, or until onion is transparent. Add the black pepper and cayenne.

7. Add the beer or water and all but 1 cup of the corn kernels. Bring to a boil, then reduce heat to low and simmer for 10 minutes.

8. Place the corn mixture and the peeled chile in a food processor or blender and process until smooth.

9. Meanwhile, place the milk and bay leaves in a large saucepan and heat to just below a boil. Turn the heat off and let the bay leaves steep in the milk for 10 minutes. Remove the bay leaves and discard.

10. Stir the corn mixture into the milk. Add the extra corn kernels. Heat gently and serve hot.

Each serving (8 oz) contains approximately 181 calories, 10.7 grams protein, 2.2 grams total fat, 4 mg cholesterol, 140 mg sodium.

Mexico City-Style Chicken Soup Buffet
Serves 12

This soup works well for casual company. Set out the beans, salsa, and guacamole as condiments to add to each bowl of soup, as desired. The warmed tortillas are for dipping. You may want to use canned beans as a time saver. If so, use three cans, which would equal about 4½ cups of cooked beans, and use water or beer for the extra liquid.

BEANS

   1½ cups dried black beans
   6 cups water
   6" strip kombu seaweed (optional)
   1 tsp chili powder
   1 tsp ground cumin
   ½ tsp ground coriander
   ½ tsp dried oregano
   ¼ tsp cayenne
   2 TB low sodium soy sauce

SOUP

   2 pounds chicken pieces, with bones, without skin
   8 cups chicken broth or Homemade Chicken Stock (see page 44)
   1 red onion, diced
   4 cloves garlic, finely minced
   1 TB pasilla chile powder or chili powder
   1 TB extra virgin olive oil
   salt or VegeSal to taste
   black pepper to taste

GUACAMOLE

   2 ripe avocadoes
   ½ tsp ground cumin
   salt or VegeSal to taste

SALSA

1 recipe Fresh Salsa (see page xx) or salsa of choice, as needed

TORTILLAS

12 corn tortillas

1. Soak beans as in Minestrone di Abruzzi, page 13.

2. Drain beans and add to a 3-4 quart saucepan. Add fresh water and kombu. Cook for 1 hour. Remove kombu and discard. Cook for 30-60 minutes more, or until the beans are tender. Set aside.

3. Meanwhile, wash chicken and pat dry. Place chicken broth in a pot. Bring to a boil, add chicken, reduce heat to low, and simmer for 15 minutes.

4. Remove the chicken from the pot using cook's tongs. Let cool. When cool enough to handle, shred the chicken, with your fingers or a fork. Return the shredded chicken to the pot of chicken broth. Discard the bones.

5. Meanwhile, in a sauté pan, sauté the onion, garlic, and pasilla chile powder in the olive oil over medium heat for 5 minutes. When done, add to the pot of chicken soup. Taste and add salt and pepper to taste. Keep hot.

6. Drain the beans, reserving about $^1/_2$ cup of the bean cooking water. Transfer to the sauté pan. Add the spices and soy sauce. Simmer for 15 minutes, adding the bean water as needed. Taste and adjust seasonings. Keep warm.

7. To make the guacamole, cut the avocados in half and remove the pits. Rinse the halves of avocado under water briefly. This will help keep the avocado from turning brown. Spoon out the flesh into a mixing bowl. Mash with a fork. Add cumin. Taste and add more cumin and salt to taste.

In place of the soy sauce you can use Dr. Bronner's Balanced Protein Seasoning, which is available at natural food stores. Mix it with 2 TB boiling water, stir, and add to beans.

8. Make the Fresh Salsa or place store bought salsa in a serving bowl.

9. Warm the tortillas stovetop in a non-stick skillet until pliable, or in the microwave—wrap the tortillas in wet paper towels and cook on high power for 30-60 seconds, depending on the number of tortillas you are cooking.

10. Serve the soup, allowing your guests to spoon in the beans, salsa, and guacamole. Some may prefer to eat the beans as a side dish. Tortillas are for dipping and pushing!

Each serving (14.5 oz) contains approximately 379 calories, 31.6 grams protein, 14.1 grams total fat, 63 mg cholesterol, 368 mg sodium.

FISH

SWORDFISH WITH GINGER TOMATO CONCASSÉ | Serves 6

I've been on a ginger kick lately, and have found that one of the best and most unexpected combinations is ginger and tomatoes. What I've learned about ginger in all its applications is that it must be subtle to be good. When too strong, it dominates and lets no other flavor share its spotlight. When light, it dances well with many partners.

2 TB chopped shallots
2 tsp grated fresh ginger
$^1/_4$ cup dry white wine
1 TB extra virgin olive oil
$^1/_4$ tsp salt or VegeSal
black pepper to taste
5 medium-size ripe tomatoes
2 pounds swordfish
garlic oil spray or other vegetable oil spray as needed
1 tsp grated fresh ginger
1 clove garlic, finely minced

1. Preheat the oven to Broil.

2. Sauté the shallots and ginger in the white wine over low heat until the liquid is almost gone.

3. Meanwhile, cut away the outer membrane of each tomato and discard the pulp and seeds (or save for another purpose). To do this, place each tomato on the chopping block on its end. Start cutting through the skin at the stem end and carve down in strips all around the tomato. You want only the skin and thick fleshy membrane, not the pulp. Once you have done this with all the tomatoes, you will have a pile of strips. Now dice the strips.

4. Add the diced tomato and olive oil to the cooked shallots and ginger and set aside.

5. Spray a broiler rack with some oil. Wash swordfish and pat dry. Lightly spray the fish with the garlic oil spray. Sprinkle the ginger and garlic evenly over the fish.

6. Broil for 8-9 minutes, turning once halfway through (if you have a convection oven you don't have to turn the fish).

7. Meanwhile, add salt and pepper to the concassé of ginger and tomatoes and stir to mix.

8. Transfer the cooked swordfish to serving plates and serve with a few spoonfuls of concassé on each steak.

Each serving contains approximately 225 calories, 30.6 grams protein, 8.4 grams total fat, 59 mg cholesterol, 232 sodium.

RED SNAPPER AND VEGETABLES IN ORIENTAL MARINADE, BAKED IN PARCHMENT PAPER
Serves 8

Y ou can substitute any kind of fish you'd like for the red snapper. Even a combination, such as a few scallops, a shrimp or two, and a couple ounces of sea bass per packet would be great. Don't get too carried away and overfill the packets, though. It's harder to fold them when they're bulging!

---

5 TB dry sherry
1 TB water
2 tsp low sodium soy sauce
8 cloves garlic
1 TB Olio Santo (see page 10) or extra virgin olive oil
24 sprigs fresh cilantro
2 carrots, cut into sticks or rounds
4 scallions, sliced into rounds
8 mushrooms, sliced
24 spinach leaves, washed, chopped, and stemmed
1 pound red snapper, cut into 1" cubes

1. Preheat oven to 450°F.

2. To make the sauce, place sherry, soy sauce, garlic, and Olio Santo in a bowl and stir.

3. Divide rest of ingredients into 8 equal portions.

4. Cut out a piece of parchment paper for each of the 8 packets. See page 50 for detailed instructions on folding parchment paper.

5. To fill, place $1/8$th of the fish and vegetables plus 1 TB sauce in the center of one-half of each packet. Fold per instructions on page 50. Place each packet on a cookie sheet and bake for 10-12 minutes.

Each serving contains approximately 114 calories, 16.2 grams protein, 2.6 grams total fat, 29 mg cholesterol, 55 mg sodium.

HALIBUT BAKED WITH PASILLA-MOLE AND MARSALA
Serves 4

A lthough Mole sauce has come to be associated with the traditional Mexican celebration dish made of chiles, peanuts, and chocolate (see Puebla-Style Mole Sauce, page 118 for my version), "mole" is actually a suffix, meaning sauce, as in "guacamole." This "Pasilla-Mole" is a purée of pasilla chiles and sun-dried tomatoes with fresh basil leaves. It is a deep maroon color and adds a very robust flavor plus moisture to the halibut fillets.

---

1 cup sun-dried tomatoes
1 pasilla chile
hot water to cover
4 cloves garlic
1/2 cup fresh basil leaves, patted dry
2 TB extra virgin olive oil
2 pounds halibut fillets
1/4 cup marsala wine or dry sherry

1. Preheat oven to 425° F.

2. Soak sun-dried tomatoes and the pasilla chile in hot water until soft, about 15 minutes.

3. Meanwhile, place garlic and basil leaves in a food processor or blender and process until chopped.

4. Drain the water from the sun-dried tomatoes and pasilla chile. Remove the stem and seeds from the pasilla and discard.

5. Place sun-dried tomatoes, pasilla chile, and olive oil in the food processor with the garlic and basil. Process until creamy, then set aside.

6. Wash fish and pat dry. Take out a shallow baking sheet and add fish in a single layer.

7. Using a rubber spatula, smear the pasilla-mole on 1 side of the fish. Turn fish over and repeat with the other side.

8. Pour marsala over the fish and bake for 15-20 minutes.

Each serving contains approximately 292 calories, 35 grams protein, 8.8 grams total fat, 124 mg cholesterol, 182 mg sodium.

TACOS DEL MAR WITH CORNMEAL AND PUMPKIN SEED COATING

Makes 8 fish tacos

Fish Tacos are a southern/Baja California classic. They are usually made by dipping cubed, mild fish in a beer batter, deep frying, and then dressing them with a mayonnaise and sour cream based Tartar Sauce. My version is much lighter, and carries all the flavor and sensations of the original. If you've never had a Fish Taco before, you'll wonder where you've been all these years! If you have, you'll be pleasantly surprised that you can now enjoy them guilt-free!

FISH
1/2 cup raw pumpkin seeds (also knows as pepitas)
1 tsp grated lime peel
2 cloves garlic
1 tsp chili powder
1/2 tsp black pepper
6 TB cornmeal
1-1 1/2 pounds sea bass
1 lime

TORTILLAS AND TOPPINGS
8 corn tortillas
1 cup grated zucchini
1 cup grated red cabbage
1/2 cup red onion, finely diced

1. Preheat oven to 500° F.

2. Place pumpkin seeds in a food processor or blender and process to a fine powder.

3. Add grated lime peel, garlic, chili powder, black pepper, and cornmeal. Pulse to mix well.

4. Place pumpkin seed mixture in a plastic produce bag.

5. Wash fish and pat dry. Cut it into 1 1/2" cubes. Place in a mixing bowl.

6. Squeeze lime juice over cubed sea bass. Add to the plastic bag with the pumpkin seed mixture, coating each piece of fish thoroughly.

7. Place coated fish on a lightly oiled cookie sheet. Bake for 7-9 minutes.

8. Meanwhile, warm the tortillas stove top in a non-stick skillet until pliable, or in the microwave—wrap tortillas in wet paper towels and cook on high power for 30-60 seconds, depending on the number of tortillas you are cooking. When fish is done, serve immediately. Keep tortillas covered so they'll stay warm. Serve garnishes in separate bowls. Top with Light Tartar Sauce (see recipe below).

Each taco (using 1 pound of fish and all the coating) contains approximately 159 calories, 14 grams protein, 4.14 grams total fat, 23 mg cholesterol, 50 mg sodium.

LIGHT TARTAR SAUCE
Serves 8

This is a purposefully thin tartar sauce, ideal for drizzling onto Fish Tacos. If you want it to be thicker, start with "yogurt cheese" instead of the nonfat plain yogurt.

1 cup nonfat plain yogurt or yogurt cheese
1 clove garlic

To turn regular yogurt into "yogurt cheese," put a paper filter in the top of your coffee maker. Add the yogurt. Place over a glass, so that it is suspended and the part where the liquid drips from is not blocked. Cover the yogurt loosely and refrigerate. Liquid will drip from the yogurt (this is called the whey and can be used as the liquid in bread baking or pizza making, or thrown away), turning the yogurt into a cheese-like substance. The longer you let it drain, the more dense the yogurt cheese will be. Drain at least 1 hour. Leaving it overnight will produce the richest results.

2 TB capers, rinsed
1 TB red onion, chopped
1/2 cup fresh cilantro
1/4 tsp salt or VegeSal
1/8 tsp cayenne

1. If using regular yogurt, place all the ingredients in a food processor or blender and process until well mixed. Or, if using yogurt cheese, mince the cilantro with a chef's knife, then stir all ingredients together in a mixing bowl.

2. Refrigerate briefly to enhance flavors. Serve with Fish Tacos.

Makes enough for 16 Fish Tacos.

Each serving contains approximately 17 calories, 1.9 grams protein, 0 grams total fat, 0.5 mg cholesterol, 49 mg sodium.

GRILLED SEA BASS ON A BED OF MEXICAN CORN RELISH
Serves 6

As with most of the seafood recipes in this book, you may substitute another type of fish. If you can't get sea bass, try flounder, cod, yellowtail, or snapper, any fish that is mild in taste and thick enough to grill. The recipe makes just enough relish to cover 6 servings of fish. If you want to serve enough relish to cover the entire dinner plate, make double the amount of relish.

FISH
2 pounds sea bass
2 TB sherry vinegar or white wine vinegar
1/4 cup dry sherry
1 tsp Olio Santo (see page 10) or extra virgin olive oil
1/2 tsp paprika
1/4 tsp cayenne

RELISH

> 2 TB diced Anaheim (mild) or Poblano (hot) chiles,
> or 2 from a can of green chiles
> 3 ears fresh corn
> 3 cloves garlic, finely minced
> 1 medium red onion, diced
> 1 red bell pepper, diced
> 1 TB Olio Santo (see page 10) or extra virgin olive
> oil
> 4 tomatillos, husked and diced
> 1/2 tsp ground cumin
> 1 TB fresh lemon juice
> 1 tsp low sodium soy sauce

1. Preheat the oven to Broil or prepare a stovetop or outdoor grill. If using fresh chiles, preheat the oven to Broil even if using a grill for the fish.

2. Wash fish and pat dry. Place in a shallow baking dish large enough to hold all the fish in a single layer.

3. Mix together the vinegar, sherry, oil, paprika, and cayenne in a small bowl. Pour over fish. Turn twice to coat well on both sides of the fish. Marinate for about 1 hour.

4. To make the relish, either roast the fresh chiles, or use the ones from a can. To roast the fresh chiles, cut them in half lengthwise. Remove the seeds and stems. Place, cut side down, on a lightly oiled cookie sheet and broil for 10 minutes, or until the chile is blackened. Place charred chile in a bowl. Cover with a plate so the chile steams in its own heat for 15 minutes. When cooled, peel away blackened skin and discard. Dice chile.

5. Husk the corn and cut the corn off the cob.

6. Sauté the garlic, onion, and bell peppers in the olive oil for 5 minutes, or until the onion is clear.

7. Add the corn kernels, tomatillos, chiles, and cumin and cook for 5 minutes more.

8. Add the lemon juice and soy sauce to taste. Turn off heat, cover, and keep hot.

9. When ready, grill/broil the fish for 8-10 minutes, depending on thickness of the fish. Turn once halfway during cooking. (If you are using a convection oven you do not have to turn the fish.)

10. To serve, spoon one-sixth of the corn mixture onto each dinner plate. Top with a piece of the grilled fish. Serve immediately.

Each serving contains approximately 278 calories, 39 grams protein, 7.5 grams total fat, 121 mg cholesterol, 162 mg sodium.

POULTRY

BREAST OF CHICKEN STUFFED WITH WATERCRESS, BASIL AND TOMATOES
Serves 4

I once made this dish for a luncheon of 90 women. Making anything for 90 people is a lot of work, but this dish is much easier to prepare than its elegant presentation implies.

> 4 half skinless, boneless chicken breasts, pounded to
> 1/4" thick
> 1 cup dry white wine
> 2 TB extra virgin olive oil
> 3 cloves garlic, finely minced
> 2 tsp Dijon-style mustard
> 1/4 tsp dried Italian herbs
> 1/2 cup fresh watercress, leaves only
> 1/2 cup fresh basil, torn into small pieces
> 2 pieces whole grain bread, made into breadcrumbs
> 2 medium tomatoes, diced

1. Preheat oven to 350° F.

2. To pound chicken, place each breast between 2 sheets of plastic wrap. Pound with a meat pounder until breast is of uniform thickness. (It's best to start in the center and work out, pounding the chicken, rather than pressing it.) Place the pounded breasts in a single layer in a baking dish and set aside.

3. To make the marinade, place wine, olive oil, garlic, mustard, and herbs in a bowl and mix well. Pour two-thirds of the marinade over the chicken breasts, refrigerate and marinate for at least 30 minutes.

4. Meanwhile, tear pieces of bread and place them into a food processor or blender and process until they are crumbs. Pour out onto a dinner plate.

5. Mix watercress and basil in a bowl and set aside.

6. When ready to assemble chicken, toss the watercress and basil with the remaining marinade. Remove one chicken breast and spoon about 1 TB of the watercress/basil mixture onto one-half of the flattened chicken. Add the same amount of diced tomatoes. Fold one-half of the chicken over the mixture. Pick up and carefully coat with breadcrumbs, being careful not to disassemble it.

7. Return each filled and coated chicken breast to the baking dish. Repeat with each chicken breast, then bake for 35-40 minutes.

Each serving contains approximately 283 calories, 30 grams protein, 8.8 grams total fat, 70 mg cholesterol, 132 mg sodium.

GARDEN TURKEY BURGERS WITH FRESH TOMATO SLICES
Serves 8

Turkey burgers are so often tasteless grey patties, with just the slightest resemblance to a real burger. I've remedied this problem with soaked and pureed sun-dried tomatoes and other robust flavorings. Grated zucchini lends additional color, and is a great way to add more vegetables to your diet and use up a summer crop's excesses.

3 TB red wine
3 TB hot water
6 sun-dried tomatoes
$^1/_4$ medium (to equal 3 TB minced) yellow onion
2 cloves garlic, finely minced
1 egg white
$1^1/_2$ TB Worcestershire sauce
$1^1/_2$ pounds ground turkey
1 average (to equal 1 cup grated) zucchini, grated
salt or VegeSal (optional) to taste
black pepper (optional) to taste
8 hamburger buns
8 slices fresh tomato

1. Preheat oven to Broil or prepare a stovetop or outdoor grill.

2. Pour red wine in a small mixing bowl. Add hot water and sun-dried tomatoes. Let soak for about 15 minutes.

3. Meanwhile, place the onion and garlic in a food processor or blender and process till minced.

4. When fully re-hydrated and soft, add the sun-dried tomatoes and half the wine/water mixture they were soaking in to the mixture in the food processor. Process until just about liquified.

5. Add egg white and Worcestershire sauce to the food processor and process again until well mixed.

6. Place ground turkey in a large mixing bowl. Add the sun-dried tomato mixture and the grated zucchini to the ground turkey and mix well.

7. Form 8 burgers. To make uniform-size burgers, assuring they will cook evenly, use a biscuit cutter to form each burger.

8. Spray a broiler pan with vegetable oil spray. Cook in the oven for 8 minutes, turn, and cook for 7 minutes more. Or, cook on a barbecue or on a stovetop ridged grill for about the same amount of time.

9. After the burgers are done, heat the buns in a broiler or on the grill.

10. Assemble burgers and serve with a slice of tomato and the following relish and mustard.

Each serving contains approximately 226 calories, 21 grams protein, 7.4 grams total fat, 67 mg cholesterol, 102 mg sodium.

RED PEPPER AND PEPPERONCINI RELISH
Makes enough for 8 burgers

I recommend doubling this recipe each time you make it. It is fabulous with the Garden Turkey Burgers, and also with omelettes, tossed with pasta, and alongside barbecued swordfish.

9 pepperoncini, stems removed, minced
1/2 red bell pepper, finely minced
2 TB minced red onion
1 clove garlic, finely minced
1 tsp apple cider vinegar

1. Combine all ingredient in a bowl, stir, and serve.

RED WINE AND CAPER MUSTARD
Makes enough for 8 burgers

Why go to all the trouble of making mustard from scratch when you can just "doctor" some up? Simply add flavorful ingredients to your favorite type of mustard, as I've done below. Leftovers can be kept in the refrigerator indefinitely.

4 tsp red wine
1 TB capers, rinsed and minced
4 TB mustard, such as brown, Dijon-style or yellow

1. Combine all ingredients in a bowl, stir, and serve.

ITALIAN "FRIED" CHICKEN
Serves 8

What would summer be without a picnic of fried chicken?! This chicken tastes so authentically fried, you'll begin picking off the skin, thinking it's too fat filled. By coating the chicken pieces in yogurt, then dipping them in a flour mixture, you're essentially re-creating a "skin" that just happens to be fat free. The cornmeal gives it that "Southern fried" flavor, while the spices take it to Italy!

1/2 cup + 2 TB whole wheat flour
1/2 cup + 2 TB cornmeal
1/2 tsp salt or VegeSal
1 tsp black pepper
1 rounded tsp dried basil
1/2 rounded tsp dried marjoram
1/4 rounded tsp dried oregano
1/4 rounded tsp dried thyme
1/8 tsp dried rosemary
1 cup nonfat plain yogurt or buttermilk
8 half (about 8 oz each) chicken breasts, with bones, without skin
vegetable oil spray as needed

1. Preheat oven to 400° F.

2. In a large bowl, combine the whole wheat flour, cornmeal, and spices and stir well. Pour out onto a dinner plate and set aside.

3. Place yogurt or buttermilk in a bowl. If using yogurt, stir to thin it out. Set aside.

4. Rinse chicken breasts well and pat dry. Spray the rack of a roasting pan with a little vegetable oil spray.

5. Using a fork or rubber spatula, dip or brush each chicken breast with the yogurt. If using buttermilk, dip each breast, coating it well.

6. Coat each chicken breast with the flour/spice mixture, then place on the roasting rack, meaty side up. Spray the top of each chicken breast with vegetable oil spray.

7. Bake for 40-45 minutes.

Each serving (with ¹/₂ tsp oil sprayed on each breast) contains approximately 111 calories, 11.27 grams protein, 1.7 grams total fat, 20 mg cholesterol, 156 mg sodium.

MARINATED MEXICAN CHICKEN ■ *Serves 4*

Add a steaming platter of fresh corn-on-the-cob, a tossed green salad, and a few ice cold beers, crickets for background sound, and the smell of night blooming jasmine. Summer nights have never been better!

---

¹/₂ cup fresh lime juice
1 TB extra virgin olive oil
3 cloves garlic, finely minced
1 red onion, diced
1 tsp dried oregano
¹/₂ tsp ground cumin
4 half skinless, boneless, chicken breasts
¹/₂ recipe Fresh Salsa (see recipe below)

1. Place lime juice, olive oil, garlic, onion, and spices in a bowl and stir well to mix.

2. Place the chicken in a single layer in a shallow baking dish. Pour the marinade over the chicken, coat both sides well, and cover.

3. Refrigerate for 2-3 hours, turning occasionally, or overnight.

4. Preheat an outdoor grill or the broiler.

5. Grill the chicken for about 3-4 minutes per side. (If you use bone-in chicken, cook it for about 9 minutes per side.)

6. Arrange the chicken breasts on a platter and top with a few spoonfuls of Fresh Salsa (see recipe below).

Each serving contains approximately 217 calories, 29.4 grams protein, 5.3 grams total fat, 68 mg cholesterol, 222 mg sodium.

FRESH SALSA ■ *Makes 2¹/₂ cups*

Californians use salsa for everything from the morning's eggs to baked potatoes, sandwiches and salads. Everyone has their family secret for the best salsa. Some claim you must add serrano chiles, not jalapeños. Others say vinegar is more authentic than lime juice, or a squeeze of orange juice is the trick, or a dash of cayenne, a pinch of oregano. All are delicious suggestions, and yet what I've found is the most important factor in any salsa recipe is the tomatoes. They must be ripe and full flavored. Summer, then, is the time for the best homemade salsa. Any type of ripe tomato will work, romas, Sweet 100's—even the type of tomatoes that are yellow when ripe.

---

8 medium-size ripe tomatoes
1 small red onion, diced
¹/₂ cup fresh cilantro leaves, minced
3 cloves garlic, finely minced
1 jalapeño chile, seeded, de-veined, and minced (optional)
apple cider vinegar or fresh lime juice to taste
¹/₂ tsp ground cumin
¹/₂ tsp salt or VegeSal
black pepper to taste

1. To peel the tomatoes, first make an "X" in the bottom of each with a paring knife. This will give you a place to start peeling. Immerse them in a pot of boiling

water for a few seconds. Immediately plunge them into cold water to stop the cooking. You don't want to cook them, just loosen their skins, so don't leave them in the hot water longer than 20 seconds.

2. Peel tomatoes. Cut them in half around their centers. Squeeze out seeds and discard. Dice tomatoes and place in a large bowl.

3. Add red onion, cilantro, garlic, and chile, if using. Stir in a little vinegar or lime juice, cumin, salt, and pepper. Taste and adjust seasonings.

4. Serve immediately, or cover and refrigerate for 1 hour and serve.

Contains approximately 100 calories per cup.

VEGETABLE MAIN DISHES

TAMALE CORNBREAD PIE *Serves 12*

I make this pie when I've had a frustrating day and need a little "chopping therapy!" Many of my students have told me they like this recipe because it is a one-dish meal, and makes enough for two nights. If you're going to use this pie for more than two nights worth of meals, I suggest you use the optional tablespoon of lemon juice or vinegar suggested in the cornbread recipe. It will help it to keep better. I call for fresh tofu in this dish as the protein component. You can substitute leftover chicken or any kind of cooked bean, like kidney or pinto, that has held its shape. This cornbread recipe is somewhat sweet and contrasts with the spiciness of the tamale pie. Notice that it contains no eggs, yet it's still quite light without them.

FILLING
  1 TB extra virgin olive oil
  3 jalapeño chiles, seeded, de-veined, and finely minced (optional)
  1 large red onion, diced
  6 cloves garlic, finely minced
  1 large red bell pepper, diced
  1 large green bell pepper, diced
  4 medium-sized tomatoes, diced, or 1 14-oz can, tomatoes, drained and diced
  3 ears corn, husked and cut off the cob or 1$^1/_2$ cups frozen and defrosted corn
  2 zucchini, diced
  4$^1/_2$ tsp chili powder
  1$^1/_2$ tsp ground cumin
  $^3/_4$ tsp dried basil
  $^1/_2$ (scant) tsp dried coriander
  $^1/_2$ tsp dried oregano
  1 cup chopped fresh cilantro
  8 oz fresh, firm tofu, crumbled

CORNBREAD TOPPING
  $^3/_4$ cup whole wheat flour
  1$^1/_2$ cup cornmeal
  $^3/_4$ tsp baking soda
  $^1/_4$ tsp salt or VegeSal
  3 TB canola oil
  $^1/_4$ cup honey
  1 TB lemon juice or vinegar (optional)
  1 cup low-fat milk or plain soy milk

1. Preheat oven to 350°F.

2. Sauté all filling ingredients over medium-high heat for about 10 minutes, or until peppers are cooked, but not mushy.

3. Meanwhile, make the cornbread. Place dry ingredients in one bowl and wet ingredients in another bowl.

4. When filling is done, pour into a 9" x 12" baking dish.

5. For the cornbread topping, add dry ingredients to wet ingredients, stirring just enough to mix. Spoon over filling, spreading evenly with a rubber spatula.

6. Bake for 30-35 minutes.

Each serving contains 215 calories, 6.7 grams protein, 7.0 grams total fat, 0.8 mg cholesterol, 125 sodium.

LIGHTLY CURRIED VEGETABLE BURRITOS `Serves 8`

Kids have a knack for eating these. They know just what to do with a messy, sauce-oozing burrito—pick it up, and eat it. Do not put it down until it's all gone—that's the secret.

¹/₂ green bell pepper, diced
¹/₂ red bell pepper, diced
1 medium red onion, diced
4 cloves garlic, finely minced
1 tsp curry powder
1 TB sesame oil (not toasted) or canola oil
4 cups chopped vegetables, such as broccoli, coarse-ly chopped; zucchini, diced; cauliflower, coarse-ly chopped; carrots, diced; potatoes, steamed until tender and diced; asparagus tips or green beans cut into 1" lengths
4 cups red leaf or butter lettuce, cut into shreds
8 flour tortillas, preferably whole wheat flour
8 tsp crumbled feta cheese, rinsed

1. Sauté green and red peppers, onion, garlic, and curry powder in the oil for about 5 minutes.

2. Add the chopped vegetables and shredded lettuce, cover, lower heat, and steam for 10 minutes.

3. Meanwhile, warm the tortillas, stove top in a non-stick skillet until pliable or in the microwave—wrap tortillas in wet paper towels and cook on high power for 30-60 seconds depending on the number of tortillas you are cooking.

4. Spoon about ¹/₂ cup of the vegetables in a strip down the middle of the warm tortilla. Sprinkle on the feta cheese.

5. If using a regular size flour tortilla, fold 1 side over the filling, then roll, starting from the bottom, towards

the top. One end will be open. If you are using the burrito-size (larger) tortillas, fold both sides over the filling, then roll, starting from the bottom, towards the top. Serve immediately.

Each serving contains approximately 202 calories, 6 grams protein, 5.7 grams total fat, 3 mg cholesterol, 218 mg sodium.

SEASONED BLACK BEAN TOSTADAS `Serves 8`

Top these bean tostadas with the following Summer Squash and Tomatillo Salsa (recipe below). You can also use a biscuit cutter to cut out smaller sizes from the tortillas and make 16 appetizer-size tostadas.

BEANS
1¹/₂ cups black beans
6" strip kombu seaweed (optional)
3 cups water
2 cloves garlic, finely minced
¹/₂ medium red onion, finely diced
1 tsp ground coriander
1 tsp ground cumin
¹/₂ tsp dried oregano
1 TB chili powder
1 serrano chile, seeded, de-veined, and finely minced (optional)
1 TB canola oil
2 TB low sodium soy sauce

TORTILLAS
8 corn or flour tortillas
vegetable oil spray as needed

1. Soak beans as in Minnestrone de Abruzzi (see page 13).

2. Cook the soaked beans in the 3 cups of fresh water with kombu, if using, for 1 hour. Remove kombu and discard. Cook beans for ¹/₂ hour or until tender.

In place of low sodium soy sauce, use 1 TB + 1 tsp Dr. Bronners Balanced Protein Seasoning mixed in 2 TB hot water.

3. Sauté garlic, onion, spices, and chile, if using, in the canola oil for 5 minutes, or until onion is clear.

4. Drain cooked beans, reserving about 1 cup of the bean water. Using the back of a fork or potato masher, mash the beans.

5. Add the beans to the sauté pan with the garlic and spices. Add the soy sauce. Cook over medium heat for 15 minutes, adding bean water for moisture, as needed.

6. To cook the tortillas, lightly spray a non-stick skillet or pancake griddle with vegetable oil spray. Add tortillas and cook, turning occasionally, for 5 minutes or until they are crisp.

7. Spoon beans onto tortillas and top with the following salsa.

Makes 8 tostadas or 16 tostada appetizers.

Each tostada or 2 tostada appetizers contain approximately 194 calories, 5.2 grams protein, 3.2 grams total fat, 0 mg cholesterol, 72 mg sodium.

SUMMER SQUASH AND TOMATILLO SALSA | Serves 8

This beautiful summer salsa is versatile enough to be used with beans, grilled fish, or chicken.

1 small tomato
2 tomatillos, husks peeled away
1/2 zucchini, finely diced
1 small crookneck squash, finely diced
1 small carrot, finely diced
1 clove garlic, finely minced
1/2 red onion, finely diced
2 TB minced fresh cilantro
1 TB fresh lime juice
salt or VegeSal to taste

1. Prepare tomato as in recipe for Fresh Salsa (see page 89). Reserve water.

2. Add the tomatillos to the reserved water, bring to a boil, reduce heat to low, and simmer for 7-10 minutes, or until they are soft.

3. Place the tomato and the tomatillo in a food processor or blender and process until smooth.

4. Transfer tomato/tomatillo puree to a bowl. Add the vegetables, lime juice, and salt to taste. Refrigerate for up to 1 hour.

Makes enough Salsa for 8 tostadas or 16 tostada appetizers.

Each 4 TB serving (with 1/4 tsp VegeSal) contains approximately 18 calories, 0 grams protein, 0 grams total fat, 0 mg cholesterol, 46 mg sodium.

EGGPLANT PARMIGIANA | Serves 8

I gave this recipe to my friend Diane five years ago, and she still makes it regularly for company, always to rave reviews. You can substitute 2 pounds of zucchini for the eggplant, and proceed exactly as described for the eggplant. You might also want to flour and brown some skinless, boneless chicken breasts in a non-stick skillet with a little oil, and layer them in with the vegetables before baking.

1 recipe Liza's Spaghetti Sauce (see page 19)
1 large (2 pound) eggplant, cut into 1/4" slices
8 oz part-skim milk mozzarella cheese, shredded
1/4 cup freshly grated Parmesan cheese

1. Preheat oven to 350° F. Make a batch of Liza's Spaghetti Sauce (see page 19) and let simmer or defrost a batch and simmer.

2. Place eggplant slices on a lightly oiled baking dish or cookie sheet. Bake for 20-25 minutes, or until tender. Remove from oven.

3. To assemble the parmigiana, cover the bottom of a casserole or individual-sized baking dishes with a few spoonfuls of spaghetti sauce, then add 1 layer of eggplant slices. Cover with mozzarella, then more sauce.

4. Begin another layer of eggplant, cover with more mozzarella, then sauce. If you have enough for another layer, continue as directed.

5. End by sprinkling the last layer of sauce with the Parmesan cheese.

6. Bake, covered, for 25 minutes, or until done and bubbling.

Each serving contains approximately 216 calories, 12.2 grams protein, 9.4 grams total fat, 18 mg cholesterol, 427 mg sodium.

BOHEMIAN PIZZA `Serves 12`

This pizza is a combination of summer's finest vegetables—a sort of ratatouille made with the addition of roasted, rather than stewed, bell peppers. It would be wonderful served over a bed of rice, yet is a little more casual—just like the season—if used as a topping for pizza. I like it without any cheese on top, but a little feta or goat cheese is good, too.

1 recipe Pizza Dough (see page 19)
1 red bell pepper
1 green bell pepper
1 yellow bell pepper
1 large red onion, quartered and sliced into "C's"
4 cloves garlic, finely minced
1 bay leaf
1 medium (1¹/₂ pounds) eggplant, peeled and cut into cubes
1 tsp dried basil
1 tsp dried marjoram

1 TB extra virgin olive oil
4-6 TB dry red wine
1 medium zucchini, sliced into 3 equal sections, then quartered lengthwise
1 medium summer squash, cut into large pieces
3 large ripe tomatoes, cut into chunks
¹/₄ cup chopped fresh parsley
16 fresh basil leaves, cut into shreds
2 oz freshly grated Parmesan cheese
4 oz feta cheese, rinsed or goat cheese (optional)

1. Preheat oven to Broil. Make Pizza Dough (see page 19) and let rise.

2. Roast peppers as in Calzone with Roasted Red Pepper Sauce (see page 56). Save any juices in the bowl. Cut peppers into strips and set aside.

3. Reduce oven temperature to 500° F.

4. Sauté the onion, garlic, bay leaf, eggplant cubes, and herbs in the olive oil and red wine over medium heat for 10 minutes.

5. Add the zucchini and squash. Simmer, covered, for 5 minutes. If more liquid is needed, add a little more wine or water. (This mixture is going on pizza, you don't want it to be too liquid or it will sog the crust.)

6. Add the tomatoes and roasted peppers and cook 1 minute. Remove from heat and set aside. Do not cover.

7. When the dough has risen, punch it down, form it into a ball, and divide the dough into 2, 4, 8, or 16 equal pieces. Form into the size pizzas you want using a rolling pin.

8. Sprinkle the grated Parmesan cheese evenly over the dough, leaving a margin around the outer edge with no cheese.

9. Spoon on the vegetables, spreading them evenly, then sprinkle with fresh parsley and fresh basil.

10. Sprinkle with the feta or goat cheese, taking care to cover the fresh herbs.

11. Bake for 8-10 minutes, or until the cheese is melted.

Each serving (assuming 2 15" pizzas, 6 slices each, 12 7 oz servings) contains approximately 251 calories, 9.2 grams protein, 8.8 grams total fat, 8 mg cholesterol, 135 mg sodium.

Zucchini Cakes with Herbed Tomato Sauce
Serves 4

Grated and seasoned zucchini is folded into beaten egg whites, formed into patties, griddled, and topped with a subtle herb and fresh tomato sauce. The dish is light and nourishing, and makes use of summer's most prolific vegetables—zucchini and tomatoes. It's also good with peeled and grated eggplant in place of the zucchini.

SAUCE
1 yellow onion, diced
1 TB extra virgin olive oil
$^1/_8$-$^1/_4$ tsp cayenne
$^1/_4$ tsp dried oregano
$^1/_4$ tsp dried basil
$^1/_4$ tsp dried thyme
1 pinch dried rosemary
3 large ripe tomatoes, chopped
1 cup dry white wine
1 cup sliced carrots, about 3 carrots
2 TB low sodium soy sauce

CAKES
1 pound zucchini
2 TB unbleached flour
$^1/_2$ tsp granulated garlic or garlic powder
$^1/_2$ tsp salt or VegeSal
$^1/_2$ tsp black papper
4 egg whites

1. To make sauce, sauté the onions in the olive oil in a sauce pan for 5 minutes, or until transparent.

2. Add the herbs and cook for 2 minutes more.

3. Add the chopped tomatoes, white wine, and carrots. Bring the mixture to a boil, reduce heat to low, and simmer, covered, for 25 minutes, or until the carrots are soft.

4. Place mixture in a food processor or blender and process until smooth. Return purée to the pan and simmer.

5. Meanwhile, make the zucchini cakes. Grate the zucchini, add them to a large mixing bowl, and toss with the flour, granulated garlic, salt, and pepper. Set aside.

6. Beat the egg whites till stiff. Fold the egg whites into the zucchini mixture.

7. Heat a non-stick griddle or large skillet and spray with a little vegetable oil spray. When the griddle is hot, turn the heat down to medium, and spoon on the zucchini mixture, or form the zucchini mixture into patties and add to the heated griddle.

9. Cook for 3-5 minutes per side, or until light golden.

10. Serve immediately, topped with some of the sauce.

Makes 12 cakes (there will be leftover sauce).

Each serving contains approximately 59 calories, 2.5 grams protein, 1.3 grams total fat, 0 mg cholesterol, 199 mg sodium.

PASTAS

Nouveau Pasta
Serves 4

I actually devised this recipe "tongue in cheek." I thought I'd include every trendy food item I could in one dish. To my surprise, it was absolutely delicious—a "keeper," as we say in our household! The vegetables are sautéed in wine rather than oil to balance the presence of feta cheese and avocado. Cooking in this manner will keep the dish light and healthy.

5 ripe roma tomatoes
8 oz. dried pasta
3 cloves garlic, finely minced
1 small red onion, sliced into rounds
1 Anaheim chile, seeded, de-veined, and sliced into
    $^1/_2$" strips
$^1/_4$ cup dry white wine
$^1/_2$ avocado, diced
$^1/_2$ cup chopped fresh cilantro or parsley
$^1/_4$ cup feta cheese, rinsed and crumbled

1. Bring a large pot of water to a boil.

2. Prepare tomatoes as in Fresh Salsa (see page 89).

3. Cook pasta in the boiling water for 10 minutes, or until al dente.

4. Sauté the garlic, onion, and chile in the white wine until cooked but not limp.

5. Drain the pasta and toss with the sautéed mixtures, the tomatoes, diced avocado, cilantro or parsley, and feta cheese. Serve immediately.

Each serving contains approximately 331 calories, 11.2 grams protein, 6.6 grams total fat, 6 mg cholesterol, 100 mg sodium.

PASTA CRUDO WITH FRESH BASIL AND ALMONDS `Serves 6`

My sister Mary came home from a trip to New York with the idea for this recipe. She'd had it in a restaurant her husband was photographing for a travel magazine. We tried to re-create it in my kitchen, but it was Christmas time and the basil and tomatoes, which we paid a fortune for, were dreadful. (This is why we cook seasonally!) You could taste the potential, though, so the minute I got my hands on some sun-ripened tomatoes and basil, I made it again. It's fabulous!

8 oz dried medium-size shell pasta
$^1/_2$ cup raw, whole almonds
6 cloves garlic
12 oz fresh tomatoes
1 cup fresh basil leaves
$^1/_4$ tsp salt or VegeSal
black pepper to taste
$1^1/_2$ TB extra virgin olive oil

1. Bring a large pot of water to a poil. Prepare tomatoes as in Fresh Salsa (see page 89).

2. Cook pasta in boiling water for 10 minutes, or until al dente.

3. Meanwhile, place almonds, garlic, and basil in a food processor or blender. Pulse to chop. (You want texture, not a powder or mush, so watch carefully as you pulse.)

4. Cut tomatoes in quarters, add to the food processor, and pulse until chopped. Season to taste with salt and pepper.

5. Drain pasta well and toss with the olive oil. Add the sauce and toss well. Serve immediately.

Each serving contains approximately 276 calories, 8.4 grams protein, 10.4 grams total fat, 0 mg cholesterol, 98 mg sodium.

PASTA WITH GRILLED CHICKEN, ROASTED PEPPERS, GARLIC, AND TOMATOES AND PEANUT GINGER SAUCE `Serves 6`

The secret to this recipe is to take out the bowl you will be serving the pasta in and fill it with the vegetables as they are roasted. In this way, you will retain a fairly clean kitchen and create an easy flow to making this unforgettable pasta.

SAUCE
> *1 shallot*
> *1 clove garlic*
> *1½ tsp grated fresh ginger*
> *2 TB peanut butter* (peanuts are better)
> *½ tsp cayenne*
> *3 TB lemon juice*
> *1 TB low sodium soy sauce*

PASTA
> *1 large red bell pepper* = 2 peppers are better
> *8 cloves garlic*
> *8 oz dried spinach linguine or fettucine*
> *4 medium tomatoes*
> (1) *2 large half boneless, skinless chicken breasts*
> *2 TB chopped fresh cilantro or parsley*

1. Pre-heat oven to Broil.

2. To make the sauce, combine all ingredients in a food processor or blender. Purée until smooth and set aside. (The sauce can be made up to 1 week in advance.)

3. Roast pepper as in Calzone with Roasted Red Pepper Sauce (see page 56). Cut pepper into strips and place in a large pasta serving bowl.

4. Separate the garlic cloves from the head. With skin on, broil the garlic cloves for 10 minutes. When cool, remove skin, dice, and add to the pasta bowl.

5. Remove stems from the tomatoes with a paring knife. Cut tomatoes in half through their middle (not through stem) and broil, cut side down, for 7-9 minutes. When cool, remove skins with tongs, squeezing out seeds as you pick up the tomatoes. Add tomatoes to the pasta bowl. They should be very soft—almost mush.

6. Meanwhile, bring a large pot of water to a boil. Cook pasta in boiling water for 10 minutes, or until al dente.

7. Broil the chicken breasts, about 5 minutes per side. (If you use a convection oven, you don't need to turn the chicken breasts.) When done, slice into strips and keep warm.

8. Drain pasta well and add to pasta bowl. Toss with vegetables, sauce, chicken strips, and chopped cilantro or parsley. Serve immediately.

Each serving contains approximately 248 calories, 16.9 grams protein, 4.64 grams total fat, 24.3 mg cholesterol, 142 mg sodium.

CLASSIC MARINARA SAUCE WITH EGGPLANT SLICES AND SPAGHETTI
Serves 6

Just as every wardrobe needs a basic white shirt, every cook's repertoire needs the recipe for this classic sauce. It mixes and matches with any food—pasta, fish, chicken, and roasted or steamed vegetables. It's simple enough to know by heart, so you can make it wherever you go. I've suggested baked eggplant slices be tossed with the spaghetti and sauce, but you can omit them if you like.

EGGPLANT AND PASTA
> *1 small eggplant*
> *vegetable oil spray as needed*
> *8 oz dried spaghetti*

SAUCE
> *3 pounds ripe roma tomatoes*
> *2 TB extra virgin olive oil*
> *10 cloves garlic, peeled and very thinly sliced*
> *¼ cup chopped fresh basil or 1 TB dried basil*
> *¼ cup chopped fresh parsley*
> *salt or VegeSal to taste*
> *black pepper to taste*

1. Preheat oven to 350° F.

2. Slice the eggplant and lay the slices on a lightly oiled cookie sheet. Spray the tops of the slices with a little oil. Bake for 20 minutes, turn, spray with oil and bake

> You can substitute 1 28-oz can Italian whole tomatoes or 1 35-oz box of tomatoes, such as Pomi brand, for the fresh tomatoes.

for 20 minutes more, or until tender yet not dried out. Place in a bowl and cover to keep warm.

3. Meanwhile, prepare tomatoes as in Fresh Salsa (see page 89). Chop and set aside.

4. Place oil and garlic slices in a 3-4 quart saucepan. Cook over low heat, stirring occasionally, until the garlic is golden but not brown. (Do not let the garlic burn. Slow, gentle cooking will result in mild, sweet flavored garlic, which is vital to the success of this sauce.)

5. Add chopped tomaotes to the saucepan and increase heat to high. (If using canned tomatoes, carefully squeeze them into the pot to break them apart. Add the liquid from the can too. If using boxed tomatoes, simply pour them into the saucepan. They are already crushed or puréed.)

6. Add *dried* basil, if using. Bring to a boil and cook, uncovered, stirring occasionally, until the sauce is thick. This should take about 10 minutes. If using boxed tomatoes, just bring to a boil, reduce heat to low, and cook, uncovered, for about 10 minutes.

7. Meanwhile, bring a large pot of water to a boil and cook the pasta for 10 minutes, or until al dente.

8. Add fresh herbs to the tomatoes 1-2 minutes before the sauce is done. Remove from heat and season with salt and black pepper.

9. Drain pasta well and toss with the sauce. Add eggplant slices and a little more sauce and toss again. Serve immediately.

Each serving contains approximately 243 calories, 7.6 grams protein, 5.5 grams total fat, 9 mg cholesterol, 112 mg sodium.

SPAGHETTI WITH UNCOOKED TOMATO SAUCE
Serves 4

All these years and all these recipes, this is still my husband's favorite dish I ever made.

8 oz. dried spaghetti
4-6 roma tomatoes
3 cloves garlic, finely minced
3 TB Olio Santo (see page 10) or extra virgin olive oil
¼ cup chopped fresh basil
¼ cup fresh lemon juice
¼ tsp crushed red peppers (optional)
2-4 TB freshly grated Parmigiano Reggiano

1. Bring a large pot of water to a boil. Cook pasta in boiling water for 10 minutes, or until al dente.

2. Prepare tomatoes as in Fresh Salsa (see page 89). Chop into cubes and place in a large pasta serving bowl.

3. Add the minced garlic, olive oil, basil, and lemon juice. Stir.

4. Drain pasta and add to pasta bowl. Toss with tomato sauce.

5. Add the crushed red peppers, if using, and the Parmesan cheese. Toss and serve immediately.

Each serving contains approximately 287 calories, 8.4 grams protein, 10 grams total fat, 2.3 mg cholesterol, 70 mg sodium.

VEGETABLE SIDE DISHES

TOMATO BASIL PHYLLO TARTS
Serves 8

In my opinion, the season's best food combination is ripe tomatoes and fresh basil leaves. Here is another way to enjoy this perfect pairing.

12 sheets (14" x 18") from 1 package phyllo dough
2 yellow onions, diced
4 cloves garlic, finely minced

1 TB extra virgin olive oil
¹/₄ tsp black pepper
vegetable oil spray as needed
2 large tomatoes, thinly sliced
8 fresh basil leaves, sliced into shreds
4 TB Parmigiano Reggiano

1. The day before, take the phyllo dough out of the freezer and place it in the refrigerator overnight. On the day, remove it from the refrigerator and leave it at room temperature for 1 hour. Or, take the dough straight from the freezer and leave it at room temperature for 3-4 hours.

2. Preheat the oven to 350° F.

3. Sauté onions and garlic in the olive oil over a very low heat. Cook them until they are a nice golden hue, about 30 minutes. (This process is called carmelizing and it is done to sweeten the onions.) When the onions are done, add the black pepper.

4. Unwrap the phyllo dough right before you are ready to assemble the tart. Unroll it so it is completely unfolded. Take out a pair of kitchen shears and an 8" x 13" ceramic or glass baking sheet.

5. Spray the baking sheet with vegetable oil spray.

6. Peel off 1 sheet of phyllo dough and lay it in the baking pan. Spray with vegetable oil spray. Do the same with 3 more sheets of phyllo dough. If some of the sheets tear—no big deal. The next or previous sheets will cover the tear.

7. Add half the onion mixture, half the tomatoes, half the basil, and half the Parmigiano cheese.

8. Add 4 more sheets of phyllo dough, spraying each sheet with vegetable oil spray before adding the next. Work quickly, without interruptions and your dough will not dry out.

9. Add the remaining half of the onion mixture, tomatoes, basil, and cheese.

10. Add 4 more sheets of phyllo dough, exactly as before. Finish a spray of oil.

11. Tuck the overlapping pieces into the edges of the pan.

12. Cut the tart into squares. Be sure to cut through all the layers.

Serve within 20 minutes. This tart will not wait as the liquid from the vegetables will begin to make the dough too soggy.

13. Bake for 30-35 minutes, or until lightly golden on top.

Each serving contains approximately 381 calories, 7.6 grams protein, 5.3 grams total fat, 40 mg cholesterol, 302 mg sodium.

CHARD-STUFFED TOMATOES
Serves 8

I have a group of students who come to every one of my cooking classes. They're wonderful people who are never shy about telling me if my recipes suit them and their families! During the class when I made these tomatoes, they actually refused to try them. "I hate stuffed tomatoes." "What is this, airplane food?" "I've never had a stuffed tomato I've liked." They began leaving without a bite, the little brats! I wouldn't let them leave. They would try them. A showdown in my very own kitchen! Finally, Nancy B. took a bite. "Hey, you guys, they're delicious!" They all put down their purses and happily ate their stuffed tomatoes. Nancy B. loves to tell this story—especially since she makes this recipe all the time!

8 medium tomatoes
1 large yellow onion, diced
6 cloves garlic, finely minced
2 TB dry sherry
¹/₄ tsp dried marjoram
2 bunches Swiss chard
6 TB freshly grated Parmesan cheese
black pepper to taste
crushed red peppers to taste (optional)

1. Preheat oven to 375° F.

2. Choose tomatoes that will stand upright. Cut their tops off, forming the lids to the stuffed tomatoes.

3. Using a grapefruit spoon, hollow out each tomato. Reserve the insides.

4. Sauté the onion and garlic in the sherry for 5 minutes, or until the onions are clear. Add the marjoram.

5. Dice and add the insides of the tomatoes.

6. Wash Swiss chard well. Chop into bite-size pieces.

7. Add chard to the sauté pan, cover, and cook for 5-10 minutes, or until wilted.

8. Remove from the heat and stir in 2 TB of the Parmesan cheese, pepper, and crushed red pepper to taste.

9. Fill each tomato with some of the chard mixture. Top each with ¹/₂ TB of the cheese and the lids.

10. Place in a baking pan and bake for 15-20 minutes.

Each serving contains approximately 73 calories, 4.3 grams protein, 1.9 grams total fat, 3 mg cholesterol, 108 mg sodium.

Morrocan Vegetable Sauté

Serves 8

Eggplant can soak up a lot of oil. In this recipe, a mixture of water and soy sauce is added to the vegetables throughout their cooking time, instead of more oil. The result is a side dish full of flavor, not grease!

2 TB low sodium soy sauce
1 cup water
2 red bell peppers
1 large (about 1¹/₂ pounds) eggplant
1 TB extra virgin olive oil
4 cloves garlic, finely minced
1 TB Hungarian paprika
1 TB ground cumin
¹/₄-¹/₂ tsp cayenne
¹/₂ cup chopped fresh parsley
¹/₄ cup chopped fresh cilantro (optional)

1. Preheat oven to Broil. In a small bowl, mix soy sauce and water and set aside.

2. Roast peppers as in Calzone with Roasted Red Pepper Sauce (see page 56). Save juices in bowl. Dice peppers and add them to a large non-stick skillet.

3. Peel the eggplant, cut into ¹/₂" cubes, and add to the skillet. Stir in olive oil, garlic, paprika, cumin, and cayenne.

4. Cook, uncovered, for 20-25 minutes over medium heat, stirring occasionally. When you need more moisture in the pan, add a little of the water/soy sauce until it has all been added over the 25 minutes of cooking.

5. Five minutes before serving, add the chopped parsley and cilantro, stirring well to incorporate.

6. Serve hot or warm.

Each serving contains approximately 52 calories, 1.7 grams protein, 2.2 grams total fat, 0 mg cholesterol, 201 mg sodium.

Chard with Cumin and Lime

Serves 6

You can't eat too many greens! This simple preparation can also be used for spinach, bok choy, or green cabbage.

2 bunches Swiss chard
¹/₂ yellow onion, diced
2 cloves garlic, finely minced
¹/₂ tsp ground cumin
1 TB extra virgin olive oil
squeeze from a half of a fresh lime

1. Wash the chard well. Cut off and discard the stems and the thick parts of the stem that grow into the leaf. Chop into bitesize pieces. Do not dry the leaves. Set aside.

2. In a large sautépan, sauté the onion, garlic, and cumin in the olive oil for 5 minutes or until the onion turns clear.

3. Add the chard and cook, covered, for 10 minutes, until the chard wilts.

4. Right before serving, squeeze the half a lime over the cooked chard. Toss well and serve immediately.

Each serving contains approximately 56 calories, 3 grams protein, 2.7 grams total fat, 0 mg cholesterol, 93 mg sodium.

SUGAR SNAP PEAS, BROCCOLI, AND ZUCCHINI TOSSED WITH CHINESE MARINADE
Serves 8

I f you have leftovers of the marinade, toss it with tuna for tomorrow's lunch and serve it in pita bread with a few bean sprouts, shredded red cabbage, and tomatoes.

MARINADE
2 tsp grated fresh ginger
2 cloves garlic, finely minced
1 TB sesame oil (not toasted) or canola oil
3 TB fresh lime juice
3 TB rice vinegar
1 TB low sodium soy sauce
3 TB finely minced green onions
2 TB finely minced fresh cilantro or parsley
1/4 tsp black pepper

VEGETABLES
20-25 sugar snap peas, strings removed
1 bunch broccoli, cut into small florets
2 zucchini, sliced into 1/2" thick rounds

1. To make the marinade, sauté the ginger and garlic in the oil over medium heat for 2 minutes.

2. Add the lime juice, vinegar, and soy sauce and bring the mixture to a low boil.

3. Add the green onions, cilantro, and black pepper and simmer for 5 minutes.

4. Meanwhile, place the vegetables in a steamer basket and steam for 7 minutes, or until cooked but not mushy.

5. When ready to serve, toss the vegetables with the marinade. Serve immediately.

Each serving contains approximately 66 calories, 3.3 grams protein, 2.6 grams total fat, 0 mg cholesterol, 126 mg sodium.

SWEETS

BANANA WALNUT FROZEN YOGURT
Serves 8

T he basis for this dessert is nonfat yogurt, but because of the bananas, the result-ing texture is actually more like ice cream than soft frozen yogurt. Garnish with a few fresh berries, mint leaves, or walnut halves.

4 whole peeled, frozen bananas, sliced
8 oz nonfat plain yogurt
2 tsp vanilla
2 TB maple syrup
1/2 cup walnuts, chopped

1. Place sliced bananas in a food processor or blender. Purée until smooth, making sure there are no lumps of banana.

2. Add the yogurt, vanilla, and maple syrup. Process until well blended.

3. Add walnuts and pulse until incorporated into mixture.

4. Pour into the container of an ice cream maker and proceed according to manufacturer's instructions. Or, if you don't have an ice cream maker, pour mixture into a mixing bowl, cover, and place in freezer. It should be the first consistency within 45 minutes. Eat this dessert soon after taking it from the freezer. If it becomes too hard, let it sit out for about 20 minutes and it will return to the right consistency.

Each serving contains approximately 122 calories, 3.1 grams protein, 4.3 grams total fat, 0.5 mg cholesterol, 22 mg sodium.

STRAWBERRY ORANGE FROZEN YOGURT *Serves 8*

This fruit yogurt is also good frozen in plastic popsicle containers. Let them freeze solid—they'll soften while you eat.

1 large peeled and frozen
  banana, sliced
2 cups nonfat vanilla yogurt
2 cups sliced fresh strawberries
1 tsp grated orange peel
4-6 TB honey

1. Place sliced banana in a food processor or blender. Process until slices are broken up.

2. Add all other ingredients and process until very smooth.

3. Pour into the container of an ice cream maker and proceed according to the manufacturer's instructions.

4. Serve when set to the consistency you like.

Makes about 1 quart.

Each serving (4.5 oz) contains approximately 105 calories, 3.6 grams protein, 0.2 grams total fat, 1 mg cholesterol, 45 mg sodium.

RASPBERRY CABERNET SAUCE OVER VANILLA FROZEN YOGURT *Makes about 2 cups*

I got the idea for this sauce from a chef who in turn got it from another chef. It's a beauty, and can be used to top fresh or poached fruit, ice cream, frozen yogurt, waffles, or pancakes. I like to strain out the raspberry seeds, but this step is not necessary. If you do choose to strain them out, don't use so fine a strainer that you strain out the pulp of the berries too. That pulp is where the pectin of the fruit is and is needed to thicken the sauce. A food mill—the type you'd use to remove the seeds and skin from tomatoes for sauce—works well. The sauce will keep for about 4 weeks in the refrigerator.

1 bottle reasonably good Cabernet Sauvignon
12 oz raspberries, or frozen and defrosted
1 cup maple syrup
favorite brand of vanilla frozen yogurt as needed.

1. Bring Cabernet, raspberries, and maple syrup to a boil, then reduce heat and simmer, uncovered, for about 20 minutes, or until reduced by about one-half, to measure about 2 cups.

2. Strain mixture through a straner or food mill to remove the raspberry seeds, but not the pulp.

3. Let cool to room temperature and serve over vanilla frozen yogurt.

Each 2 TB contain approximately 67 calories, 0.2 grams protein, 0 grams total fat, 0 mg cholesterol, 4 mg sodium.

NECTARINE BLUEBERRY SUMMER BAKE **Serves 8**

A s with all fruit desserts, the amount of sweetening you add to the nectarines and blueberries in this recipe depends on how ripe the fruit is. The riper it is, the more natural sugar is present, and the less you'll need to add.

FRUIT

5 (2 cups sliced) nectarines
1 cup blueberries, fresh or frozen and defrosted
2-3 TB honey or maple syrup
¹/₄ tsp almond flavoring

TOPPING

¹/₄ cup unsalted macadamia nuts
1 cup whole wheat pastry flour or 1 cup + 2 TB unbleached flour
¹/₂ cup oats
1¹/₂ tsp baking powder
¹/₄ tsp salt
1 egg white
¹/₂ cup honey or maple syrup
1 TB almond oil or canola oil
¹/₄ tsp almond flavoring
2 TB shredded unsweetened coconut

1. Preheat oven to 325° F.

2. Cut the nectarines in half, then quarters. (Do not peel the nectarines.) Cut the quarters into ¹/₄" slices.

3. Toss the sliced nectarines and blueberries together in a mixing bowl.

4. Add the honey and almond flavoring, tossing well to coat all the fruit. Taste and add more honey, if needed.

5. Toast the macadamia nuts in the oven for 15 minutes, or until light golden. (If you find macadamia nuts salted, rinse the salt away under hot water, and re-toast them in the oven for 15 minutes, or until light golden.) Cool, chop and set aside.

6. To make the topping, place the flour, oats, baking powder, salt, and chopped macadamia nuts in a medium-size mixing bowl. Mix together well and set aside.

7. Lightly beat the egg white. Add the honey, oil, and almond flavoring and beat until well mixed.

8. When ready to assemble the topping, lightly spray an 8" x 10" baking pan or pie pan with vegetable oil spray.

9. Add the fruit on the bottom of the baking pan. Shake to spread it evenly over the bottom of the pan.

10. Add the flour mixture to the wet ingredients and stir until just mixed, no more.

11. Spread the batter over the fruit. Smooth, then sprinkle on the coconut.

12. Bake for 20-25 minutes.

Each serving contains approximately 232 calories, 4.2 grams protein, 6 grams total fat, 0 mg cholesterol, 76 mg sodium.

PLUM TART WITH ALMOND PASTRY **Serves 12**

T his is an easy tart to make because you don't roll out the dough. Instead, you pat it into the tart pan. The tart looks very rustic if you simply cut the plums in half instead of in crescents, and line the pastry crust with them, although cooking time will be a little longer. I've also done this tart with bing cherries and with apricots, using the appropriate jams for the glaze.

PASTRY

¹/₂ cup slivered raw almonds
1¹/₄ cups unbleached flour
¹/₄ tsp salt
6 TB frozen sweet butter, cut into small pieces
1 TB honey

FILLING

2 pounds plums
¹/₄ cup plum jam
1 TB Amaretto
1-2 TB honey

1. Preheat the oven to 325° F.

2. To make the almond pastry crust, toast the almonds in the oven for about 15 minutes, or until light golden and aromatic. Remove from oven and let cool.

3. Place the toasted almonds in a food processor or blender and process to a fine meal or powder.

4. Add the flour and salt and pulse to mix well with the almonds.

5. Add the butter and honey and process until the dough comes together into a ball.

6. Pat the dough evenly into the bottom and up the side of an 11" tart pan. (To make the dough even with the top of the tart pan, roll a rolling pin over the top to cut off the excess.)

7. Place the lined tart pan in the freezer for 30 minutes. Increase the oven temperature to 375° F.

8. After chilling the tart shell, bake for 10-15 minutes, or until light golden. Remove from the oven to cool. Reduce oven temperature to 350° F.

9. Wash the plums well, cut in half or crescents. Discard the pit.

10. Heat the plum jam, Amaretto, and honey in a saucepan. Let the jam melt, then boil for 2 minutes, or until thickened. Strain the glaze, if desired, through a sieve.

11. Brush the bottom of the tart shell with some of the jam glaze.

12. Arrange the plums in the shell so they overlap a bit to allow them to shrink while baking, yet still cover the entire pastry crust.

13. Brush the rest of the jam mixture over the top of the fruit.

14. Bake, uncovered, for 30 minutes, then cover with foil and bake for 15-25 minutes more.

15. Let cool for 15 minutes and serve.

Each serving contains approximately 211 calories, 3.2 grams protein, 9.3 grams total fat, 15.5 mg cholesterol, 95 mg sodium.

MEXICAN CHOCOLATE PUDDING WITH RASPBERRIES   *Serves 8*

There is a fitness spa in San Diego County called Cal-a-Vie. It's sumptuous country French setting soothes and relieves you from the rigors of five hours of exercise per day. Located far from town, the solitude allows you to enjoy the sounds of the country while being pampered with massage, hydrotherapy, and seaweed wraps for four hours in the afternoon. And all the day long, healthful, energizing food is served to you from their very creative kitchen. Heaven on earth! I was asked to be guest chef one afternoon, and I served my Tacos Del Mar with Light Tartar Sauce (see recipe page 84) and this Mexican Chocolate Pudding. It's a rich, creamy pudding made of silken tofu—do not make it with fresh tofu—cocoa, and sweetener. Cinnamon lends a Mexican flavor, and raspberries a fresh summer feel. For a variation, add 2 TB of Kahula in Step 2.

---

2 boxes Mori-Nu silken tofu, firm
¹/₄ cup cocoa powder
¹/₂ cup maple syrup
¹/₂ tsp cinnamon
12 oz fresh or frozen raspberries

1. Place silken tofu in a food processor or blender and process until very creamy.

2. Add cocoa powder, maple syrup, and cinnamon. Process until thoroughly mixed, taking care to scrape down the sides of the bowl so that all the cocoa powder is incorporated into the mixture.

3. Meanwhile, clean/defrost the raspberries. Cover the bottom of 8 individual ramekins or custard dishes with the raspberries, reserving 8 for garnish.

4. Spoon chocolate pudding over the raspberries, garnish the reserved raspberries, and refrigerate, covered, for 1 hour.

Each serving contains approximately 103 calories, 4.25 grams protein, 2 grams total fat, 0 mg cholesterol, 27.4 mg sodium.

FALL

Californians are always hearing that we have no seasons. I disagree. Living on the coast in California for 19 years, I know that we actually have five seasons, and two of them occur during the traditional autumn months of September through December. Our real summer starts in August and runs throughout September and October. Although it's called Indian Summer, it's our only summer! Before that, we have June gloom, the low clouds and haze that plague us from May through July. But in Indian Summer, hot Santa Ana winds blaze through the county. While the rest of the country is bundling up, we can't even think of wool. Our gardens are still producing, and we are blessed with the produce of summer while sensing the ever-so-slight-scent of approaching autumn. Finally in November the air bites back, and we know autumn has officially arrived. The oven's warmth and pleasing aromas of baking pies and roasting chickens are welcomed. It's my favorite time of the year to cook—no hurry, just the joy of being warmed from the inside out by the foods of the season.

SUGGESTED MENUS

BACK TO SCHOOL
Turkey Loaf with Fresh Tomatoes
Clay Baked Autumn Vegetable Roast
Green Salad with Balsamic Vinaigrette (see page 76)
Fudgy Brownies

HALLOWEEN
Butternut Squash Soup with Cayenne and Pepitas
Dark Meat Chicken Salad with Fig Vinaigrette
Pear Crisp

THANKSGIVING
Green Salad with Ginger Vinaigrette (see page 7)
Acorn Squash Stuffed with Wild Rice, Fennel, and Carrot Pilaf And/Or Aromatic Roast Chicken (or Turkey) with Herbes de Provence
Yukon Gold Mashed Potatoes with Roasted Garlic
Stewed Kale with Chianti Vinegar
Double Crust Apple Pie

DINNER I
Rose Geranium Leaf and Sage Honey Biscuits
Marinated and Broiled Curried Chicken Breast
Wilted Chard with Warm Curry Dressing
Sake-Baked Pears

DINNER II
Green Salad with Jalapeño Vinaigrette
Puebla-Style Mole Sauce with Chicken Strips
Timbales of Rice and Barley Pilaf

DINNER III
Green Lettuce and Dressing from Indian Summer Salad
Grilled Mahi-Mahi with Pistachio Salsa
Store-bought Vanilla Frozen Yogurt*

DINNER IV
Pasta with Wild Mushroom Cream Sauce
Parisian Baguette
Salad with No Oil Herbed Vinaigrette (see page 40)
Chocolate Dipped Almond and Pine Nut Biscotti

DINNER V
Oak Leaf Lettuce and Creamy Parsley Marjoram Dressing
Spicy Eggplant Casserole
Short Grain Brown Rice*
White Chocolate Custard with Ginger

DINNER VI
Watercress and Tomatoes with Yogurt Dressing (see page 75)
Acorn Squash Enchiladas
Almond-Crusted Orange Roughy

* Recipe not included

APPETIZERS AND BREADS

MUSHROOMS STUFFED WITH WALNUT PARSLEY PESTO `Serves 5`

Hungarian paprika actually provides taste, not just color. It's available in most grocery stores in a red tin. If you can't find it, make the recipe with plain paprika, and when you do locate it and re-make the pesto, you will be able to taste the difference and discern the flavor that Hungarian paprika can lend to a dish.

PESTO
¹/₂ cup raw walnuts
1 slice whole grain bread, torn in pieces
1 clove garlic
¹/₄ cup fresh parsley leaves
¹/₄ cup fresh cilantro leaves
1 tsp Hungarian paprika
1 TB rice vinegar or white wine vinegar
2 TB finely chopped red onion
salt or VegeSal to taste

MUSHROOMS
20 large (not jumbo) mushrooms
1 tsp extra virgin olive oil
2 TB red wine

1. Place walnuts, bread, garlic, parsley, cilantro, paprika, and vinegar in a food processor or blender. Process until mixture becomes a paste.

2. Transfer to a bowl. Stir in red onion, season to taste with salt, and set aside.

3. Wash mushrooms well. Remove stems and reserve for another use.

4. Add olive oil to a large non-stick skillet. Add mushrooms and cook over medium heat for 3 minutes. Turn and cook for 3 minutes more. Add red wine and

increase heat to high. Cook until lightly browned, then transfer to a plate and let cool.

5. Spoon a little of the pesto into each mushroom. Arrange on a platter and serve warm or at room temperature.

Each mushroom contains approximately 33 calories, 1.1 grams protein, 2.3 grams total fat, 0 mg cholesterol, 39 mg sodium.

ROSE GERANIUM LEAF AND SAGE HONEY BISCUITS `Makes 12 biscuits`

Rose geranium leaves lend a lovely spicy-rose taste to foods. While we're accustomed to smelling rose, tasting it causes the senses to do a double take! I have used rose geranium leaves to flavor breadsticks, muffins, berries, and yogurt spreads, as well as these biscuits. Since the leaves are slightly "furry," be sure to chop them finely. The sage honey works quite well in combination with the rose geranium, but if you can't find it, eucalyptus, clover, or wild flower honey will work well too. Drizzle additional honey onto the hot biscuits, if desired. These biscuits are great teamed with Broiled Breast of Chicken on Wilted Chard Leaves with Warm Curry Dressing (see recipes page 119).

1 cup whole wheat flour
1 cup unbleached flour
4 tsp baking powder
4 rose geranium leaves, finely minced
¹/₂ tsp black pepper
¹/₄ tsp salt or VegeSal
³/₄ cup low-fat milk or plain soy milk (if soured, add ¹/₂ tsp baking soda to dry ingredients)
¹/₄ cup canola oil
2 TB sage honey

1. Preheat oven to 400° F.

2. Mix dry ingredients in one bowl and wet ingredients in another.

3. Combine the two mixtures and mix well.

4. Turn out onto a lightly floured surface and knead briefly.

5. Using a rolling pin, roll out to a thickness of ¹/₂"-³/₄". Flour a biscuit cutter and cut out 12 biscuits, or cut into squares, triangles, or diamonds with a sharp knife. (A dull knife or unfloured biscuit cutter will pinch the edges together, inhibiting rising.)

6. Place on a lightly oiled cookie sheet and bake for 8 minutes.

Each biscuit contains approximately 130 calories, 2.9 grams protein, 5 grams total fat, 0.6 mg cholesterol, 163 mg sodium.

PARISIAN BAGUETTE
Makes 2 loaves

There is nothing like the aroma, texture, and taste of homemade bread. Save any leftovers to make croutons.

1³/₄ cups water
2 packages yeast
1¹/₂ cups whole wheat flour
2¹/₂ cups unbleached flour
1-2 tsp salt or VegeSal

1. Heat water to bath water temperature (105°-115° F.) Add yeast and let sit for 5 minutes, or until the mixture begins to foam. If it hasn't foamed within 5 minutes, that means your yeast is no good. Discard and begin again with a fresh package.

2. Meanwhile, place the flours and salt in a medium-sized bowl. When the yeast has foamed, add it to the flours and stir until the dough comes together into a ball.

3. Turn out onto a lightly floured surface and knead for 5 minutes. To knead, gather the dough together into 1 lump. Then fold dough over in half toward you. Lightly press down on the dough with the heels of your hands as you smear the seam of the fold back into the dough. Turn the dough a quarter turn and repeat the procedure. While kneading, very gradually add a little extra flour to the work surface so the dough does not stick. Knead until dough is smooth, elastic, and shiny, about 5 minutes.

4. Shape the dough into a ball and place it in a lightly oiled bowl. Turn to coat the dough with oil on all sides.

5. Cover the bowl with plastic wrap or a damp towel and let rise in a draft-free place until double in size, 45-60 minutes. (You know the dough has risen enough when an indentation left by your finger in the dough doesn't rise back up at you.)

6. Punch down dough and form into 2 baguettes. Place in a baguette pan or on a lightly oiled cookie sheet, cover with a damp towel or plastic wrap, and let rise again for 30 minutes. (You may omit this second rising if you'd like—the bread will be a little denser.)

7. Meanwhile, preheat oven to 400° F.

8. Bake loaves for 35-45 minutes.

Makes 2 loaves, or about 24 slices.

Each slice contains approximately 74 calories, 2.6 grams protein, 0.3 grams total fat, 0 mg cholesterol, 135 mg sodium.

ROASTED CURRY ALMONDS
Serves 8

Most flavored nuts found in tins are quite greasy, so I like to dry roast my own in the oven. Also, by doing them myself I am assured of the freshness of the nuts.

1 cup raw, whole almonds
2 tsp low sodium soy sauce
¹/₄ tsp granulated garlic or garlic powder

¹/₄ tsp curry powder
¹/₄ tsp ground dried ginger
¹/₂ tsp ground cumin

1. Preheat oven to 350°F.

2. Place almonds in a bowl and add soy sauce, stirring well to coat each almond.

3. Sprinkle on seasonings and stir to distribute evenly.

4. Place in a single layer on a cookie sheet and bake for 20-25 minutes. Stir half way through.

5. Let cool—they will become crisper as they come to room temperature.

Each serving (1 oz) contains approximately 93 calories, 3.4 grams protein, 8.4 grams total fat, 0 mg cholesterol, 55 mg sodium.

SEMOLINA SCALLION CRACKERS
Makes about 60 cut-out crackers

S emolina flour is derived from durum wheat, which is higher in protein than other strains of wheat. Pasta and couscous are made from it, so you may already be familiar with its pale yellow color and nutty taste. The flour is very sandy in texture, yet it works up into an incredibly smooth dough. Look for it in gourmet grocery stores, natural food stores, or Italian markets.

³/₄ cup semolina flour or unbleached flour
³/₄ cup whole wheat pastry flour or ³/₄ cup + 1 TB unbleached flour
¹/₂ tsp salt or VegeSal
3 TB Olio Santo or extra virgin olive oil (see page 10)
3 (about ¹/₂ cup) scallions, cut into rounds
4-6 TB water

1. Preheat oven to 350°F.

2. Mix flours together in a mixing bowl. Add salt, oil, and scallions and stir to mix. Use the back of a fork to cut the oil into the flours.

3. Add water until the dough just comes together.

> Make a double batch and freeze extras, or store in a sealed plastic bag in the pantry.

4. Turn dough out onto a lightly floured surface and "knead" for a minute or two. Let the dough rest while you lightly oil cookie sheets.

5. Roll out dough to about ¹/₈" thick. Roll from the center out toward the edges, making sure dough is of equal thickness all over. You can bake this sheet whole (it will take about 1¹/₂ times as long to bake) or cut out shapes with a cookie cutter or the rim of a glass.

6. Place on cookies sheets and bake cut-out crackers for 8-12 minutes. Let cool and serve. If you baked the whole sheet, rather than cut-outs, break into pieces and serve.

Each serving (8 crackers) contains approximately 123 calories, 3.1 grams protein, 5.6 grams total fat, 0 mg cholesterol, 68 mg sodium.

CASHEW SUNFLOWER AIOLI WITH STEAMED POTATOES AND GREEN BEANS
Makes about ¹/₂ cup

T his aioli, or mayonnaise, made from nuts and seeds, is marvelous with all kinds of steamed or blanched vegetables, and as a sandwich spread. Take a look at the nutritional analysis below and see how it compares to standard mayonnaise. I think you'll be pleasantly surprised!

¹/₄ cup raw cashews
¹/₄ cup raw sunflower seeds
2 TB fresh lemon juice

¹/₄ TB extra virgin olive oil
¹/₄-¹/₂ cup water
4-6 potatoes
8 oz green beans

1. To make the aioli, place the cashews and sunflower seeds in a food processor or blender and process to a powder.

2. With the machine running, add the lemon juice and oil. Scrape down the sides of the bowl and process again.

3. Add as much water as desired, up to ¹/₂ cup, depending on the consistency you want and process until well blended. Refrigerate while you prepare the potatoes and beans.

4. Scrub the potatoes well and cut them into halves, quarters, or eighths—whichever is bite-size, which will depend on the size of the potato.

5. Rinse the green beans. Snip off the ends, if desired.

6. Place potatoes in a steamer basket and steam for 20-25 minutes, or until tender.

7. To blanch the green beans, bring a large pot of water to a boil. Immerse the green beans for 30 seconds until their color brightens. Immediately refresh in cold water. Drain.

8. Arrange the potatoes and green beans on a platter. Serve with a bowl of Cashew Sunflower Aioli for dipping.

Each serving (1 TB) contains approximately 46 calories, 1.4 grams protein, 9.1 grams total fat, 0 mg cholesterol, 1 mg sodium.

Each 1 TB of canola mayonnaise contains approximately 104 calories, 0.1 grams protein, 12 grams total fat, 4 mg cholesterol, 55 mg sodium.

SALADS

DARK MEAT CHICKEN SALAD WITH FIG VINAIGRETTE

Serves 6

Since it is often easier to find dried figs, I created this recipe using them. But it can also be made with fresh figs, when they are available. The directions are the same, but you will not need to add the water.

DRESSING
5 dried black mission figs
¹/₂ cup dry red wine
3 TB sherry vinegar
2-4 TB orange or tangerine juice
6 TB extra virgin olive oil
¹/₄ cup water

CHICKEN SALAD
4-8 potatoes
1 bunch red Swiss chard
1 head romaine lettuce
1 large beet
6-8 chicken thighs, with bones, without skin

1. Preheat the oven to 425°F.

2. To make the dressing, cut the stems off the figs and quarter them. Place in a small saucepan, along with the dry red wine. Simmer for about 10 minutes, or until the figs are softened.

3. Place the fig/wine mixture, sherry vinegar, and 2 TB of the orange juice in a food processor or blender. Process until well blended.

4. Taste, and if you want it a little sweeter, add the other 2 TB of orange juice.

5. With the machine running, add the olive oil. Check the consistency. If it is too thick, add up to $^1/_4$ cup water. Set aside.

6. Meanwhile, quarter but do not peel the potatoes. Bake for 35 minutes. Remove from oven and keep warm. Increase oven temperature to Broil.

7. Wash and dry the red chard and lettuce and tear it into bite-size pieces.

8. Grate the beet and toss with the chard and lettuce.

9. Broil the chicken thighs for 15-18 minutes, or until done.

10. Toss the greens with the dressing. Arrange the baked potato quarters around the edges of the greens, and nestle 1 or 2 chicken thighs per person in the greens. Serve immediately.

Makes 2 cups of dressing—there will be leftovers.

Each serving of chicken salad contains 360 calories, 24.5 grams protein, 3.8 grams total fat, 67 mg cholesterol, 267 mg sodium.

Each serving (2 TB) of dressing contains approximately 67 calories, 0.2 grams protein, 5.1 grams total fat, 0 mg cholesterol, 1 mg sodium.

LENTIL SALAD WITH CREAMY WALNUT MISO DRESSING   *Serves 8*

Often when I'm home alone for dinner, this is what I'll make—not because my husband doesn't like to eat it, but because I could eat it seven nights in a row!

BEANS
1 cup dried lentils, rinsed
2$^1/_4$ cups water
3" strip kombu seaweed (optional)
6 sun-dried tomatoes, not re-hydrated, chopped
2 TB chopped fresh parsley

GREENS
12 cups mix of romaine, arugula, radicchio, and other strong tasting lettuce

DRESSING
$^1/_3$ cup raw walnuts
2 scallions
$^1/_4$ cup walnut or canola oil
$^1/_4$ cup water
2 TB mellow white miso
2 TB sherry vinegar

1. Preheat the oven to 325° F.

2. Place lentils, water, kombu, and sun-dried tomatoes in a saucepan. Bring to a boil, reduce heat to low, and simmer, covered, for 30-40 minutes, or until the lentils are done, but still hold their shape.

3. Meanwhile, clean the lettuce, tear into bite-size pieces, and arrange 8 serving plates, using about 1$^1/_2$ cups of lettuce for each.

4. To make the dressing, toast the walnuts in the oven for 10-15 minutes, or until lightly browned and aromatic.

5. Place walnuts in a food processor or blender. Process to a powder. Add the scallions and process well.

6. Add all other dressing ingredients and process until creamy. If too thick, add more water.

7. Remove the kombu from the cooked lentils and discard. Stir in the chopped parsley.

8. Serve by mounding a heaping $^1/_3$ cup of lentils over the lettuce on each plate, then drizzle with 2 TB of dressing.

Each serving of beans with greens contains approximately 111 calories, 8.9 grams protein, 0.6 grams total fat, 0 mg cholesterol, 16 mg sodium.

Each serving (2 TB) of the dressing contains approximately 116 calories, 1.6 grams protein, 11.45 grams total fat, 0 mg cholesterol, 158 mg sodium.

OAK LEAF LETTUCE WITH CREAMY PARSLEY MARJORAM DRESSING `Serves 4`

This is a variation on an herb vinaigrette. By adding the tomato, the consistency changes to thick and creamy, the color to a lovely pastel pink, and the flavor takes on a certain smoothness.

DRESSING
1/2 cup extra virgin olive oil
1/4 cup apple cider vinegar
1/2 large tomato
2 TB water
3 TB fresh parsley
1 TB fresh marjoram
1 sprig fresh lemon thyme (optional)
1 clove garlic
salt or VegeSal to taste
black pepper to taste

SALAD
1 head oak leaf lettuce
2 scallions, cut into rounds
1/2 cucumber, sliced into rounds

1. To make the dressing, combine all ingredients in a food processor or blender and process until creamy.

2. Add salt and black pepper to taste. Refrigerate until ready to serve.

3. Wash and spin dry the lettuce. Tear into bite-size pieces and place in a large salad bowl.

4. Slice the scallions and cucumber and add to the lettuce.

5. Toss about 1/2 cup of the dressing with the lettuce. Serve immediately.

Makes 1 1/2 cups dressing—there will be leftovers.

Each serving of salad contains approximately 21 calories, 1.7 grams protein, 0.3 grams total fat, 0 mg cholesterol, 7 mg sodium.

Each serving (2 TB) of dressing contains 82 calories, 0.1 grams protein, 9 grams total fat, 0 mg cholesterol, 24 mg sodium.

NEW NIÇOISE SALAD WITH JALAPEÑO VINAIGRETTE `Serves 8`

The Niçoise salad originated in the south of France near Nice, and traditionally includes tuna, hard boiled eggs, capers, beans, potatoes, and tomatoes. I've always found tuna and eggs to be so filling that it was hard to eat all the vegetables, so I omitted the egg in favor of the vegetables. I also gave the salad a Southwest flavor, with salmon instead of tuna, the addition of chiles, and a spicy vinaigrette dressing. I think you'll agree that this is a delicious autumn luncheon salad, maintaining the integrity of the original version while improving upon it with new choices. The single jalapeño chile in the dressing makes it exciting, yet not fiery. If you like it hotter, add some of the seeds of the jalapeño, but go slowly!

DRESSING
3/4 cup extra virgin olive oil
1/4 cup sherry vinegar
1/4 cup fresh lime juice
2 cloves garlic
1 jalapeño chile pepper
1 tsp capers, rinsed
1 tsp Dijon-style mustard (with jalapeños, if possible)
1/2 cup fresh cilantro or parsley, finely minced

SALAD
1 1/2 pounds fresh salmon steaks
4 small red potatoes, steamed, cooled, and sliced

*4 Anaheim chiles, roasted, peeled, sliced, and cooled
    or canned green chiles, sliced lengthwise*
4 roma tomatoes, quartered
1 small red onion, sliced into rounds
24 green beans, lightly steamed and chilled
1 head romaine lettuce, washed and spun dry

1. Preheat oven to Broil.

2. To make the dressing, place all the ingredients in a food processor or blender. Blend until creamy. Or, place ingredients in a jar with a lid and shake until creamy.

3. Prepare all the vegetables as directed.

4. Broil the salmon for about 8 minutes total, turning halfway through. (If you use a convection oven you do not need to turn the fish.) Cool and arrange on 8 serving plates.

5. Tear the lettuce into bite-size pieces and add to the 8 plates. Arrange other ingredients on top.

6. Drizzle 1 TB of Jalapeño Vinaigrette over each salad before serving.

Makes 8 luncheon salads, but enough dressing for 12 salads.

Each serving of the salad contains approximately 285 calories, 3.6 grams total fat, 18.9 grams protein, 38 mg cholesterol, 61 mg sodium.

Each serving (1 TB) of dressing contains approximately 61 calories, 6.7 grams total fat, 0 mg cholesterol, 3 mg sodium.

INDIAN SUMMER SALAD WITH VERY LOW-FAT AVOCADO DRESSING
Serves 4

Indian Summer nights call for late dinners, after the sun has gone down and the sprinklers have come one. This complete dinner salad can be made stovetop, or with the help of the outdoor grill—no hot ovens necessary. Try this light meal when Indian summer comes to your part of the country.

SALAD
2 1/2 cups water
1/4 cup raw wild rice
2 bay leaves
3" strip kombu seaweed (optional)
1/4 cup raw short grain brown rice
1/2 cup dried lentils, rinsed
2 bunches spinach
1 ear corn, husked
3 oz (about 10) mushrooms, preferably shiitake
*2 tomatoes, thickly sliced into rounds, then cut in
    half*

DRESSING
2 cloves garlic
1/4 small red onion
1/4 cup fresh parsley leaves
1 medium avocado
4 TB nonfat plain yogurt
3 TB rice vinegar or white wine vinegar
1 TB balsamic vinegar
1 TB low sodium soy sauce or white miso
2 TB water

1. Bring the water to a boil. Add the wild rice, bay leaves, and kombu. Return to a boil, reduce heat to low, and cook, covered, for 10 minutes.

2. Add the short grain brown rice and lentils and cook, covered, for 30 minutes more. Remove and discard the bay leaves and kombu.

3. Meanwhile, make the dressing. Place the garlic, onion, and parsley leaves in a food processor and process until finely minced, or finely mince by hand. Add avocado to the food processor and purée until smooth, or mash with a fork.

4. Add the yogurt, vinegars, soy sauce, and 2 TB water. Process or stir until well blended and creamy. Refrigerate until ready to use.

5. Wash spinach and spin dry, and remove and discard discolored leaves. Tear into bite-size pieces and arrange on 4 dinner plates.

6. The ideal way to cook the corn and mushrooms is on a grill, either stovetop or outdoor. Heat the grill and lightly spray the vegetables with vegetable oil spray.

Cook the corn for about 4 minutes, turning each minute or so, or until it changes color slightly. Cook the mushrooms for about 2 minutes per side. Cut the corn off the cob and slice the mushrooms. Or, if you don't have a stovetop or outdoor grill, cut the corn off the cob and slice the mushrooms before cooking. Sauté with a little oil for about 5 minutes, until the mushrooms begin to give up their juices.

7. Place the corn kernels and mushroom slices on top of the spinach leaves.

8. Add the tomato slices around the edges.

9. Add a scoop of the cooked rice and lentils to the top of the salad.

10. Pour 2 TB of the dressing on top and serve immediately.

Serves 4 as a main dish salad, 8 as a side dish salad. Makes 1³/₄ cup dressing—there will be leftovers.

Each main dish salad contains approximately 221 calories, 13.1 grams protein, 1.5 grams total fat, 0 mg cholesterol, 0.5 mg sodium.

Each 2 TB of dressing contains approximately 26 calories, 0.6 grams protein, 2 grams total fat, 0 mg cholesterol, 51 mg sodium.

SOUPS

TWENTY MINUTE BLACK BEAN AND SHERRY SOUP
Serves 8

This recipe takes advantage of canned beans and canned chicken broth to save time, although you can use homemade and frozen versions of both. The seasonings and fresh vegetables are what give it that "cooked all day" appeal.

1 medium yellow onion, diced
2 cloves garlic, finely minced
1 jalapeño chile, diced (optional)
¹/₂ TB extra virgin olive oil
1 tsp ground cumin
¹/₂ tsp chili powder
2-15 oz cans black beans
2-15 oz cans chicken broth or Homemade Stock (see page 44)
1 TB sherry
salt or VegeSal to taste
8 TB chopped tomatoes, fresh or canned
8 TB chopped fresh cilantro or parsley

1. In a 4-quart saucepan, sauté onion, garlic, and jalapeño in the olive oil until soft.

2. Add cumin and chili powder and cook for 1-2 minutes longer.

3. Rinse the beans. Add beans and chicken broth to the pot. Bring to a boil, reduce heat to low, and simmer for 5-10 minutes.

4. Pour soup into a food processor or blender and purée in batches. Return puréed soup to saucepan.

5. Stir in sherry and season with salt to taste. Heat for 1 minute.

6. Ladle into soup bowls, add the tomatoes and cilantro to the top of each, and serve.

Each serving contains approximately 142 calories, 8.75 grams protein, 2.4 grams total fat, 0.5 mg cholesterol, 39 mg sodium.

BUTTERNUT SQUASH SOUP WITH CAYENNE AND PEPITAS
Serves 8

Butternut is my favorite of the squashes that begin appearing in the grocery store in the fall, and continue throughout the winter months. It is naturally sweeter than acorn squash, with a more buttery flavor than any of the others. This soup, so creamy and delicately spiced, is truly memorable.

When preparing this soup for Halloween, use a hollowed-out pumpkin as a soup tureen, or use smaller hollowed-out pumpkins as individual soup bowls.

---

1 large butternut squash or 2-3 yams (to equal 3 cups)
2 cloves garlic, finely minced
1 medium yellow onion, diced
1 TB extra virgin olive oil
1 tsp grated fresh ginger
¹/₂ tsp ground cumin
pinch cayenne
low sodium soy sauce to taste
1 cup canned chicken broth or Homemade Chicken Stock (see page 44)
1 cup evaporated skim milk or low-fat milk or plain soy milk
2 TB pepitas (pumpkin seeds) as garnish (optional)

1. Preheat oven to 350° F.

2. Poke holes all over the butternut squash. Bake squash for 60-90 minutes, until very soft. Let cool, cut in half lengthwise, and scrape out the strings and seeds and discard. Or bake unpeeled yams for 1 hour at 425° F. or until soft.

3. Meanwhile, sauté garlic and onion in olive oil in a 3-4 quart saucepan for 5 minutes, or until onion is clear. Add seasonings

4. When squash is cool enough to handle, scoop the flesh away from the skin and purée it in a food processor or blender. Add the garlic and onion mixture, and enough broth and milk to make the mixture creamy. Make sure to purée it long enough to liquify the onions.

5. Return soup to the saucepan and heat for 1 minute. Serve immediately, topping each bowl of soup with a few pepitas as garnish, if desired.

For a vegetarian option to the chicken stock, use 1 cup water and 1 tsp Bernard Jensen's Broth Powder, found in well-stocked natural food stores.

Each serving contains approximately 67 calories, 22 grams protein, 2.6 grams total fat, 0 mg cholesterol, 46 mg sodium.

HEARTY MINESTRONE Serves 8

When my husband and I light the first fire of the season, we like to eat dinner in the living room in front of the fireplace. More often than not, our meal is a bowl of this minestrone, a thick slice of bread, and a glass of red wine.

---

³/₄ cup dried garbanzo beans
5 cups water
6" strip kombu seaweed (optional)
1 bay leaf
4 cloves garlic, finely minced
1 medium yellow onion, diced
2 stalks celery, diced
1 carrot, diced
1 green bell pepper, diced
1 cup canned tomato purée
3 TB dry red wine
¹/₄ tsp dried thyme
¹/₄ tsp dried summer savory
¹/₂ tsp dried marjoram
¹/₂ tsp dried basil
¹/₂ tsp dried rosemary
2 zucchini, sliced into rounds
¹/₄ cup dried pasta, short shape
crushed red peppers as needed (optional)
¹/₄ cup freshly grated Parmesan cheese

---

1. Soak beans at least 8 hours in enough water to cover the beans plus 2" or quick soak by placing beans in a saucepan, with enough water to cover plus 2" and bring to a boil. Turn off heat and let sit for 1¹/₂ hours.

2. Drain beans and place in an 8-quart Dutch oven. Add 5 cups fresh water, kombu, bay leaf, garlic, onion, celery, carrot, and green pepper. Bring to a boil, reduce heat to low, and simmer, covered, for 60-90 minutes, or until garbanzos are tender.

3. When the beans are tender, add the tomato purée, red wine, herbs, zucchini, and dried pasta.

4. Cook for 15 minutes more, then ladle into bowls. Top with crushed red peppers, if desired, and a sprinkling of Parmesan cheese.

Each serving (10.5 oz) contains approximately 146 calories, 7.2 grams protein, 2.2 grams total fat, 2 mg cholesterol, 77 mg sodium.

BLACK BEAN CHILI   `Serves 12`

Once you measure out all the seasonings for this, you'll be surprised how much there is—it's a bowlful! As often as I make this chili, the more I think they should sell chili powder by the six-pack!

---

2 cups dried black beans
8 cups water
6" strip kombu seaweed (optional)
1 bay leaf
2 large yellow onions, diced
5 cloves garlic, finely minced
4 tsp ground cumin
4 tsp paprika
4 tsp dried oregano
1 tsp cayenne
3 TB chili powder
1-28 oz can crushed tomatoes with purée
1 TB red wine vinegar
salt or VegeSal to taste

If you can't find crushed tomatoes with added purée, use 1-28 oz can whole tomatoes, drained of liquid and re-filled with purée to the top (approximately ½ of a 16-oz can of tomato purée).

1. Soak beans at least 8 hours in enough water to cover the beans plus 2", or quick soak by placing beans in a saucepan, with enough water to cover plus 2", and bring to a boil. Turn off heat and let sit for 1½ hours.

2. Drain beans and place in an 8-quart Dutch oven. Add 8 cups fresh water, kombu, bay leaf, onions, and garlic. Bring to a boil, reduce heat to low, and simmer, covered, for 1 hour. Remove and discard kombu. Cook for 30-60 minutes more, or until the beans are tender.

3. Add the seasonings, tomatoes, and red wine vinegar. Cook for 20-30 minutes more.

4. Taste, and add salt as needed. Serve hot.

Each serving (10.3 oz) contains approximately 132 calories, 7.9 grams protein, 1 gram total fat, 0 mg cholesterol, 168 mg sodium.

LENTIL SOUP   `Serves 8`

Lentils, along with split peas, mung beans, and aduki beans, do not need to be soaked. Lentils should cook up in 40-60 minutes. If they don't get tender within that time, it may be because you added something acidic or salty to the pot before they had a chance to soften. This means you shouldn't add tomatoes, lemon or lime juice, vinegar, soy sauce, or salt until after the beans are as soft as you want them. Second, if the beans are very old, they take longer to cook. If you've had a batch of lentils in your pantry for more than two years, throw them out and buy a fresh batch. You'll save yourself lots of time by not having to stare into a pot of hard lentils!

---

2 cups dried lentils, rinsed
8 cups water
1 bay leaf
6" strip kombu seaweed (optional)
3 cloves garlic, finely minced
1 medium yellow onion, diced
3 stalks celery, diced
3 carrots, diced
2 TB dry red wine
3 TB fresh lemon juice
salt or VegeSal to taste

1. Place lentils, water, bay leaf, kombu, garlic, onion, celery, and carrots in an 8-quart Dutch oven. Bring to a boil, reduce heat to low, and simmer, covered, for 45 minutes.

2. Check to make sure the lentils are tender. If not, let them cook another 15-20 minutes. Remove and discard kombu.

3. Add red wine and lemon juice. Taste, and add salt as needed. Serve hot.

Each serving (10.6 oz) contains approximately 169 calories, 14.2 protein, 0.6 grams total fat, 0 mg cholesterol, 100 mg sodium.

ROASTED PEPPER AND WHITE BEAN SOUP `Serves 8`

I love the confetti look of this soup from the variously colored bell peppers. Along with red, yellow, green, and orange bell peppers, you may find purple ones, too. Although they are an unusual color, I don't suggest them for this soup. They are not very flavorful, and they turn green when cooked—yes, those expensive purple peppers turn into the far cheaper green peppers with just a little heat!

2 cups dried white beans
8 cups water
6" strip kombu seaweed (optional)
2 bay leaves
6 cloves garlic, finely minced
1 yellow onion, diced
3 stalks celery, diced
2 carrots, sliced into rounds
2 red bell peppers
1 green bell pepper
1 yellow or orange bell pepper
1 TB Olio Santo (see page 10) or extra virgin olive
    oil (optional)
pinch dried sage

¹/₄ tsp dried rosemary
1 tsp dried basil
salt or VegeSal to taste

1. Soak beans at least 8 hours in enough water to cover the beans plus 2", or quick soak by placing beans in a saucepan, with enough water to cover plus 2" and bring to a boil. Turn off heat and let sit for 1¹/₂ hours.

2. Drain beans and place in an 8-quart Dutch oven. Add 6 cups fresh water, kombu, bay leaves, garlic, onion, celery, and carrots. Bring to a boil, reduce heat to low, cook for 1 hour. Remove and discard kombu. Cook for 1 hour more, or until beans are very soft.

3. Meanwhile, preheat the oven to Broil.

4. Roast peppers as in Calzone with Roasted Red Pepper Sauce (see page 56). Save juices in a bowl. Dice the peppers and add to the bowl.

5. Add the oil to the peppers and set aside.

6. When the beans are completely soft, remove the bay leaves and discard. Purée the soup in batches in a food processor or blender.

7. Return the soup to the pot. Add sage, rosemary, and basil. Taste, and add salt as needed.

8. Stir in roasted peppers and juices and simmer for 10 mintues. Serve hot.

Each serving (13 oz) contains approximately 227 calories, 12.5 grams protein, 2.6 grams total fat, 0 mg cholesterol, 102 mg sodium.

FISH

GRILLED MAHI-MAHI WITH PISTACHIO SALSA `Serves 6`

This Asian-influenced dish offers an array of colors, flavors, and textures atop mild-flavored fish. Mahi-mahi is a Pacific Ocean fish. If it's not available, substitute sea bass, snapper, or halibut.

FISH

> *2 pounds mahi-mahi*
> *$^1/_2$ tsp toasted sesame oil*
> *3 TB rice vinegar*
> *2 tsp grated fresh ginger*

SALSA

> *4 medium-size ripe tomatoes*
> *$^1/_2$ red onion, diced*
> *2-3 TB fresh cilantro, minced*
> *$^1/_2$ tsp toasted sesame oil*
> *salt or VegeSal to taste*
> *a squeeze or two from a fresh lime, if needed*
> *$^1/_2$ cup shelled, roasted, unsalted pistachios*

1. Wash fish and pat dry. Place on a plate or in a ceramic or glass baking dish large enough to hold all the fillets in a single layer.

2. Mix together the toasted sesame oil, rice vinegar, and fresh ginger and pour over the fish. Turn the fish to coat it with marinade on both sides. Cover and refrigerate for 30-60 minutes.

3. Prepare an outdoor or stovetop grill or preheat the oven to Broil.

4. Prepare tomatoes as in Fresh Salsa (see page 89). Chop into cubes and place in a medium-size mixing bowl. (You should have about 2 cups.)

5. Add the red onion, cilantro, and toasted sesame oil to the tomatoes. Stir, taste and season with salt. If preferred, add a squeeze of lime juice. However, if the tomatoes are ripe and full flavored, you shouldn't need it.)

6. Shell the pistachios if you couldn't find them already shelled. Rub the shelled nuts in a clean kitchen towel to remove as much of their papers as possible. Set aside. Do not add the pistachios to the tomatoes yet or they will become soggy.

7. Cook the fish for 8-10 minutes, depending on thickness, turning once halfway through. (If you are broiling in a convection oven, you do not need to turn the fish.)

8. Stir the pistachios into the salsa.

9. Serve fish topped with the salsa.

Each serving of fish contains approximately 177 calories, 28.6 grams protein, 5.9 grams total fat, 103 mg cholesterol, 106 mg sodium.

Each serving (4 TB) of salsa contains approximately 45 calories, 1.6 grams protein, 3 grams total fat, 0 mg cholesterol, 51 mg sodium.

SALMON WITH SUN-DRIED TOMATO AND ONION CHUTNEY `Serves 6`

T his chutney's sweet and tart flavors go especially well with the distinctive taste of salmon.

> *1 large yellow onion, halved and thinly sliced crosswise*
> *1 TB extra virgin olive oil*
> *$^1/_2$ cup marsala wine or dry sherry*
> *$^1/_4$ cup sun-dried tomatoes*
> *2 TB pine nuts*
> *1 tsp grated lemon peel*
> *1 tsp grated orange peel*
> *2 pounds salmon*
> *1 TB red wine vinegar*

1. Preheat oven to 325°F.

2. To make the chutney, sauté the onion slices in the olive oil over low heat for 15 minutes.

3. Meanwhile, heat the marsala wine to boiling in the microwave or stovetop. Remove from heat, add the sun-dried tomatoes, and let them soak for 15 minutes.

4. Toast the pine nuts in the oven for 10 minutes, or until light golden. Set aside. Increase the oven temperature to Broil.

5. When the sun-dried tomatoes are plumped, slice them. Add the marsala wine they were soaking in to the onions and continue to sauté.

6. Add the sun-dried tomatoes, lemon peel, and orange peel. Cook for 5-10 minutes over low heat.

7. Wash salmon and pat dry. Place on a lightly oiled broiler rack. Broil the salmon for 8-10 minutes, turning once halfway through. (You don't need to turn the fish if you are using a convection oven.)

8. Add the red wine vinegar and pine nuts to the sauté pan and stir.

9. Serve the salmon immediately with some of the chutney spooned over the top.

Each serving contains approximately 235 calories, 31.2 grams protein, 8.2 grams total fat, 69 mg cholesterol, 109 mg sodium.

ALMOND CRUSTED ORANGE ROUGHY ▌ *Serves 6*

T he crusty almond coating gives form to the tender orange roughy fillets. This coating will also work well with a red snapper fillet or a thick sole fillet.

2 pounds orange roughy fillets
2-4 TB cognac
1/2 cup raw almonds
1/4 cup flour (rice flour, unbleached flour, or semolina flour)
1 tsp grated lemon peel
vegetable oil spray as needed
lemon wedges as needed

1. Preheat oven to 325°F.

2. Wash fish fillets and pat dry. Arrange in a baking dish large enough to fit all the fillets in a single layer.

3. Pour the cognac over the fish. Turn the fish to coat with the cognac on both sides.

4. Cover and refrigerate for at least 30 minutes.

5. Meanwhile, toast almonds in the oven for 15 minutes. When done, increase the oven temperature to 400°F.

6. Grind almonds to a powder in a food processor or blender.

7. Combine powdered almonds with flour of your choice. Mix well and place the mixture on a dinner plate.

8. Dip the marinated fish in the almond/flour mixture, coating on both sides.

9. Lightly spray a broiler rack with vegetable oil spray. Place fillets on the rack. Cover loosely with aluminum foil and bake for 10 minutes, or until done.

10. Serve immediately with lemon wedges to squeeze over the fish.

Each serving contains approximately 258 calories, 34 grams protein, 8.4 grams total fat, 56 mg cholesterol, 98 mg sodium.

POULTRY

PUEBLA-STYLE MOLE SAUCE WITH CHICKEN STRIPS ▌ *Serves 8*

I n the Mexican culture, mole sauce is made for weddings, coming of age ceremonies, birthdays—any festivity that needs to be celebrated in style. Traditionally, it takes days to prepare and includes an impressive arms length array of ingredients. My version excludes some of the less healthful ingredients, such as lard and white sugar, yet retains the native richness and variety of flavors mole is savored for. Additionally, the following is quick to prepare since all you need to do is roast the vegetables, measure out the remaining ingredients, and purée them all in the food processor or blender.

1 pasilla chile
$^1/_2$ white onion
1 Anaheim chile
4 cloves garlic, unpeeled
1 medium tomato
2 tomatillos, husks peeled off
$^1/_2$ cinnamon stick or 1 tsp ground cinnamon
$^1/_4$ tsp ground cumin
$^1/_4$ tsp ground coriander
2 TB raw sesame seeds
2 TB raw, whole almonds
1 TB peanut butter
1 TB cocoa
1 TB low sodium soy sauce
$^1/_2$ TB honey
1 tsp black pepper
$^3/_4$ cup chicken broth or Homemade Chicken Stock
    (see page 44)
8 half skinless, boneless chicken breasts

1. Preheat oven to 400° F. Bake pasilla chile in oven for 3-5 minutes or until it is puffed up. Watch it carefully because you don't want to burn it. When cooled, remove seeds and stem and discard. Place chile in a food processor or blender. Or, you can soak the chile in hot water for 10-15 minutes, or until plumped. When plumped, remove seeds and stem and discard. Place chile in a food processor or blender. Increase oven temperature to Broil.

2. Cut onion in quarters. Place on a lightly oiled cookie sheet. Slice Anaheim chile in half lengthwise and remove and discard seeds and veins. Add chile and unpeeled garlic to the cookie sheet. Cut tomato and tomatillos in half and place, cut sides down, on cookie sheet. Broil for 8 minutes. When done, peel skins from garlic, tomato, and tomatillos and discard. Place vegetables in the food processor along with the pasilla chile.

3. If using a cinnamon stick, grind in a coffee/spice grinder. Add ground cinnamon, cumin, and coriander to the food processor. Process until smooth.

4. Add sesame seeds, almonds, and peanut butter. Process until smooth.

5. Add cocoa, soy sauce, honey, and black pepper. Process again.

6. Add chicken stock to food processor. Pulse to mix.

7. Meanwhile, place each chicken breast between 2 sheets of plastic wrap. Pound with a meat pounder until breast is of uniform thickness—$^1/_2$" thick.

8. Pour half of the Mole Sauce into a small saucepan and heat gently.

9. Pour the other half of the Mole sauce into a shallow bowl. Coat chicken in the mole sauce.

10. Place chicken breasts on a lightly oiled rack 6" from heat source and broil for 5 minutes on each side. (For a convection oven, broil for 7 minutes total—do not turn.)

11. Transfer chicken to cutting board. Slice on the diagonal. Serve immediately with the remaining sauce spooned over the top.

Each serving contains approximately 206 calories, 30.8 grams protein, 6 grams total fat, 74 mg cholesterol, 147 mg sodium.

MARINATED AND BROILED CURRIED CHICKEN BREAST SERVED ON WILTED CHARD LEAVES WITH WARM CURRY DRESSING *Serves 8*

T he mellow flavors of curry with basil, the sweetness of cooked garlic and scallions, the rustic tastes of balsamic vinegar and red wine all combine to dress up the down-home qualities of chicken and greens.

CHICKEN
    1 tsp extra virgin olive oil
    $^1/_4$ cup lemon juice
    1 tsp curry powder
    1 TB chopped fresh mint (optional)
    6 cloves garlic, finely minced
    8 half skinless, boneless chicken breasts

CHARD AND DRESSING

1 TB whole grain mustard
1 tsp curry powder
2 TB balsamic vinegar
3 TB dry red wine
2 cloves garlic, finely minced
2 scallions, chopped into rounds
2 TB extra virgin olive oil
2 TB chopped fresh basil leaves or 2 tsp dried basil
*3 bunches red or white swiss chard, well washed,
    and chopped*

1. To make the marinade, combine the olive oil, lemon juice, curry powder, fresh mint, if using, and garlic. Pour over chicken breasts, turn to coat, and marinate for 1 hour or overnight.

2. Preheat the oven to Broil.

3. To make the Warm Curry Dressing, place the mustard, curry powder, vinegar, red wine, garlic, and scallions in a saucepan. Using a wire whisk, blend ingredients together, over a low heat.

4. Slowly stir in the olive oil. Add basil, remove from heat and keep warm.

5. Broil the chicken for 8-10 minutes, turning once halfway through. (For a convection oven, broil for 6 minutes—do not turn.)

6. Meanwhile, place chard in steamer basket and steam for 8 minutes.

7. Toss the steamed chard with the Warm Curry Dressing in a mixing bowl. Serve the chicken breast nestled inside the dressed chard.

Each serving contains approximately 220 calories, 30.7 grams protein, 7 grams total fat, 68 mg cholesterol, 460 mg sodium.

TURKEY LOAF WITH FRESH TOMATOES   *Serves 8*

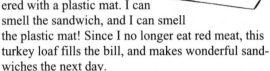

I guess I've always been "food oriented." One of my strongest grammar school memories is of me eating a meatloaf sandwich at my desk, which was covered with a plastic mat. I can smell the sandwich, and I can smell the plastic mat! Since I no longer eat red meat, this turkey loaf fills the bill, and makes wonderful sandwiches the next day.

---

3 cloves garlic, finely minced
1 large yellow onion, diced
1 medium green bell pepper, diced
2 TB canola oil
2 large ripe, unpeeled tomatoes
1 TB Worcestershire sauce
³/₄ cup wheat bran or oat bran or bread crumbs
¹/₂ cup chopped fresh parsley
1 tsp dried basil or 1 TB minced fresh basil
2 pounds ground turkey
¹/₃ cup salsa of choice

1. Preheat oven to 350°F.

2. Sauté garlic, onion, and bell pepper in the canola oil until cooked but not limp.

3. Place tomatoes in a food processor or blender and purée.

4. Add Worcestershire sauce and process again.

5. In a large bowl, mix together the wheat or oat bran or bread crumbs, parsley, and basil. Add the sautéed vegetables and stir well.

6. Add the ground turkey and mix well to combine.

7. Form into a loaf and place in a 9" x 5" x 3" loaf pan.

8. Top with tomato purée and bake for 90 minutes. (If you halve the recipe, use an 8" x 3" x 3" pan and bake for 60 minutes.)

Each serving contains approximately 299 calories, 29.2 grams protein, 9.9 grams total fat, 90 mg cholesterol, 136 mg sodium.

AROMATIC ROAST CHICKEN WITH HERBES DE PROVENCE
Serves 8

Autumn is my favorite season of the year, and I admit that I always rush it. I can't wait for nature to bring on the fall colors and clouds and chill. I prematurely wear autumn clothes and cook autumn foods, absolutely certain I feel a little crispness in the air. When I was young I would swelter in the San Fernando Valley's heat while wearing my new wool jumper with knee socks to match. And now that I'm older, I swelter in my kitchen, roasting chickens during San Diego's hot Santa Ana winds!

1 lemon, unpeeled
^{1}/$_2$ yellow onion, unpeeled
^{1}/$_2$ head garlic, broken into cloves, unpeeled
2 tsp Herbes de Provence
4-4^1/$_2$ pound whole chicken
1 cup dry sherry or dry white wine
crushed red peppers as needed
water as needed

1. Preheat oven to 500° F.

2. Dice lemon and onion and place in a bowl. Add unpeeled garlic cloves and Herbes de Provence. Mix well.

3. Remove giblets and neck from body cavity. Cut away extra fat from neck and tail openings, making sure you don't cut so much away that you can't close the openings.

4. Rinse bird well, inside and out. Pat dry.

5. Stuff bird with lemon mixture. Close openings by using toothpicks or metal skewers.

6. Place bird on its side on a rack set in a roasting pan. Pour about ^{1}/$_2$ cup sherry or white wine over the bird. Sprinkle generously with crushed red peppers. Turn on the other side and repeat, leaving the bird on its side. Add water to the sherry that has accumulated in the roasting pan tray until the tray is filled about halfway. (This will keep the fat that drips into the pan from splattering too much inside your oven. It also "perfumes" the oven while flavoring the bird.)

7. Place the roasting pan on a rack in the middle of the oven.

8. Roast for 20 minutes, then turn the bird onto its other side, baste, and roast for 20 minutes more.

9. Turn the bird breast side up, baste, and roast for 20 minutes (12 minutes if you're using a convection oven).

10. Remove roasting pan from the oven, cover chicken with a tent of aluminum foil, and let sit for 10-15 minutes so the juices can soak back into the meat.

11. Remove foil tent, carve, and serve immediately.

Each serving (with skin) contains approximately 183 calories, 23 grams protein, 7.9 grams total fat, 71 mg cholesterol, 65 mg sodium.

A Guide to Roasting Chicken

This chart is for conventional oven use. For convection oven use, take off 15-20% from the total time listed. Cooking temperature for both is 500°F.

Size of chicken	Total amount of time to cook
1^1/$_2$-2 pounds	35-40 minutes
2^1/$_2$-3 pounds	45-50 minutes
3^1/$_2$-4 pounds	55-60 minutes
4^1/$_2$-5 pounds	65-70 minutes

VEGETABLE MAIN DISHES

COUNTRYSIDE BEANS AND GREENS `Serves 4`

W hen there's no time to soak and cook dried beans, I use canned. I like the Eden brand that is cooked with kombu. When shopping for the porcini mushrooms called for in this recipe, also known as "cêpes," you'll most likely find them dried. After you reconstitute them, don't throw away the soaking water—it is extremely rich, and is used in this recipe to add moisture and flavor to the sauté pan without adding fat. Porcini mushrooms are very sandy, so take all the precautions mentioned in the instructions below to remove the grit.

$^1/_2$ cup boiling water
$^1/_4$ oz dried porcini or Chilean mushrooms
6 cups spinach or swiss chard
10 standard or 6 shiitake mushrooms, sliced
1 15-oz can or $1^1/_2$ cups cooked navy beans (small white beans)
4 cloves garlic, finely minced
$^1/_4$ yellow onion, diced
1 TB extra virgin olive oil
$^1/_4$ tsp crushed red peppers
$^1/_2$ tsp dried basil
$^1/_4$ tsp dried oregano
$^1/_3$ of a 15-oz can or $^1/_2$ cup cooked garbanzo beans
salt or VegeSal to taste
fresh Parmesan cheese, shaved as needed (optional)

1. Bring the $^1/_2$ cup of water to a boil. Rinse the dried porcini mushrooms briefly and rub off any dirt or sand. Wash the spinach or chard, remove and discard stems and discolored leaves, and slice it into shreds. Wash and slice the mushrooms and rinse the canned beans. Set all aside.

2. Add the porcinis to the boiling water and let simmer for 30 minutes.

3. Meanwhile, sauté the garlic, onion, and sliced mushrooms in the olive oil over medium heat for 10 minutes.

4. Add the crushed red peppers, basil, and oregano.

5. Remove porcini from soaking water (reserve water) and rinse away any hidden pockets of sand. Finely chop porcini and add to the sauté pan.

6. Strain the soaking water through a couple layers of cheesecloth. Add this water to the sauté pan when more moisture is needed.

7. Add the spinach or chard to the sauté pan, and cook, covered, until wilted.

8. After 5 minutes, add the beans and stir well. Cook, covered, for 5 minutes more. Taste, and add salt as needed.

9. Spoon onto dinner plates. Top with shaved Parmesan, if desired.

Each serving contains approximately 211 calories, 12.2 grams protein, 5.5 grams fat, 2 mg cholesterol, 119 mg sodium.

SPICY EGGPLANT CASSEROLE `Serves 8`

I n California, we still have eggplants and peppers on the vine well into the fall. In fact, we even have basil (last year mine lasted until December 5th), and tomatoes and corn! Season's can't always be clearly defined, so I offer this recipe as a transition dish. It's a baked casserole, appropriate for those locations that have chilly evenings, and a few summer vegetables still in the garden.

3 cloves garlic, finely minced
1 large yellow onion, diced
1 TB extra virgin olive oil
1 green bell pepper, diced

1 tsp ground coriander
1 tsp turmeric
¹/₄ tsp cayenne
2 tsp grated fresh ginger
2 bay leaves
¹/₄ cup dry red wine
1-1¹/₂ pound eggplant, peeled and cut into cubes
1-28 oz can crushed tomatoes with purée

1. Preheat oven to 325° F.

2. Sauté onion and garlic in olive oil for 5 minutes, or until the onion is transparent.

3. Add the green pepper and spices. Mix well.

4. Add the wine and eggplant cubes, stirring well so the eggplant will absorb the wine and oil.

5. Add the tomatoes. Mix well, heat through, then transfer to a casserole dish.

6. Bake, uncovered, for 1 hour. Turn off the heat of the oven and keep in a warm oven for as much as 1 hour longer, if possible.

7. Serve hot, warm, or cold in pita bread.

Each serving contains approximately 87 calories, 2.8 grams protein, 2.1 grams total fat, 0 mg cholesterol, 19 mg sodium.

LAYERED MEXICAN CASSEROLE ▐ *Serves 8*

The wonderful thing about leftovers is that you sometimes come up with a tasty dish, such as this, to use them all up. If you have leftover rice, a few tortillas, and a can of refried beans, try this yummy Mexican casserole.

1 cup cooked brown rice
5 cloves garlic, finely minced
1 jalapeño chile, finely minced (optional)

1 TB extra virgin olive oil
2 cups fresh cilantro leaves
2 cups fresh parsley leaves
4 TB fresh bread crumbs
2 TB fresh lime juice
4 TB white wine
4 TB chicken or vegetable broth
¹/₄ cup corn kernels, fresh or frozen
2 cups homemade pinto beans or 1-15 oz can of vegetarian refried beans
6-8 corn tortillas
3 tomatoes, sliced

1. Preheat oven to 350° F. If you don't have leftover rice, cook ¹/₂ cup of brown rice in 1 cup of water for 30 minutes. (This will yield a little more than 1 cup cooked rice.) Don't lift the lid or stir the rice during this time.

2. Place the garlic, chile pepper, olive oil, cilantro, parsley, bread crumbs, lime juice, white wine, and broth in a food processor or blender and process until smooth. Set aside about one quarter of this sauce for Step 7.

3. Stir three-quarters of the sauce into the cooked rice.

4. Add the corn kernels and stir.

5. Re-fry the homemade pinto beans or heat up the can of vegetarian refried beans.

6. Warm the tortillas stovetop in a non-stick skillet until pliable, or in the microwave—wrap the tortillas in wet paper towels and cook on high power for 30-60 seconds, depending on the number of tortillas you're cooking.

7. To assemble the casserole, lightly oil a 2-3 quart casserole. Begin layering the casserole with 1 tortilla, then some of the rice mixture, a tortilla, some beans, a few tomato slices, a tortilla, more rice mixture, a tortilla, beans, tomatoes. End with the tomatoes. Add the extra sauce to the top.

8. Bake for 20 minutes. If the sauce is browning too quickly, cover with a lid.

Each serving contains approximately 193 calories, 7.3 grams protein, 3.3 grams total fat, 0 mg cholesterol, 40 mg sodium.

ACORN SQUASH ENCHILADAS

Serves 6

Spiced acorn squash works especially well with the Mexican Hot Sauce. For a variation, you can replace the walnuts with chicken, prepared as the chicken in Shredded Chicken and Spinach Tacos (see page 52). Serve this recipe as a unique side dish for Thanksgiving dinner.

2 acorn squash
1 TB extra virgin olive oil
1 small red onion, diced
2 cloves garlic, finely minced
$^{1}/_{2}$ tsp ground cumin
$^{1}/_{2}$ cup raw walnuts, chopped
$^{1}/_{2}$ recipe Mexican Hot Sauce (see page 58)
12 corn tortillas

1. Preheat oven to 350°F. Poke a couple of holes in the whole acorn squashes. Bake for 50-60 minutes, or until the squashes are soft throughout.

2. Meanwhile, make a batch of Mexican Hot Sauce, or defrost a half batch and heat it up.

3. Sauté the onion, garlic, and ground cumin in the olive oil over medium heat for 5 minutes or until the onions are transparent.

4. Cut the acorn squashes in half lengthwise and let cool. When cool enough to handle, scoop out the seeds and strings, and discard. If you're in a hurry and have no time to wait for the squashes to cool, put on rubber gloves as insulation against the heat.

5. Increase the oven temperature to 375°F.

6. Place the acorn squash and the onion mixture in a food processor or blender and process until completely pureed. Stir in the walnuts.

7. To heat the tortillas to make them pliable, spray a non-stick skillet with a little vegetable spray. Cook the tortillas for a few seconds on each side.

8. To assemble the enchiladas, spoon a strip of squash purée down the center of each tortilla. Add a little Mexican Hot Sauce, fold the tortilla over the purée and place, seam side down, in a lightly oiled baking dish. Spoon on a little more Mexican Hot Sauce and spread over the tops of each enchilada.

9. Bake for 12 minutes and serve hot.

Makes 12 enchiladas.

Each enchilada contains approximately 152 calories, 3.7 grams protein, 5.7 grams total fat, 0 mg cholesterol, 19 mg sodium.

BLACK BEAN CHILI ENCHILADAS WITH TOMATILLO SAUCE

Serves 6

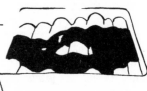

This is another recipe for the versatile Black Bean Chili, introduced in the Fall section on Soups (see page 115). The sauce I've paired it with here is made from tomatillos, also known as "husk tomatoes." They were first cultivated in Central and South America centuries ago, even before tomatoes. A papery husk encases the tomatillo from the time it emerges until it matures and falls from the plant. Peel the husk to reveal the slightly sticky, pale green, tomato-like fruit. Raw, they are sour, so they are most often cooked briefly to mellow their flavor, then puréed into a sauce.

TOMATILLO SAUCE
1 pound fresh tomatillos
1 small red onion, finely diced
2 cloves garlic, finely minced
1 tsp extra virgin olive oil
2 serrano chiles, finely minced (optional)
2 TB chopped fresh cilantro
apple cider vinegar or fresh lime juice to taste

BLACK BEAN CHILI
3 cups Black Bean Chili (see page 115)
12 corn tortillas
4 oz reduced fat sharp Cheddar cheese, grated
(optional)

1. Prepare the Black Bean Chili or defrost a batch and warm in a saucepan.

2. To prepare the Tomatillo Sauce, peel the papery husks off the tomatillos and discard. Place tomatillos in a steamer basket and steam for 10-15 minutes, or until they are soft.

3. Place tomatillos in the food processor or blender and purée until smooth. Set aside.

4. Meanwhile, sauté the onion and garlic in the olive oil for 5 minutes, or until the onion is clear.

5. Add the sautéed onion and garlic to the tomatillos in the food processor.

6. Add the minced chiles and cilantro. Stir and taste. Add up to $^1/_2$ teaspoon vinegar or lime juice.

7. Preheat the oven to 375°F.

8. Heat the tortillas until just pliable (see previous recipe).

9. To assemble the enchiladas, spoon $^1/_2$ cup of the Tomatillo Sauce onto the bottom of a 9" x 13" baking pan.

10. Coat each cooked tortilla with a little of the Tomatillo Sauce.

11. Put $^1/_4$ cup of the Black Bean Chili and 2 TB of the grated Cheddar cheese in a strip down the middle of each tortilla. Fold the seams over and place, seam side down, in the baking pan in a single layer.

12. Spoon the remaining Tomatillo Sauce over the top. Bake for 15-20 minutes, or until heated through. Serve immediately.

Each enchilada contains approximately 156 calories, 7.5 grams protein, 4.1 grams total fat, 7 mg cholesterol, 101 mg sodium.

PASTAS

PASTA WITH ROASTED GARLIC AND SUN-DRIED TOMATOES   Serves 6

This pasta dish has so much character—a rich aroma, so many distinct flavors and textures—that it's a sure bet for the most gourmet of guests.

---

1 whole head garlic
8 sun-dried tomatoes
8 oz dried linquine pasta
2 TB shallots, finely minced
4 TB sherry
1 TB extra virgin olive oil
$^1/_2$ tsp dried tarragon
$^1/_4$ tsp dried thyme
$^1/_8$ tsp dried sage
4-6 shiitake mushrooms, stems removed and discarded, caps sliced
6-8 mushrooms, sliced
$^1/_4$ cup Parmesan cheese

1. Preheat oven to 350°F.

2. To roast garlic, cut off the tops of the head so the garlic cloves are partially exposed. Make sure it sits well on the "butt" side. Place in a small baking dish and bake for 40-60 minutes, depending on the size of the head, or until the cloves of garlic are tender. (There is no need to use any oil in this process.)

3. Meanwhile, soak the sun-dried tomatoes in enough boiling water to cover for about 15 minutes, or until they are soft. Discard the water. Slice the re-hydrated sun-dried tomatoes and set aside.

4. Sauté the shallots in sherry and oil until light golden in color, about 5 minutes.

5. Add seasonings and mushrooms to the shallots and cook over low heat until mushrooms have given up their juices, about 5 minutes. Don't cook away the juices by turning the heat up too high. (Add more sherry, not oil, if you accidentally cook away too much.)

6. Add the sun-dried tomatoes to the sauté pan and keep the heat on low long enough to heat the tomatoes through, about 2 minutes. Turn off the heat, cover, and keep hot.

7. Cool the roasted garlic and remove each clove from its skin by squeezing and/or peeling. Slice or chop the garlic and add it to the vegetable mixture.

8. Bring a large pot of water to a boil. Cook pasta in the boiling water for 10 minutes, or until al dente.

9. Drain pasta and toss it with the sautéed mixture in a large serving bowl. Sprinkle with Parmesan cheese and serve immediately.

Each serving contains approximately 224 calories, 8.25 grams protein, 4.4 grams total fat, 3 mg cholesterol, 75 mg sodium.

NOODLES WITH CABBAGE AND CARAWAY `Serves 4`

This recipe is adapted from a dish served to us at The Churchill House Inn, a lovely Bed and Breakfast nestled in the Green Mountains of Vermont.

8 oz ribbon pasta
1 yellow onion, diced
2 TB extra virgin olive oil
1/2 head cabbage, sliced into shreds
1 1/2 TB caraway seeds

1. Bring a large pot of water to a boil. Cook noodles in the boiling water for 10 minutes, or until al dente.

2. Meanwhile, sauté the onion in the olive oil for 5 minutes, or until clear.

3. Add the cabbage shreds to the onions and cook over high heat, tossing to mix, for about 1 minute.

4. Drain the noodles.

5. Add the caraway seeds and the cooked noodles to the onion/cabbage mixture.

6. Toss well to blend flavors and serve immediately.

Each serving contains approximately 324 calories, 9.6 grams protein, 8.1 grams total fat, 0 mg cholesterol, 20 mg sodium.

PASTA WITH WILD MUSHROOM CREAM SAUCE `Serves 4`

Wild mushrooms vary in taste and texture, but are generally much more flavorful than the standard mushrooms we are accustomed to seeing in the grocery store. Here, I suggest dried porcinis, which offer a deep taste and meaty perfume, and cremini, or shiitake mushrooms. Cremini are a close relative of the standard mushrooms, but are slightly more flavorful. Shiitakes, most often associated with Asian cooking, are even more richly flavored—and about twice the cost! All are sautéed with shallots and tarragon. To make a cream sauce, add just a little butter and evaporated skim milk. Toss with pasta and add a scraping of Parmigiana Reggiano at the table. Perciatelli, the type of pasta called for in this recipe, is a very thick spaghetti that can be found in many grocery stores that carry the popular Ronzoni brand. It adds to the peasanty feel of this dish.

1 oz dried porcini or Chilean mushrooms
2 cups water
4 TB minced shallots
1 TB extra virgin olive oil

*10 oz fresh cremini or fresh shiitake mushrooms,
   cleaned and sliced (discard shiitake stems) or a
   combination of both*
2 TB butter
$^1/_2$ tsp dried tarragon or 2 TB minced fresh tarragon
$^3/_4$ cup evaporated skim milk
8 oz perciatelli or fettucine
Parmigiana Reggiano (optional) as needed

1. Bring the 2 cups of water to a boil. Rinse dried porcini mushrooms briefly and rub off any dirt or sand. Soak the porcinis in the boiling water for 30 minutes.

2. Meanwhile, sauté the shallots in the olive oil until light golden in color.

3. Add the sliced cremini or shiitake mushrooms and cook over medium heat, stirring occasionally. Cook for 5 minutes.

4. Bring a large pot of water to a boil. Cook pasta in boiling water for 10 minutes, or until al dente.

5. Remove porcinis from soaking water (reserve water) and rinse any pockets of sand.

6. Finely mince porcini and add them to the sauté pan, along with the dried tarragon, if using. (If using fresh tarragon, don't add it until step 9.)

7. Strain the soaking water through a couple of layers of cheesecloth. Add this water to the sauté pan when more moisture is needed. If you don't, don't throw it away! Cook some rice in it tomorrow night.

8. Melt butter in the sauté pan. Add fresh tarragon, if using.

9. Add the evaporated skim milk. Stir and let cook over high heat until it heats and thickens a bit.

10. Drain pasta, add it to the sauté pan, and toss.

11. Serve immediately, adding a little Reggiano, if needed, at the table.

Each serving contains approximately 392 calories, 14.7 grams protein, 11.4 grams total fat, 21 mg cholesterol, 180 mg sodium.

VEGETABLE SIDE DISHES

DUTCH OVEN GREEN BEANS WITH SHALLOTS AND MARJORAM
Serves 8

This recipe is designed to toss together quickly, using a Dutch oven as both mixing bowl for preparation and pot for cooking. Just mix the ingredients together, turn on the heat, put the lid on, and forget about it until it's done. If you don't like "squeaky" green beans, cook for an additional 5 minutes.

1 pound green beans
4 cloves garlic, finely minced
2 shallots, finely minced
1 TB sesame oil or canola oil
$^1/_2$ cup coarsely chopped parsley
1 TB balsamic vinegar
1 TB minced fresh marjoram or 1 tsp dried marjoram

1. Using kitchen shears or a paring knife, cut the tips and ends off the green beans.

2. Place the beans, garlic, shallots, and oil in the Dutch oven or a heavy saucepan with a tight fitting lid.

3. Add the parsley, vinegar, and marjoram to the bean mixture.

4. Turn heat to low and cook, covered, for 20 minutes.

5. Serve hot or warm.

Each serving contains approximately 31 calories, 1.1 grams protein, 1.35 grams total fat, 0 mg cholesterol, 4 mg sodium.

STEWED KALE WITH CHIANTI VINEGAR `Serves 8`

The kale and tomatoes stew together for 30 minutes, resulting in a tender, sweet dish. If you can't find Chianti vinegar, use half red wine vinegar and half white wine vinegar.

4 bunches (about 2 pounds) kale
1 large yellow onion, diced
1 TB garlic, finely minced
1 TB extra virgin olive oil
2 16-oz or 1 28-oz can(s) peeled whole tomatoes plus juices
2 tsp Chianti vinegar
black pepper to taste

1. Wash the kale well. Chop into bite-size pieces—do not dry. Set aside.

2. Sauté onion and garlic in the olive oil over low heat for about 3 minutes.

3. Squeeze the tomatoes into the sauté pan, breaking them up into small pieces with your hands or a wooden spoon.

4. Add the kale. Cook, covered, for 25-30 minutes on low heat, stirring occasionally.

5. Right before serving, stir in the Chianti vinegar and season to taste with black pepper. Serve immediately.

Each serving contains approximately 97 calories, 4.6 grams protein, 2.3 grams total fat, 0 mg cholesterol, 230 mg sodium.

CLAY BAKED AUTUMN VEGETABLE ROAST `Serves 8`

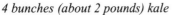

There is no end to the variations you can create with this recipe. These vegetables do go particularly well together, but if you can't locate one at the grocery store, don't let that stop you from making it—omit or substitute something else. Cubed winter squashes would be good, as would fennel, although rather dominant. Zucchini, celery, bell peppers, shallots, artichoke hearts—all are excellent candidates for this dish.

12 sun-dried tomatoes
4 carrots, cut into diagonals
2 parsnips, cut into diagonals
1 red onion, cut into half rings
1 head garlic, peeled and sliced
1 large celery root, peeled and sliced
4 potatoes, cut into wedges
1 TB fresh thyme leaves or 1 tsp dried thyme
¹/₃ cup sherry
1 TB extra virgin olive oil

1. Cover the sun-dried tomatoes with boiling water. Let them soak for 15 minutes. Slice in half and set aside.

2. Meanwhile, soak the lid of a clay casserole (sometimes called a Schlemmertopf or Rommertopf) as directed by the manufacturer for about 10 minutes.

3. Place the prepared vegetables in the bottom container of the clay casserole. Add the sun-dried tomatoes and thyme leaves.

4. Put into a cold oven. Turn the oven to 425°F. and bake for 1 hour.

5. Right before serving, heat the sherry over medium high heat for 3 minutes. Remove from heat and add the olive oil.

6. Pour the sherry/olive oil over the vegetables, toss, and serve.

Each serving contains approximately 141 calories, 2.5 grams protein, 3.6 grams total fat, 0 mg cholesterol, 41 mg sodium.

ZUCCHINI ROMANO WITH SLICED ALMONDS `Serves 8`

There are usually still some zucchini around in the early fall. They are not at their sweetest, so this preparation includes toasted almonds and the special flavor of Pecorino Romano cheese to enchance their flavor.

¹/₂ cup sliced almonds
2 pounds zucchini, cut into 1" dice
4 TB Pecorino Romano cheese, grated

1. Preheat oven to 325°F. Toast the sliced almonds in the oven for 10-12 minutes, or until they are light golden. Set aside.

2. Place zucchini in a steamer basket and steam for about 3 minutes.

3. Toss with the cheese. Top with the toasted almonds.

Each serving contains approximately 70 calories, 3.2 grams protein, 4.6 grams total fat, 3.6 gram cholesterol, 45 mg sodium.

TIMBALES OF RICE AND BARLEY PILAF `Serves 6`

Timbales (rhymes with "thimbles") refer to both a mold, or shape, and a dish made in the molds. Dishes called Timbales are most often custard-based, baked in single-serving sized molds, and inverted onto a plate. In this case, we are just using the mold shape to make a pilaf more interesting looking on the plate. Simply press the rice pilaf into a ramekin or custard dish, turn it upside down on a dinner plate, tap the sides, and remove. It should hold the shape.

¹/₄ cup raw wild rice
1¹/₂ cups chicken stock or vegetable stock or water
¹/₂ cup dry red wine
³/₄ cup raw short grain brown rice
¹/₄ cup raw barley
¹/₂ tsp ground cumin
1 bay leaf
2 TB pine nuts

1. To quick soak the wild rice, bring rice and enough water to cover plus 2" to a boil. Immediately remove from heat and let sit 30 minutes. Drain and set aside.

2. Preheat oven to 325°F.

3. Combine stock or water and red wine. Bring to a rapid boil and slowly add the soaked wild rice, brown rice, barley, cumin, and bay leaf.

4. Reduce the heat to low, and simmer, covered, for 35 minutes. (Do not lift the lid or stir.)

5. Meanwhile, toast the pine nuts in the oven for 10 minutes, or until light golden in color. When cool, chop, then set aside.

6. Check the pilaf—there should be no moisture in the pan and the grains should be soft.

7. Remove and discard bay leaf and stir in the toasted pine nuts.

8. Serve by pressing the pilaf into ramekins or custard dishes. Invert onto plates. Remove ramekin. The pilaf should remain in the ramekin shape.

Each serving contains approximately 159 calories, 4.4 grams protein, 2.1 grams total fat, 0.1 mg cholesterol, 102 mg sodium.

YUKON GOLD MASHED POTATOES WITH ROASTED GARLIC

Serves 8

In this recipe, I use a whole head of buttery roasted garlic and just enough olive oil to provide the creaminess and comfort that mashed potatoes are treasured for. The use of yellow-flesh potatoes lends the butter color one expects of mashed potatoes.

1 head garlic
6 medium Yukon Gold or Yellow
    Finn potatoes
2 tsp Olio Santo (see page 10) or extra virgin olive
    oil
4 TB chopped fresh parsley
salt or VegeSal to taste
black pepper to taste

1. Preheat oven to 350°F.

2. To roast garlic, cut off the tops of the head so the garlic cloves are partially exposed. Place in a small baking dish and bake for 40-60 minutes, or until the cloves of garlic are tender.

3. Quarter but do not peel the potatoes. Place in a large saucepan, cover with water, and bring to a boil. Reduce heat to low and simmer until tender, 30-40 minutes.

4. Peel the paper skins from the garlic and discard.

5. Place the peeled garlic and drained potatoes in a mixing bowl. Whip until fluffy.

6. Add oil, parsley, salt, and black pepper to taste. Whip to mix and serve immediately.

Each serving contains approximately 182 calories, 3.8 grams protein, 1.3 grams total fat, 0 mg cholesterol, 80 mg sodium.

ACORN SQUASH STUFFED WITH WILD RICE, FENNEL, AND CARROTS

Serves 8

If you have vegetarian friends or family for Thanksgiving, they will welcome this as their main dish. The wild rice, fennel, and carrot pilaf is excellent not only as stuffing for the acorn squash, but on its own as a side dish.

$^1/_2$ cup raw wild rice
4 TB pecans
4 acorn squash
4 cups water
16 shallots, sliced into rounds
8 cloves garlic, finely minced
2 tsp dried thyme
1 tsp dried marjoram
$1^1/_2$ cups raw long grain or short grain brown rice
2 cups carrots, grated
2 cups fennel, diced
$^1/_2$ cup chopped fresh parsley
low sodium soy sauce to taste

1. Preheat oven to 325°F.

2. To quick soak the wild rice, bring rice and enough water to cover plus 2" to a boil. Immediately remove from heat and let sit 30 minutes. Drain and set aside.

3. Toast the pecans in the oven for 12-15 minutes. Remove from oven. Increase oven temperature to 350°F.

4. Poke holes in the whole acorn squashes. Bake for 30-45 minutes. When they are tender enough to slice, remove them from the oven, slice in half lengthwise, and remove and discard seeds and strings. Place the halved squashes, cut side down, in a baking pan filled with about 1" of water. Cook for 30 more minutes, or until done. Remove from oven, drain water, and set aside.

5. Meanwhile, bring the 4 cups of water to a boil.

6. Sauté the shallots and garlic in the oil. Add the herbs, soaked wild rice, and brown rice and cook over medium high heat, stirring, until rice is slightly golden.

7. Add the boiling water to the sauté pan. Return to a boil, reduce heat to low, and simmer, covered, for 20 minutes.

8. Add carrot and fennel to the rice mixture—do not stir, otherwise your pilaf will be gummy. Cook, covered, for 15-20 minutes more, or until all the liquid is absorbed and the grains are done.

9. Stir in the parsley, toasted pecans, and soy sauce. Spoon into acorn squash and serve immediately, or set aside and re-heat just before serving.

Each serving contains approximately 320 calories, 7.2 grams protein, 6.3 grams total fat, 0 mg cholesterol, 22 mg sodium.

SWEETS

PEAR CRISP Serves 8

I like to make a double batch of the crisp part of this recipe and freeze it. That way, each time I have a pear or two left in the fruit bowl, I can make a few last minute crisps for dessert. Try this recipe with apples also, but bake them for 10 minutes longer.

CRISP
1/2 cup raw almonds
1/4 cup raw cashews
1/2 cup raw walnuts
1 cup oats
1/2 tsp ground cinnamon
1/4 tsp fresh nutmeg
4 TB maple syrup
2 TB unbleached flour or whole wheat flour
1/2 tsp vanilla

FILLING
3-4 pears
1/4 tsp ground cinnamon
1/8 tsp fresh nutmeg
1 TB maple syrup
1/4 tsp vanilla

1. Preheat the oven to 325°F.

2. To make the crisp, toast almonds and cashews in the oven for 15 minutes, or until light golden in color.

3. Increase oven temperature to 350°F.

4. Place toasted almonds, cashews, and raw walnuts in a food processor or blender. Pulse to chop, or chop by hand.

5. Add nuts to a bowl with all the other crisp ingredients. Mix thoroughly. Set aside.

6. Slice pears and add the rest of the filling ingredients to the pears, tossing to mix.

7. To assemble, fill a pie pan or half of each of 8 custard cups or ramekins with the pear filling. Top with crisp mixture.

8. Bake for 15-20 minutes.

Each serving contains approximately 198 calories, 4.5 grams protein, 8.1 grams total fat, 0 mg cholesterol, 2 mg sodium.

DOUBLE CRUST APPLE PIE Serves 12

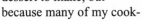

I have given the most detailed instructions for this pie, not because it's a horribly difficult dessert to make, but because many of my cooking students needed this much guidance. Don't be put off by the lengthy steps—you'll want each one of them if you're making a pie for the first time, or even if it's been awhile since your last pie baking session.

DOUBLE CRUST

2¹/₄ cups unbleached flour
12 TB (1¹/₂ sticks) sweet butter, frozen
6-8 TB ice cold water

FILLING

3 pounds (10-12) apples, preferably Golden
* Delicious*
¹/₂ cup brown sugar or date sugar
1 cinnamon stick or 1 tsp ground cinnamon
¹/₂ tsp fresh nutmeg
2-4 TB unbleached flour or whole wheat pastry flour

7. Divide the dough in half. Form each half into a flat circle, about 1"-1¹/₂" thick. Wrap each in plastic wrap and refrigerate for 1-2 hours. (This more fully and evenly hydrates the dough, and allows the gluten that did develop to relax.)

The basic caution in making a pastry crust is not to develop the gluten (the protein in the flour) by working with the dough too much, or by adding too much water. You can tell if you've done this if your dough is sticky, like glue. (The resulting crust will be tough, not light and flaky.) At the same time, you have to make sure the flour is coated with the fat, so the water doesn't join with the flour to make glue, or "glue-ten." Pure fats, like lard and Crisco, produce the flakiest crusts because they don't contain any moisture, and therefore can't encourage gluten development. These fats, however, are not healthful. The fat that produces the second flakiest crust is butter, which has the added benefit of lending the pie its buttery flavor and aroma. Oil produces a crumbly, rather than flaky, crust because oils have more coating power than solid fats. Oil "drowns" the flour particles, and can't then, produce the layers characteristic of a flaky crust.

8. Peel and slice the apple very thinly and place in a bowl.

Two Methods for Making Pastry

By Hand

1. Begin by mixing up the flours well in a mixing bowl if you are using 2 types of flour (see boxed tip).

2. Grate the frozen butter into the bowl with the flour.

3. Blend the butter into the flour using your hands. You want to "smear" the butter into the flour.

4. Add 2 TB of ice water and mix into the flour/butter mixture.

5. Add 2 more TB of ice water. The dough should be coming together pretty well.

6. Add just enough more water, a tsp at a time, so that the dough does come together.

By Food Processor

1. Add the flours to the work bowl of the food processor. Pulse to mix well, if using both types of flour (see boxed tip).

2. Cut the frozen butter into quarters lengthwise, then dice. Add to food processor.

3. Pulse (on-off half-second clicks) 10-15 times to break up the butter roughly.

4. Add 6 TB of the ice water and pulse 8-10 more times. Remove the cover and feel the dough—it should look like a bunch of small lumps, and will just hold together in a mass when you press a handful together. Do not overmix (it shouldn't mass on the blade of the machine.) If too dry, add 1 TB more water. Feel again. If too dry, add droplets more until it is the right consistency.

5. Turn the dough out onto the work surface. Press it into a rough mass.

6. Blend, or "smear" the dough with the heel of your hand, a bit at a time, in front of the pile of dough.

Substitute 1½ cups unbleached white and 1 cup whole wheat pastry flour for the 2¼ cups unbleached flour.	**9.** Add the sugar, cinnamon, and nutmeg to the sliced apples. Stir well, coating each piece of apple with some of the sugar/spice mixture. Add the 2 TB of flour. (Add up to 4 TB if the mixture is too wet). Toss well to distribute throughout.

10. Preheat oven to 350° F.

11. To assemble the pie, cut out 2 12" long pieces of wax paper or parchment paper. Remove 1 package of pastry dough from the refrigerator. Unwrap, flour each side, and place it between the pieces of wax or parchment paper.

12. Start rolling the dough out from the center toward the edge, maintaining the dough's round shape. When rolling, ease the pressure near the edge of the dough. Turn the dough over a few times during this process so you are rolling on the other piece of paper. Roll dough out to about ⅛" thick and 2" larger than the pie pan. You may need to sprinkle the dough with a little extra flour to keep it from sticking to the paper.

13. Peel off 1 side of the paper. Lift the dough with the 1 sheet of paper and transfer it to the pie tin. Lay it, paper side up, on top of the pie tin. Peel away the second sheet of paper and press the dough lightly into the tin.

14. Poke the bottom and sides of the dough with the tines of a fork. Trim the edge to about a ½" overhang all around.

15. Transfer the lined pie tin to the refrigerator while you roll out the second piece of dough just as you did the first.

16. Add the filling, shaking the pan to settle all the apples.

17. Place the top crust on the pie the same way you did the bottom crust. Trim the top crust so it is even all around with a ½" to 1" overhang.

18. Roll the free edges of pastry dough from the bottom and top crusts together and down towards the rim of the pie tin. You want the edge of the crust to sit on top of the rim of the pie tin. (Take care not to leave the edge below the rim or it will be baked to the pie tin.) Finish the edge by pinching all around with your thumb and forefinger. Cut vents in the top of the pie.

19. Bake for 60-75 minutes.

Each serving contains approximately 293 calories, 3.3 grams protein, 12.3 grams total fat, 31 mg cholesterol, 103 mg sodium.

FUDGY BROWNIES
Makes 16 brownies

U nusual as these ingredients may appear, they create a luscious brownie. Natural ingredients are used to lower the fat in these brownies, while adding nutrition. The way a kid can go through a plate of brownies, you want them to be as wholesome as possible. Why not bake these next time it's your turn to send in school snacks?

10 oz semi-sweet chocolate bits
8 Medjool dates, pitted
¼ cup + 1 TB maple syrup
¼ cup canola oil
4 egg whites or 2 eggs
1 tsp vanilla
1 cup + 2 TB unbleached flour or 1 cup whole wheat pastry flour
½ tsp baking soda
¼ tsp salt
½ cup walnuts, chopped (optional)

1. Preheat oven to 350° F.

2. Melt the chocolate bits in a double boiler over simmering water. Do not let the water come to a boil and do not let the bottom of the double boiler touch the hot water.

3. Coarsely chop the dates. Place in a food processor or blender and process until broken up.

4. Add the maple syrup, canola oil, egg

Medjool dates are large, moist dates. If you can't find these, use 12 of the standard dates found in a grocery store. Make sure to remove their pits too!

You can replace the eggs with ¹/₂ of a 10.5-oz box of Mori-Nu silken tofu, firm, and reduce the oil to 2 TB total, or you can replace the eggs with ³/₄ cup cottage cheese, and reduce the oil to 2 TB total.

whites, and vanilla. Process to a creamy mixture. (Or, if you are using one of the options suggested in the boxed tips, add the maple syrup, silken tofu or cottage cheese, canola oil, and vanilla. Process to a creamy mixture.)

5. Add the melted chocolate to the food processor or blender and process well. Scrape down the sides of the bowl and process again.

6. Place flour, baking soda, and salt in a mixing bowl.

7. Add the dry ingredients to the chocolate mixture in the food processor. Mix well, taking care to scrape down the sides of the bowl. Add the walnuts and pulse to mix them in.

8. Spray 2 8" x 8" pans lightly with vegetable oil spray. Spoon the batter into the pans and smooth the tops.

9. Bake for 20-25 minutes. Let cool thoroughly before serving for fullest flavor.

Each serving (made with whole eggs) contains approximately 141 calories, 3.6 grams protein, 12.8 grams total fat, 26 mg cholesterol, 71 mg sodium.

CHOCOLATE CHIP COOKIES *Makes 100 cookies*

Before I was 14, my entire culinary education came from the back of a Tollhouse semi-sweet chocolate chips package. My best friend Lynn and I always got the urge to make cookies when it felt the slightest bit autumny outside. Somehow, making them took half the afternoon. We measured, we tasted, we stirred, we tasted, we added the dry ingredients, we tasted—you get the idea! Baking cookies was actually eating cookie dough. Maybe we baked 10 on a good day. The following

recipe would have passed our discerning—and frequent—taste tests. The dough is a little runnier than the original Tollhouse recipe, but it bakes up just fine.

2¹/₄ c + 3 TB whole wheat pastry flour or 2¹/₂ cups + 3 TB unbleached white flour
1 tsp baking soda
¹/₂ tsp salt (optional)
1 tsp vanilla
2 large egg whites
1 cup maple syrup
¹/₂ c + 2 TB canola oil
10 oz semi-sweet chocolate chips
¹/₂ cup raw walnuts, chopped

1. Preheat oven to 375° F.

2. Combine dry ingredients in one bowl and stir well.

3. Combine wet ingredients in another bowl and stir well. Add dry ingredients to wet ingredients, then add chips and nuts and stir well.

4. Spoon teaspoonfuls of the dough onto lightly oiled cookie sheets. Bake for 8 (for chewy cookies) and 10 (for crispy cookies) minutes.

Makes 100 silver dollar-size cookies.

Each cookie (silver dollar-size) contains approximately 48 calories, 0.7 grams protein, 2.8 grams total fat, 0 mg cholesterol, 12 mg sodium.

Each cookie (silver dollar-size) made from the traditional Tollhouse Cookie recipe contains approximately 81 calories, 1.1 grams protein, 4.8 grams total fat, 13 grams cholesterol, 52 mg sodium.

SAKE-BAKED PEARS *Serves 8*

Nothing could be simpler to make, yet more elegant to serve than these pears!

1 lemon
8 firm-ripe pears (any type)

1 cup sake or dry white wine
½ cup maple syrup
1 TB grated orange peel
1 cinnamon stick

1. Preheat oven to 350°F.

2. Prepare a bowl of water large enough to hold the pears. Squeeze the lemon into the water.

3. Peel the pears using a potato peeler or paring knife. Leave the stems intact, if possible, and drop each pear into the bowl of acidulated water, which will keep the pears from turning brown.

4. Combine the sake or white wine, maple syrup, orange peel, and cinnamon stick.

5. Drain the pears and arrange them on their sides in a baking dish just large enough to hold them in a single layer. Pour the sake mixture over the pears. Cover the dish tightly and bake the pears in the middle of the oven for 30 minutes.

6. Turn the pears over gently and bake for 20-30 minutes more.

7. Serve warm or chilled with some of the liquid drizzled over each pear.

Each serving contains approximately 169 calories, 0.65 grams protein, less then 1 gram total fat, 0 mg cholesterol, 7 mg sodium.

CHOCOLATE DIPPED ALMOND AND PINE NUT BISCOTTI
Makes 64 Biscotti

Biscotti are twice-baked Italian cookies. Each Sunday after church, my mom would take my sisters and me to the Italian store. Mom would shop for bread, prosciutto, cheeses, and olives. We'd head straight for the big glass jar of biscotti. They were hard as nails, barely sweet, with a whisper of anise. My biggest problem with recreating those biscotti wasn't

the texture—you can scratch glass with mine! It was the anise flavor. Anise extract was too licorice-y; cloves didn't work; what could it be? The answer lies in a 1½ tsp of fennel seeds!

⅓ cup raw whole almonds
⅓ cup raw pine nuts
2¼ cups whole wheat pastry flour or 2½ cups unbleached flour
1½ tsp baking powder
½ tsp baking soda
½ tsp salt
1½ tsp fennel seeds
2 tsp grated lemon peel
1 tsp vanilla
½ cup maple syrup or honey
2 egg whites
2 TB canola oil
6 oz semi-sweet chocolate, broken into small pieces

1. Preheat oven to 325°F. Toast almonds in the oven for 15 minutes, and the pine nuts for 8 minutes. When done, remove from oven and let cool. Keep oven on.

2. Stir together the flour, baking powder, baking soda, salt, fennel seeds, and grated lemon peel.

3. Coarsely chop the cooled almonds. Add almonds and pine nuts to the dry ingredients.

4. Add vanilla, maple syrup, egg whites, and canola oil to a mixing bowl, mixer, or food processor and stir (or process) until smooth.

5. Combine the wet ingredients from the food processor with the dry ingredients. Stir as well as you can. (This is a dry dough, so you will need to turn it out onto a work surface and knead it until all the dry ingredients are incorporated into the dough.)

6. Divide the dough into 8 equal pieces.

7. Roll out each piece into a log ½" in diameter and 9" long. Continue with the other 7 pieces of dough.

Substitute half of a 10.5-oz box of Mori-Nu silken tofu, firm, for the 2 egg whites and 2 TB canola oil. Use a food processor to mix, per Step 4, and add the tofu at the same time you add the vanilla and maple syrup. Process until very smooth. When baking the second time, let bake for 60 minutes or until crisp.

8. Spray a cookie sheet with vegetable oil spray or line with parchment paper. Bake logs for 20-25 minutes.

9. Remove from oven and reduce oven temperature to 200°F. Let logs cool on cookies sheets.

10. Using a serrated-edged knife, cut each log on the diagonal into 8 slices. Arrange biscotti on cookie sheets (you don't have to re-spray with vegetable oil spray; you can use the same parchment paper over again). You can crowd the cookies on the sheets.

11. Bake for 40 minutes, or until crisp.

12. Cool biscotti on the cookie sheets.

13. Meanwhile, melt chocolate pieces in a double boiler over simmering water. (If you let the chocolate melt slowly, stirring often, it will not thicken.) Do not let the water come to a boil and do not let the bottom of the double boiler touch the hot water. Also, do not let any water drip into the chocolate.

14. When melted, remove double boiler from heat. Wipe bottom of any water. Dip each biscotti in the chocolate. Coat half of each biscotti, then place on cookie sheets lined with parchment (you can use the same ones you baked with if they are not browned) or wax paper. Refrigerate for about 20 minutes to let chocolate set.

Each biscotti contains approximately 47 calories, 1.2 grams protein, 2.3 grams total fat, 0 mg cholesterol, 31 mg sodium.

Each biscotti made with the tofu alternative contains approximately 44 calories, 1.2 grams protein, 1.9 grams total fat, 0 mg cholesterol, 29 mg sodium.

CRANBERRY ORANGE BREAD   Serves 12

A slice of this sweet loaf is wonderful with a cup of cinnamon spiced tea.

---

2 cups whole wheat pastry flour or 2¼ cups
*   unbleached flour*
1½ tsp baking powder
½ tsp baking soda
½ cup raw walnuts, chopped
1 TB grated orange peel
¾ cup orange juice
½ cup + 2 TB maple syrup
1 cup cranberries, fresh or frozen, defrosted
1 egg white
2 TB canola oil

1. Preheat oven to 325°F.

2. Place flour, baking powder, baking soda, and walnuts in a bowl and set aside.

3. Place orange peel, orange juice, maple syrup, and cranberries in a small saucepan. Bring to a boil, reduce heat to low and simmer for 5 minutes. Remove from heat and let cool.

4. In a large mixing bowl, beat egg white lightly and add canola oil.

5. Add cooled cranberry mixture to the egg white/oil mixture. Stir to mix well.

6. Add the dry ingredients to the wet ingredients and stir only enough to mix.

7. Pour into a lightly oiled 9" x 5" x 3" loaf pan or a 6-cup capacity bundt pan and bake for 45-60 minutes.

Each serving contains approximately 133 calories, 4.3 grams protein, 5.6 grams of total fat, 0 mg cholesterol, 79 mg sodium.

WHITE CHOCOLATE AND GINGER CUSTARD   Serves 6

I took a cooking class with Perla Meyers, another seasonal cook, and she did a chocolate mousse cake with a white chocolate and ginger sauce. It was fabulous!

Here is my version of those wonderful flavors.

2 cups evaporated skim milk
1" piece fresh ginger, peeled and sliced
4 oz white chocolate, broken into small pieces
4 egg yolks
¹/₄ cup sugar
1 oz bittersweet or semi sweet chocolate

1. Preheat oven to 325° F.

2. Place the milk and ginger in a small saucepan. Bring the milk to a boil, turn heat off, and let sit for 15 minutes for the ginger to infuse its flavor in the milk.

3. Meanwhile, melt the white chocolate. Add the white chocolate pieces to a double boiler set over a pot of barely simmering water. Do not let the water in the pot come to a boil. (White chocolate has a much lower melt point than milk or dark chocolate, so you have to be very careful not to get the heat too high. You may need to turn the burner off from time to time to keep the temperature low enough.)

4. Once the chocolate has melted, beat the egg yolks with the sugar until the yolks are a pale yellow color.

5. When the milk and ginger are done, pour the milk through a strainer into the egg and sugar mixture, stirring well.

6. Stir in melted white chocolate.

7. Pour the whole mixture through a strainer into a pitcher or measuring cup.

8. Fill 6 ³/₄-cup custard cups or ramekins two-thirds full, pouring from the pitcher.

9. Set the ramekins in a baking pan and fill the baking pan with water so it comes halfway up the ramekins. (This is to ensure that the custards do not get too hot while baking.)

10. Bake for 40-45 minutes. (Custards are done when the center still jiggles slightly and a knife inserted halfway between the edge and center comes out clean, or if you touch the surface of the custard, your finger comes away clean.)

11. Remove from the oven and immediately grate the bittersweet chocolate over the top of each custard. Let custards cool to room temperature.

12. Serve at room temperature, or refrigerate to set, about 1 hour, and serve cold.

Each serving contains approximately 258 calories, 9.8 grams protein, 11.7 grams total fat, 142 mg cholesterol, 105 mg sodium.

GLOSSARY TO INGREDIENTS

The following will introduce you to the more unusual ingredients used throughout the book:

FLOURS—Unbleached flour, whole wheat flour, whole wheat pastry flour, oat flour, and semolina flour.

Unbleached flour is white flour that has been allowed to age over a few months time. It whitens naturally and becomes easier to handle. I use it instead of all-purpose flour, which is artificially aged and bleached. Chemicals are used in these processes and often dough conditioners are added to improve the handling quality, rather than the more natural yet costly "leave it sit" technique. In baking, I use unbleached flour in tandem with whole wheat flour to dilute the heaviness of the whole wheat. Since unbleached flour is a processed grain, without the bran and germ, I rarely use it alone. Note: When unbleached flour is suggested as a substitute for whole wheat pastry flour, the proportion is 1 cup plus 2 TB unbleached flour to 1 cup whole wheat pastry flour.

Whole wheat flour and whole wheat pastry flour contain the fiberful bran and nutritious germ of the original grain of wheat. They are different in every other way, though, and need to be used suitably for best results. Whole wheat flour is high in gluten and is often called "bread flour." Gluten is the stretchy substance that develops with kneading and "catches" the bubbles the yeast forms, causing the bread to rise.

Whole wheat pastry flour, made from a softer wheat, does not contain much gluten, and is used for cakes, cookies, and quick breads where a soft, tender crumb is desired. If you use whole wheat bread flour for a cake, it will be too dense; if you use whole wheat pastry flour for a yeasted bread, it won't rise very much. It's good to know that unbleached flour is also high in gluten, so it can be paired with whole wheat pastry flour for a lighter, yet more nutritious yeasted bread.

Oat flour is very soft, almost powder-like. It is made from grinding whole oats, and can be purchased in natural foods stores. If you can't find it, make your own by processing old-fashioned oats in the food processor to a powder or flour. Note: 1¼ cups of old-fashioned oats will make about 1 cup of oat flour.

Semolina flour is derived from durum wheat, which is higher in protein than other strains of wheat. The flour is sandy in texture, but works up into an incredibly smooth dough. Pasta is typically made from semolina flour as is couscous. I use it in a few baked goods recipes to add moisture and an open crumb to the recipe. Semolina flour is a refined food, lacking the bran and germ of the original grain, so I use it sparingly. If you can't find it in a gourmet store, Italian market, or natural foods store, replace it with the suggested alternative in the individual recipes.

I buy all my flour in the bulk bins from natural foods stores that have a high turnover. It's not only cheaper that way, but is fresher, too. I store my flours in large glass jars with metal and gasket airtight lids. These jars effectively seal the contents from weevils, moths, and other bugs.

GINGER—The best way to prepare fresh ginger is to grate it, unpeeled, with a hand-held grater. The peel stays on one side of the grater, and can be easily discarded, while the pulp you will use drops away from the underside of the grater. First, cut away any shriveled or "hairy" parts that may hamper grating. Store ginger in the same place you store potatoes, garlic, and onions—in a basket or ventilated drawer.

HONEY—See SWEETENERS below.

KOMBU—Kombu is a seaweed that aids in the digestion of beans. Add a 6" strip of kombu to every 2 cups dried beans during the first hour of cooking. Remove the kombu after one hour and discard (or you can leave it in if you want—it will break apart, but will not alter the taste of the beans). Kombu is listed as an optional ingredient in the recipes that call for it, but in the recipe instructions it is assumed that you're using it. Since Americans don't consume sea vegetables regularly, it's good to know a way to incorporate such a valuable food into our regular diet. All sea vegetables are extremely high in minerals. Kombu is particularly high in calcium, potassium, magnesium, and iodine. It also boasts a high amount of anti-oxidants, which help eliminate the radioactive and chemical wastes we are exposed to. The Orientals, who have been using kombu and other sea vegetables for centuries, claim they are good for arthritis, heart problems, high blood pressure, endocrine, and nervous disorders.

MAPLE SYRUP—See SWEETENERS below.

MISO—I use red, yellow, and white miso in a number of recipes in this book. Miso looks like creamy peanut butter, but is actually a blend of naturally fermented soybeans and grains. It is high in minerals, essential amino acids, and vitamin B-12, if made traditionally. Like yogurt, unpasteurized miso is loaded with lactic acid bacteria and enzymes that aid in digestion and food assimilation. Miso adds flavor to a dish, and is often used in place of a bouillon cube or flavored stock.

The darker the color of the miso, the stronger the flavor. White miso is best in salad dressings and dips. Its light, pineapple flavor is my "secret ingredient" in many recipes. Red, yellow, and brown misos can be good in salad dressings and dips, but are best in soups. When adding miso to a soup, ladle out a cup of the broth, stir in the miso until dissolved, then return to the soup pot. You add miso at the end of the cooking process (as opposed to bouillon cubes or stock, which are added first) because cooking kills off much of the beneficial bacteria.

The one drawback to miso is that it is high in sodium. But since miso's flavor is so concentrated, you only need to use small amounts. All the recipes where I use it are well within an acceptable sodium range for one meal. Store miso in the refrigerator. It will last indefinitely. Miso can be found at a natural foods store or Oriental grocery. My favorite brand is Westbrae, which comes in Mellow White, Mellow Yellow, Mellow Red, and Mellow Brown. To order, write to Westbrae Natural Foods, Commerce, CA 90040.

SALT—When I use salt in the recipes, I specify "salt or VegeSal." VegeSal is half salt and half vegetable crystals, with all the bright, flavor-enhancing qualities of salt. Each time you use VegeSal instead of salt, you are reducing your sodium intake by 50 percent. It can be found in natural foods store, and even in many large chain groceries. It is made by the Gaylord Hauser Co., Modern Products, Inc., Milwaukee, WI 53209 (414) 352-3333.

SESAME OIL—I call for both sesame oil and toasted sesame oil in the recipes. There is a tremendous differ-

ence between the two. Sesame oil is simply the oil extracted from raw sesame seeds. It has a very slight aroma and taste of sesame seeds, but nothing overwhelming. Toasted sesame oil, on the other hand, is extracted from roasted sesame seeds, and has a very strong, smoky flavor. I clearly state "not toasted sesame oil" in the recipes that call for sesame oil, and "toasted sesame oil" in the recipes where I want its distinctive taste. I do this because a few of my students have mistakenly used toasted sesame oil where the lighter flavored oil was called for and ruined their dinners!

SOY SAUCE—"Low sodium soy sauce" is specified in the recipes because it is widely available. However, I prefer to use something called Bragg Liquid Aminos, which can be found in natural foods stores, or ordered from Live Food Products, Inc., Box 7, Santa Barbara, CA 93102, (805) 968-1020 or FAX them at (805) 968-1001. The sole ingredient in Bragg's is soybeans. It contains no added salt, as low sodium soy sauce does, or wheat, as some soy sauces and tamari sauces do (many people are sensitive to too much wheat). No preservatives or additives of any kind are added. It does contain all 22 amino acids, which are the building blocks of protein, so Bragg's offers a little nutrition with each teaspoon you use. The naturally occuring sodium contained in Bragg's, about 100 mg per $\frac{1}{2}$ tsp, is the same as low sodium soy sauce, but its other attributes make Bragg's the soy sauce of choice for me. If you can find it, try it!

SUN-DRIED TOMATOES—When I call for sun-dried tomatoes, I am referring to the type that comes in a cellophane bag, not in a jar packed in oil. I always rehydrate them in boiling water or other liquid, as stated in the individual recipes. The tomatoes dried and packed in oil are delicious, but they add fat where none is needed.

It's useful to know that you can make your own "sun"-dried tomatoes in the oven. Cut fresh tomatoes in half crosswise and place them, cut side up, on a cookie sheet. Put them in a 180° F oven for 12-24 hours, or until completely dehydrated.

SWEETENERS—I use maple syrup and honey as sweeteners in most of the dessert recipes. I chose these two sweeteners because they are minimally processed and because they are readily available all over the country. I call for sugar and brown sugar in only a couple of recipes where a liquid sweetener doesn't work well, but I do not advocate using sugar (or fructose, for that matter) often. Although sugar can be said to be natural since it comes from the sugarcane or beet plant, it is so highly processed, refined, and fragmented that it can hardly be called *natural* anymore. (Fructose, derived from sugar, is actually processed one step further than sugar.) Many people find sugar to be highly addictive, while maple syrup and honey are not.

Maple syrup is my favorite sweetener. Its flavor is fairly neutral and it doesn't alter the texture of baked goods as honey can. To make maple syrup, sap from the maple tree is simply boiled down to concentrate its sugar content. Its main drawback is expense, but I have found it regularly available at The Price Club, a warehouse discount store, where I buy it very inexpensively by the gallon.

Honey comes in a tremendous number of flavors, from buckwheat and orange blossom to sage and eucalyptus. Most honey, however, is a blend of many nectars. In most baked goods, the subtle flavors of the honey are lost, so I buy whatever raw, unfiltered type appeals to me. Honey is generally filtered or strained. I choose strained over filtered honey because filtering removes the nutritious bee pollen and may subject the honey to high temperatures that alter its sugar chemistry.

In a few recipes, I suggest using *date sugar* in place of brown sugar. Date sugar is simply dehydrated and ground dates. It resembles brown sugar in appearance and taste, and is perfect for fillings and toppings. It doesn't melt like sugar does, so it can't be used in doughs or batters. Find date sugar in natural foods stores and farmer's markets.

Fruit concentrates, barley malt, and rice syrup can be substituted for maple syrup or honey, if you prefer. Fruit concentrates are closely related to their fruit juice sources, with minimal processing. Barley malt and rice syrup are complex sugars that break down more slowly, and so have a gentler effect on blood sugar levels. I don't call for them in the recipes because they are not easy to find, but you can substitute the same amount of these other sweeteners for maple syrup or honey. Just remember that fruit concentrates and barley malt have distinct tastes that may interfere with the result you want, and that rice syrup is not as sweet as maple syrup or honey. To compensate, I often use fruit concentrate

and barley malt in combination, and only use rice syrup when its subtle flavor is desirable.

TOFU—There are two types of tofu: fresh and silken. They are quite different from each other, and need to be used appropriately. For instance, if you were to make the Tofu Blueberry Cheesecake with fresh tofu, the result would be a rubber bouncing disk (I know because I've done it!). The very same recipe made with silken tofu is luscious. Alternately, a stir-fry made with silken tofu will be a disaster. The silken tofu, higher in moisture than fresh, disintegrates, leaving puddles where tofu should be.

A very versatile food, tofu can be used in savory dishes as well as in desserts. Why use tofu? Tofu is much lower in overall fat than red meat, cheese, and eggs, the foods it would replace, and tofu contains no cholesterol. Additionally, the type of fat that tofu does contain is the healthier, unsaturated kind.

Fresh Tofu is porous, absorbing the flavors it is cooked with. Its texture varies from soft to firm, but it is always resilient, cohesive, and, when puréed, a bit grainy. Anytime you want to replace a meat, cheese, or egg with tofu in a savory dish like a stir-fry, lasagne, or casserole, use fresh tofu. It will hold its shape and blend well into its new environment.

Silken tofu does not absorb other flavors and is as gelatinous as a mousse. When puréed, it is smooth like a thick milk or custard. When you want to use tofu in a sweets recipe, like cheesecake, cookies, quick breads, or muffins, use silken. It adds creaminess and body.

You can make the switch to fresh tofu in any non-sweets recipe that does not rely on the meat, cheese, or egg you're replacing for its sole source of flavor. If the dish derives its flavor from some other ingredient in the recipe, like a sauce or spice or strong vegetable combination, you can successfully replace fattier ingredients with tofu, one to one. Casseroles, tacos, raviolis and even some soup recipes are good candidates for switching to tofu.

In sweets recipes, you can use silken tofu to replace eggs and much of the oil or butter. I usually replace 2 eggs and 2 TB of the oil or butter with half of a 10.5 oz package of silken tofu. Purée it well in a food processor or blender and proceed with the rest of the recipe. A word of caution: tofu doesn't work with every sweets recipe. Sometimes its barely discernible taste interferes with a delicately-flavored baked good like pound cake or vanilla layer cake.

You can use either fresh or silken tofu in dips, but you need to steam or blanch fresh tofu for a minute or two first to cook away any bacteria that might be present. This step isn't necessary if using silken tofu because its aseptic packaging completely locks out spoilage microorganisms and air. This process also keeps the tofu fresh, if unopened, without refrigeration for six months. Notice that the "use by" date stamped on each package is about six months away. Silken tofu can be found on the shelf in the grocery store. My favorite brand is Mori-Nu.

Fresh tofu, found in the refrigerated section of the market, will last unopened for about two weeks. Once its plastic covering has been cut open and it is properly cared for, it should last about a week. Both types of tofu, when opened, need to have their water changed daily or the water becomes slimy, shortening the fresh life of the tofu. Simply rinse under cool water, refill the container with fresh water, cover, and refrigerate.

VEGETABLE OIL SPRAY—I often use spray oil in the recipes. Most of the time I don't put it on the ingredient list, so keep some on hand. I prefer El Molino's Canola Mist, Garlic Mist, and Olive Oil Mist. This brand doesn't have the funny smell that the other sprays do. Find vegetable oil sprays at natural foods stores or order them from El Molino, a division of American Health Plus Corp., Pearl River, New York 10965.

CATEGORY INDEX

ALPHABETICAL INDEX